Love, Loyalty and Deceit

Love, Loyalty and Deceit

Rosemary Firth, a Life in the Shadow of Two Eminent Men

Hugh Firth and Loulou Brown

berghahn
NEW YORK · OXFORD
www.berghahnbooks.com

First published in 2023 by
Berghahn Books
www.berghahnbooks.com

Library of Congress Cataloging-in-Publication Data

Names: Firth, Hugh, author. | Brown, Loulou, author.
Title: Love, loyalty and deceit : Rosemary Firth, a life in the shadow of two eminent men /
Hugh Firth and Loulou Brown.
Description: New York : Berghahn Books, 2023. | Includes bibliographical references and
index.
Identifiers: LCCN 2023007810 (print) | LCCN 2023007811 (ebook) | ISBN
9781800739765 (hardback) | ISBN 9781800739789 (paperback) | ISBN
9781800739772 (ebook)
Subjects: LCSH: Firth, Rosemary, 1912–2001. | Firth, Raymond, 1901–2002. | Leach, E. R.
(Edmund Ronald), 1910–1989. | Ethnology—Great Britain—History—20th century. |
Ethnologists—Great Britain—Biography.
Classification: LCC GN21.F535 F57 2023 (print) | LCC GN21.F535 (ebook) | DDC
305.80092 [B]—dc23/eng/20230413
LC record available at https://lccn.loc.gov/2023007810
LC ebook record available at https://lccn.loc.gov/2023007811

British Library Cataloguing in Publication Data

A catalogue record for this book is available from the British Library

ISBN 978-1-80073-976-5 hardback
ISBN 978-1-80073-978-9 paperback
ISBN 978-1-80539-360-3 epub
ISBN 978-1-80073-977-2 web pdf

https://doi.org/10.3167/9781800739765

For all the women hidden from view behind famous, visible men

For whoever finds these letters

I have always loved Edmund, as I now realise, looking back on these letters at a period of almost desperate depression, loss of confidence in myself and doubts about my own work.

If you read these letters ever, may they show you rather how very complicated and uncertain is the human heart . . . Perhaps for this reason, they should be kept.

—Rosemary, December 1966

The reality is richer, nearer to the 'truth' than one thought: it does not destroy, but enlarges one's knowledge.

—Rosemary, August 1985

Contents

Illustrations

Acknowledgements

This book is authored by two people but has really been the work of three. Melinda, Rosemary's daughter-in-law, only refused our request that her name be on the cover because she believes the symmetry of our relationship, Hugh as Rosemary's son, Loulou as Edmund's daughter, should reflect the relationship between Rosemary and Edmund that was uncovered after their deaths.

Melinda was a dearly loved daughter-in-law – indeed, she was, in many ways, the daughter Rosemary had hoped to have in addition to her son. Rosemary would not have called herself a feminist, but she had a strong sense of the extent to which women are undervalued in many societies, including our own, and the bond she developed with Melinda was a strong one.

Melinda got to know Rosemary well over the twenty years before she died, and her insights have been invaluable. With her ability to stand back from the issues, Melinda played a key role in helping us make some of the most important choices about how to present this story, and which of the many gems to omit, in order to focus only on what is essential in the long process of whittling down the half a million words of letters and diaries we had initially selected to what follows.

Melinda's suggestions, whether about the focus of a chapter or the best wording for a phrase, often provided the way forward we needed. Underpinning the work involved in editing a mass of diaries and letters, and writing the back story to frame them, has been the evolving relationship between Loulou and Hugh, which was friendly but cautious at the start, with each wary of the other, but grew into an increasingly effective partnership as we worked together. Melinda's role in working deftly but gently to help us cement our working relationship has made this book possible and enabled the development of a deepening friendship between all of us.

There are others whose contribution has been crucial to the outcome of this project. Jen Breen not only agreed to type up the half a million words with which we decided to start working; her excitement, interest and visualisation of the unfolding story was important in sustaining our initial motivation to pursue publication. Jonathan Benthall was supportive of our project from the start, recognising the difficulty of balancing loyalty to those from whom one has learnt and gained so much, with the value of honesty about the frailties of eminent individuals. Throughout this project, he has been consistent in offering thoughtful comments and helpful advice at every stage of the process. Candida Brazil read through our first sample chapters and made extensive comments and suggestions for cuts to the enormous first draft. Her enthusiasm and advice helped us to pursue this project to publication. Anna Towlson from the London School of Economics (LSE) library was most helpful in facilitating our work untangling the tragic events that befell Betty Belshaw. Anna Livingstone has kindly given permission for extracts from her father James's notes and diaries to appear in chapter 3. Karin Koller provided us with some helpful material about her father Pio Koller to include in chapter 4, and Oliver Darlington has given us permission to use extracts of letters from Rosemary's father Gilbert to Rosemary. We would also like to acknowledge our debt to Ellen Godfrey, whose account of the trial of Cyril Belshaw, *By Reason of Doubt: The Belshaw Case*, provided us with many key reference points regarding the investigation, subsequent trial and verdict.[1]

Jonathan Benthall, Stacy Gillis, John Grieg and Judith Houston all read through and commented carefully on our first 'long' selection of letters and diary entries. Jemima Hunt's suggestions led to our focus on the triangle of relationships between Rosemary Upcott, Raymond Firth and Edmund Leach. Stephen Games of Booklaunch, Clare Passingham and Vivienne Schlossberg provided very helpful commentaries and suggestions on our second draft.

Most of the photographs of Rosemary, Raymond and Edmund in this book were taken by people whose names are unknown to the authors: some were professional photographers, many were colleagues and friends whose identities are now unknown. We are most grateful to all of them. It is not our intention to infringe any copyright; if anyone believes we may have done so, please contact us. For example, the photograph in figure 24.1 is by Joe Loudon, a colleague and friend of Rosemary's, but we have been unable to contact his descendants for permission to print it. Likewise, we have been unable to contact William Stanner's descendants for permission to reproduce the extract from his letter of 1 March 1941.

Alan Macfarlane, Gillian Craven, Sue Vernon, Miriam Darlington and Rosemary's grandchildren Nick and Emma, as well as their spouses Emily Todd and Will Vittery, all gave us their time, encouragement, suggestions and comments at different stages of the project, for which we are indebted. The interest and enthusiasm of Lisa Shaw at BBC Radio Newcastle greatly helped sustain us in the midst of the project. Tragically, Lisa died in 2021.

More recently, we have been immensely appreciative of the support that Robert Smith, our agent, has provided. He has been consistently enthusiastic,

optimistic and constructive in our drive towards publication. Aleksandar Boš-
cović was particularly helpful in exploring avenues for publication.

Everyone at Berghahn has been supportive and has made the process of publication both positive and productive. We particularly want to thank Michael Garvey, the copyeditor for our project, who has done an excellent job of helping our writing flow smoothly. We also greatly appreciate the support and help that Marion Berghahn, Tom Bonnington, Caroline Kuhtz and Sean Andersson have given us throughout the publishing process.

Note

1. Ellen Godfrey, 1981, *By Reason of Doubt: The Belshaw Case*, Vancouver: Clarke Irwin.

Important People

Rosemary's Family

Rosemary Upcott
(later Rosemary Firth)

Born in London in September 1912. Graduated in Political Economy at Edinburgh University in 1935. Anthropologist.

Blanche Upcott
(née Brodmeier)

Rosemary's mother, born in 1878, a professional artist. She exhibited at the Walker and Manchester Art galleries.

Gilbert Upcott

Rosemary's father, born in 1880, a senior civil servant who rose to become Auditor and Comptroller General at the Treasury.

Katherine, Maurice and Janet Upcott

Gilbert's younger sisters and brother, born in 1881, 1882 and 1888, respectively.

Margaret Upcott
(later Darlington)

Rosemary's elder sister, born in 1909. She married the geneticist Cyril Darlington and had five children, Oliver, Andy, Clare, Debby and Rachel.

Elizabeth Upcott
(subsequently Clay, later Kaye)

Rosemary's younger sister, born in 1914. She had one son, Christopher.

Kathryn Upcott
(Hodgkinson, née Townsend)

Rosemary's stepmother, born in New York around 1890. She met Gilbert playing bridge.

Terence Hodgkinson

Rosemary's stepbrother, born in 1913. An art historian, he became Director of the Wallace Collection.

Elizabeth Downs (née Drew)	A paternal second cousin, some ten years older than Rosemary. Rosemary stayed with Elizabeth when she spent time with Edmund in Cambridge in 1931.
Hugh Firth	Rosemary and Raymond's son, born in London, in 1946.
Melinda Firth (née Shaw)	Rosemary's daughter-in-law, born in 1955, married Hugh in 1980.

Raymond's Family

Raymond Firth	Born in Auckland in March 1901. Graduated in Economics at Auckland University, 1921. Anthropologist.
Wesley Firth	Raymond's father, born in 1873 in Rawtenstall, Lancashire, of a Methodist family. He emigrated to New Zealand in 1886 and became a carpenter and housebuilder.
Marie Firth (née Cartmill)	Raymond's mother, born in 1876 in New Zealand.
Gretta Firth	Raymond's sister, who died in 1907, aged 2½ years.
Cedric and Olive (Bobby) Firth	Raymond's younger brother, born in 1908, and his wife, who lived for much of their lives in Wellington, New Zealand.
Hugh Firth	Raymond and Rosemary's son, born in London in 1946.
Melinda Firth (née Shaw)	Rosemary's daughter-in-law, born in 1955, married Hugh in 1980.

Edmund's Family

Edmund Leach	Born in Sidmouth in November 1910. Graduated in Engineering at Cambridge University in 1932. Worked in business in

	China from 1933 to 1937, then became an anthropologist.
Celia Leach (née Buckmaster)	Edmund's wife, born in 1914, an artist and novelist.
William Edmund Leach	Edmund's father, born in 1851.
Mildred Leach (née Brierley)	Edmund's mother, born in 1873.
Louisa (Loulou) Brown (née Leach)	Edmund and Celia's daughter, born in Burma in 1941.
Alexander Leach	Edmund and Celia's son, born in 1946.

Rosemary's Closest Friends

Betty Belshaw	University teacher of English literature, born in 1920 in New Zealand, wife of Cyril Belshaw.
Burton and Marion Benedict (née Steuber)	Burton (born in 1923) was an American anthropologist, who taught at the LSE from 1958 to 1968. Marion was his wife.
Margaret (Greta) Redfield (née Park)	American anthropologist, born in 1898, a close friend of Rosemary, and wife of Robert Redfield, anthropologist.
Helen Stocks	Some eight years younger than Rosemary, she was the daughter of Mary Stocks, historian, writer and broadcaster. She worked as a research assistant for Raymond in the 1960s.
James Livingstone	Born in 1912, he was a fellow undergraduate with Rosemary at Edinburgh University from 1931 to 1935, and a lifelong friend.
Judith Freedman (née Djamour)	Judith was an Egyptian-born anthropologist, educated in Cairo, who worked in Britain and Singapore. Born in 1921, she married Maurice Freedman (born 1920), a British anthropologist.

Margaret Hardiman	Anthropologist, born in 1918. She was Rosemary's senior at Battersea College and then taught at the LSE.

Other Good Friends of Raymond and Rosemary

Audrey Richards	A student of Malinowski's at the LSE, born in 1899. She was an intellectual role model for Rosemary as an anthropologist and one of the very few women whom Edmund Leach respected.
Bronisław (Bronio) Malinowski	Born in Poland in 1884, Malinowski is regarded as the father of British social anthropology. He was Raymond's supervisor, mentor and friend.
Cycill Tomrley	Design writer, born in 1902. Rosemary's supervisor at the Board of Trade in East Anglia, 1942–45.
Cyril Belshaw	A New Zealand anthropologist, born in 1921, who lived and worked in Vancouver, Canada, from 1953 onwards.
Eileen Power	An economic historian, born in 1899, whom Rosemary first met in 1933. She subsequently married Munia Postan in 1937.
Isaac Schapera	Born in South Africa in 1905, he was a student of Malinowski's who spent most of his career at the LSE.
Munia Postan	A medieval historian, born in 1899, and close friend of Raymond's from 1924. He married Eileen Power in 1937.
William Stanner	An Australian anthropologist, born in 1905, whom Rosemary met in 1937 when he worked as a research assistant for Raymond.

Chronology

1901   Raymond William Firth born, Auckland, New Zealand.

1910   Edmund Ronald Leach born, Sidmouth, England.

1912   Rosemary Upcott (later Firth) born, London, England.

1924   Raymond emigrates to London, England, for his doctoral research.

1928   Rosemary first meets Edmund.

1928–29 Raymond undertakes his first anthropological fieldwork expedition on Tikopia.

1929–32 Raymond lives and works in Sydney, Australia.

1929–32 Edmund at Cambridge for his undergraduate degree in Engineering.

1931–35 Rosemary at Edinburgh for her undergraduate degree in Political Economy.

1933–37 Edmund lives and works in China.

1933–68 Raymond employed at the London School of Economics.

1935   Rosemary first meets Raymond.

1936   Marriage of Rosemary Upcott and Raymond Firth, London.

1938   Edmund undertakes anthropological fieldwork in Iraq.

1939–40 Raymond and Rosemary undertake anthropological fieldwork in Kelantan, Malaya (Malaysia), returning to England in 1940.

1939–41 Edmund undertakes anthropological fieldwork in Burma (Myanmar).

1939–45 Britain at war with Germany.

1940   Marriage of Celia Buckmaster and Edmund Leach, Rangoon (Yangon), Burma.

1941   Louisa (Loulou) Leach born, Maymyo, Burma.

1941   Japan invades Burma and Malay peninsula, and attacks Pearl Harbor. Japan at war with Britain and the United States until 1945. Edmund remains in Burma, fighting in the Burma campaign until 1945.

1942   Celia Leach escapes Burma with five-month-old Loulou.

1942–45   Raymond seconded full-time to Admiralty Intelligence.

1942–46   Rosemary researches supply and demand for the Board of Trade in East Anglia, and later London, as well as travelling to undertake targeted research in cities and towns across Great Britain.

1945–53   Edmund returns to England, completes his doctorate and subsequently joins the staff at London School of Economics under Raymond Firth.

1946   Hugh Firth born, London. Rosemary does not undertake paid employment again until 1961.

1948   Raymond and Rosemary make their first visit to Canberra, Australia.

1951   Raymond and Rosemary live in Canberra for half a year.

1952   Raymond undertakes his second expedition to Tikopia. Rosemary lives for seven months with her parents-in-law in Auckland, New Zealand. Rosemary and Raymond return to England.

1953   Edmund moves to Cambridge University.

1956   Rosemary meets Helen Stocks.

1959   Raymond and Rosemary live in Palo Alto, California, while Raymond is attached to the Center for Advanced Study in the Behavioral Sciences.

1961   Edmund and Celia live in Palo Alto while Edmund is attached to the Center for Advanced Study in the Behavioral Sciences.

1961   Rosemary commences teaching at Battersea College.

1966   Rosemary moves to London University.

1966   Raymond undertakes his third expedition to Tikopia.

1966–79 Edmund is Provost of King's College, Cambridge.

1968–74 Raymond retires from the London School of Economics in 1968 and begins spending lengthy periods abroad on visiting professorships in the United States and Canada.

1972–73 Rosemary and Raymond spend half a year teaching in Canberra, Australia.

1978 Rosemary retires.

1978–79 Rosemary and Raymond spend half a year in Auckland, New Zealand.

1979 Betty Belshaw, one of Rosemary's closest friends, is reported missing.

1979 Edmund retires.

1989 Edmund Leach dies, Cambridge, England.

2001 Rosemary Firth dies, London, England.

2002 Raymond Firth dies, London, England.

Introduction

Insiders, Outsiders and Discoveries

Rosemary loved many people in many different ways, but she loved two men in particular throughout most of her life.

One was her husband, Raymond Firth, regarded by some as one of the founding fathers of social anthropology.[1] She loved Raymond deeply and warmly during the sixty-five years of their married life. Yet she also retained a passionate devotion to her first love, Edmund Leach, who would subsequently become both an *enfant terrible* and the public intellectual face of social anthropology in the late 1960s. Both Raymond and Edmund were part of the process of defining the nature of this growing discipline in the first part of the mid-twentieth century.

This book is about the lives of all three – Rosemary, Raymond and Edmund – but it is written from Rosemary's perspective. This is because she left a huge volume of letters and many diaries spanning seventy years. We also have the numerous letters Edmund wrote to Rosemary in the 1930s and 1940s. Raymond left some description of his life from the 1920s to the 1940s,[2] but he wrote very little about his thoughts and feelings about his personal or professional relationships. Our focus is primarily on the life of a woman and how this intersected with the lives of two eminent men. This book is therefore also about Rosemary's aspirations, loves, marriage, struggles and achievements, and about the resolution of the conflicts she faced in her life.

Inevitably, therefore, this story is told through one particular lens, although this is supplemented by our knowledge and memory of many details of the lives of our parents.

Discovery

It was our parents' deaths that brought us together. The two of us, Loulou (Louisa) and Hugh, had known each other slightly as children, but we had not seen each other for over thirty years when we met at Hugh's mother Rosemary's funeral. It was the start of a very unusual and dramatic story.

ಎಲ

I, Hugh, had known since my early teens that my mother, Rosemary, had first met Loulou's father, Edmund Leach, in her teens some years before she met my father, Raymond. I also knew that Edmund had gone off to spend four years in China, that my mother did not wait for him to return and that she married Raymond while Edmund was out east.

Rosemary had always been very straightforward with me and her daughter-in-law Melinda about her very early love for Edmund, whom she fell in love with four years before she ever met Raymond. She was also open about her need to decide whether to wait for a man who offered no sign of engagement, or to look elsewhere. There was nothing to hide.

Not long before my mother, Rosemary, died, she had let me know that there were a number of notebooks that might be of some interest, so I had an inkling that I would find something that might catch my attention in them. I was also aware that she had many boxes of letters, including a few from her mother, many letters to and from her father written when Rosemary herself was abroad, and a box of letters my parents wrote to each other before they were married, while my mother was in Vienna.

In February 2002, seven months after the death of my mother, my father died. I saw Loulou again at his funeral and we kept in touch via Christmas cards and brief letters.

After my parents' death, I looked at the boxes of letters and found one box of over a hundred letters from Edmund, almost all from the early 1930s before he went out to China, when (as I already knew) my mother had fallen in love with him. There were some from the Second World War and a few from afterwards. Sometime later, I contacted Loulou to let her know about these early letters from her father.

When Loulou and I met again, I also showed Loulou my mother's notebooks, which I had begun to read. It transpired that they were diaries, kept intermittently and sometimes every day, from 1931 until shortly before she died. Here were her innermost thoughts and emotions: when she was a young woman managing her disappointments and hopes about Edmund's departure for China; writing about her life with a small son living with her in-laws for seven months while her husband was out of reach and incommunicado on a remote Pacific island. Here also were her reflections on sixty years of marriage – including the tough years – and her observations on the mental and physical frustrations of old age.

What I hadn't been prepared for were revelations of which I had not the least suspicion. I discovered that the close relationship between my mother and Helen Stocks,[3] whom I had known well as a family friend since the mid-1950s, had begun as a love affair between the two of them. I learnt of my father's affairs (at least those of which Rosemary was aware), as well as my mother's own flirtations and one-night stands – and the fact that she had left my father and the family home at one point in their marriage.

Most astonishing of all was the realisation that my mother and Edmund had slept with each other again, some thirty years after Rosemary and Raymond had married, and that their love remained alive until their respective deaths. Throughout her life, my mother had stayed in love with Edmund, as well as being in love in a different way with my father, the ups and downs of married life notwithstanding.

I was taken by surprise – though, on reflection, why should I have been? I had felt safe in my relationship with my parents, and my experience was of a loving family and a loving marriage – peppered with rows, quarrelling and making up afterwards, but not apparently insecure.

My mother had also been frank in talking about relationships. When I was eighteen, at a time when my parents were rowing openly, they had each talked to me in depth as part of their process of trying to resolve the issues. So I suppose I thought that I knew both my parents well, and knew about the important events in their lives. The truth is that I did know them well, and that is precisely why I was so astounded by the events we uncovered. They were well hidden in plain sight, for three of these love affairs – my father's with a younger anthropologist and my mother's with Helen and with Edmund – were with individuals I knew and liked, who visited us more or less often while I was growing up at home. So although my mother talked openly to me (both as a young adult and as an older adult) about relationships, she was in fact scrupulous about not betraying anything she thought might be damaging, either to me or to her other relationships.

☙❧

Although I, Loulou, had known about Hugh since he was born, I'd actually met him very few times until our parents died. It was then that he began to send me Christmas cards, and I reciprocated. In early 2015, nearly ten years after my mother died in 2005, Hugh cautiously suggested that I might travel to Newcastle to see some letters Rosemary and Edmund had written to each other, and the diaries Rosemary had written. When Hugh contacted me, I was still grieving the loss of my mother, whom I loved, and was also experiencing vivid memories of my relationship with my father, Edmund, who had died in 1989. These recollections were mostly unpleasant, encompassing his impatience, restlessness, frequent criticism, an inability to connect with me emotionally, and a temper I had found frightening. Nevertheless, I was curious about my father's letters to Rosemary and wanted to read them. We began to look at them together. Initially uncertain and cautious, I felt drawn to find out more. These letters gave me a very different perspective on my father.

I'd had a difficult, distant relationship with my father. After leaving Burma with my mother when I was five months old, I did not see him again until over three years later. When he arrived in England, he was ill with malaria and had suffered many bouts of dysentery and various other diseases contracted while fighting behind the lines in Burma against the Japanese. Battered, thin and worn out, he did not want to be bothered with a small, surly girl who resented his sudden presence in the household; sadly, our relationship remained negative for the rest of his life. He thought I was unintelligent, boring, unattractive and uncooperative, while I thought he was bad-tempered, impatient, uncaring and incomprehensible. I was shunted off to boarding school at the age of five, and if he was around when I was at home, I tended to keep out of his way. The nervous energy he exuded was unsettling, and his moods, like Scottish weather, changed rapidly. I had little to do with him, and I was very surprised when I discovered shortly before he died that I was to be his literary executor. It was only much later that I realised that he'd given me this work so that I could protect my mother, which he knew I would do.

In Edmund and Rosemary's letters, I read about a man who was very different to the one I had known: someone who loved, passionately, with myriads of thoughts that tumbled into each other and often clashed, with the result that he was frequently at odds with himself. Here was a dreamer who, as Rosemary says, saw stars very clearly; a maverick whom a few, including some of his students, Rosemary and my mother, loved, but whom many considered a *bête noire*. He was marmite: you either felt positively or negatively about him – you could never ignore or forget him. Trying to integrate the two perspectives – my own experience of a preoccupied, irritable and negative authority figure who paid little attention to my needs and preferences, and Rosemary's vision of a scintillating (albeit sometimes hurtful), agile, compelling, warm and attentive presence – was intensely disturbing.

In contrast to Hugh, I felt life with my parents to be very insecure and spent my childhood feeling afraid of many things, including my future as an adult. For me, the process of reading these diaries and letters was therefore unsettling and disconcerting; but as Hugh and I began to talk more about what kind of a man Edmund had been, I was gradually able to see the relationship I had had with the difficult man that was my father from a new perspective. Through the process of sharing and debating our often contradictory or inconsistent perceptions and understandings of our parents, and selecting and organising the material in the chapters that follow, I have to some extent been able to come to terms with my father, whom I had never really known. Moreover, Hugh and I have developed a close and valuable friendship as we have worked together to bring this manuscript to fruition.

Why Publish?

Diaries and letters are intensely personal documents. They reveal intimate aspects about their authors and, more often than not, unprepossessing perspectives on the authors' nearest and dearest. One may therefore wonder why it seems appropriate to publish them, especially as they reveal the individuals' shortcomings in the full glare of public attention and may therefore appear to tarnish their reputations.

We have chosen to publish them for several reasons.

There is a growing interest in the wives of important men, and the struggles and compromises that they face. Both Rosemary and Celia, Edmund's wife, were the wives of prestigious academics. Their husbands were close friends as well as colleagues. The two women had an affection for each other and shared something of their mutual challenges. All four were close-knit. We think the relationships between them are therefore of particular interest.

We also believe that the ambivalences, uncertainties and outcomes of the protagonists' aspirations and disappointments will resonate with many people. We think this account illustrates how people can negotiate and survive the messiness of their lives through a combination of loyalty, care, hard work and an attempt at mutual understanding. Moreover, the text highlights issues which touch on conundrums and tensions in very many relationships.

We think readers may gain a more rounded understanding of these individuals, our parents. They have reputations that stand by their achievements, not their human frailties, and their lives are now, after some two decades, part of history as well as memory.

Furthermore, we believe Rosemary herself expected that her letters and notebooks would be read; indeed, she herself considered publishing something of an autobiography, which might draw on this 'Pandora's box full of treasure'.[4]

We are confident that Rosemary would have approved of the publication of this book as a whole, although, out of loyalty to her husband, she would undoubtedly have edited out many details of her difficulties with Raymond which we have left in this book. Edmund would probably have told us to do whatever we wished by way of publication, and brushed aside his own contradictions and inconsistencies.

Raymond preferred privacy, but he, like Rosemary and Edmund, believed passionately in honesty. Raymond's posthumous self would, we think, have tried to dissuade us from publishing this book, but he would have listened, understood and respected our decision. Raymond mellowed as he grew older. He loved Rosemary and cared greatly for her. He steadily learnt to be more appreciative of his wife's abilities and her contribution to anthropological thinking. He would have been embarrassed by some of the events we describe in this book, but he would have understood our carefully considered decision to tell this story.

This account of the relationships between our parents, complete with the candid as well as the more favourable aspects, has been written with care and respect for them. Hugh loved both his parents equally, albeit in different ways. Loulou, although she deeply loved her mother, did not love her father. In drawing these perspectives together, we have endeavoured to present a fair and accurate portrayal of their interlocking lives. Inevitably, the process of compiling this account has been unsettling and emotional for both of us, as we have explored and distilled the details of their lives.

∽

As Ann Oakley has observed, it is often only the preservation of letters and diaries that enables us to ensure that the wives of publicly well-known men are not forgotten.[5]

Many people take their secrets with them to the grave. Rosemary was hesitant and ambivalent for many years about how much of her vast correspondence to keep or destroy.

When she was depressed in mid-life, she nearly destroyed all her letters and diaries. Yet, twenty years later, with her own forthcoming death in mind, Rosemary wrote remarks in her diary such as 'begin at the end, whoever you are who reads this', suggesting that she expected her diaries to be read by others after her death.[6] Shortly afterwards, she wrote to a friend about her uncertainty regarding 'how much of private letters, diaries and so on, to leave around for others to pick up, read, use, or destroy at their own choice; or how much to authorise others to use; or again whether to try to write something oneself'.[7] Her final decision to leave these personal letters and diaries for the use of the next generation is clear, in that, shortly before her death, she directed both her daughter-in-law Melinda and Hugh, separately, to some notebooks in her desk that held significant information about her life and relationships.

When, in 1984, Rosemary asked Edmund what he had done with her letters, and what she should do with his (he was considering authorising someone to write his biography), he said, in effect, do 'What you like – burn them all or give them all to Martha Macintyre[8] – I have kept *no* papers!'[9] Edmund's remarks were perhaps designed to hide the significance he attached to such things: in reality, he was obsessional about his retention of letters and papers, and it is certain that Rosemary's letters to Edmund were preserved until his wife Celia destroyed them sometime after his death.

Edmund's remark is significant because although he certainly had a number of sexual liaisons during his life, there are a couple of indications that he continued to hold a special candle for Rosemary, whilst retaining his love for, and loyalty to, Celia. Perhaps the most persuasive clue is the inconsistency in Edmund's behaviour towards Rosemary when they met socially. At times, when Raymond was present, Edmund appeared to ignore Rosemary; yet he paid her great attention when Raymond was away or out of the country. His untrue but forthright denial that he had kept Rosemary's letters may suggest a degree of sustained affection for Rosemary, of which she herself was unaware.

‿༒‿

There is a structural imbalance in societal expectations of women and men that profoundly affects what women could, and can, achieve. This imbalance is a thread running throughout this book. Despite Rosemary having been brought up by relatively unconventional parents, her aspirations about marriage, a career and her role as a mother were all profoundly influenced by societal expectations in Britain in the half-century from the 1920s.

Rosemary was no feminist, although she was acutely observant of the different position of women and men both in Britain and abroad. In many ways, she was a 'difficult' woman. She was clear about her own values, even if others might see inconsistencies in her application of them. Towards some people, Rosemary exhibited great thoughtfulness, care and affection. Yet she rarely hesitated in expressing her views and was often thoughtless as to how her views would be perceived by others. In consequence, she was frequently perceived as opinionated, even plain rude. Quick to dismiss opinions she thought wrong-headed, she could be quite intimidating.

When Rosemary was just fifteen, Rosemary's mother Blanche had shared something of the difficulties she had experienced early in *her* marriage to Rosemary's father Gilbert, to show Rosemary how, with good will on both sides, such difficulties could be overcome. This was something that Rosemary held on to and which greatly helped her when there were difficulties in her marriage to Raymond in the 1960s. Despite her flirtations and one-night stands, Rosemary firmly believed in the importance of loyalty to the marriage between herself and Raymond. Inconsistent though this may seem to the reader, it had its own clear logic to Rosemary. Edmund felt a similar loyalty to his wife, Celia. Their loyalty took at least two forms: a determination to do their utmost to preserve their marriages and also to ensure that the difficulties in their marriages should not become public.

Long-term relationships are complex, full of ambivalences and ups and downs. For most of their time together, Raymond and Rosemary greatly loved and respected each other. Equally, Celia and Edmund loved each other and cared for each other deeply throughout a long marriage of nearly fifty years.

Celia and Rosemary were good friends over many decades. They had many experiences in common, as the wives of eminent men who were frequently absent from the home for both short and long periods, and often absent in spirit even when they were at home and working.

All four were individuals who were capable of great compassion and understanding towards others. Rosemary believed deeply in the importance of honesty, courage and compassion. She once remarked in her diary, 'Judge us with charity, those who love us'.[10] We are all flawed human beings, and the awareness of this can, it is hoped, help us to be more understanding and less censorious of ourselves and others, in a society that is, in some respects, increasingly strident and judgemental.

'Great, Cruel, Egoistic Angel'

'That great, cruel, egoistic angel', as Rosemary once described Edmund,[11] had a profound effect upon all those with whom he was involved. His influence was equally powerful, if ambivalent or contradictory, upon each of us and anyone he met. Loulou's perception of Edmund as an impatient, irascible father was borne out by Hugh's childhood recollections of staying with Edmund, Celia and their son, Alexander: they were not happy memories. Yet, as an adult, Hugh's own experience of Edmund had been different again: Hugh found him a warm, enthusiastic, magnetic individual with a razor-sharp intelligence.

After Edmund's death in January 1989, for weeks and months Rosemary felt as if she were back in the 1930s, passionately reliving and regretting the failed fruition of a once-great love. Why had he behaved so inconsistently towards her, not only when they were young, but throughout his long professional career? For their love was sufficiently lasting to resurface after long periods when each been preoccupied with other issues, even whilst Rosemary, Raymond, Edmund and Celia were all close friends.

Inconsistent Edmund certainly was, both – by his own admission – in his work,[12] but also in his relationships. Driven by ambition instilled in him by his mother when he was young, he was capable of ignoring those who were not useful to him at any particular moment. Rosemary once commented in her diary that 'It now seems to me that E.[Edmund]'s greatest betrayal was not his jilting of me in regard to engagement for marriage, but his casting off one who had become so intimate intellectually, emotionally and culturally, so to speak. His overweening ambition and vanity made him find excuses to throw me off' – not once, but twice.[13]

What Rosemary did not say was that Edmund could not bear any competition. Loulou was told many times by her mother, Celia, that Edmund would not tolerate any rivals, and he made quite sure that his family had absolutely nothing to do with his work as an anthropologist. The rigidity of this distinction between work and family life – and the great wariness, which almost amounted to a taboo, on any discussion about difficulties in family relationships – contrasted dramatically with the ethos in the Firth household.

Insiders and Outsiders

Rosemary, Raymond and Edmund were inextricably linked through love, friendship and their careers; yet each of them was distinctive in some respect. Each was, to some degree, destined to be an observer, either by inclination, by geography or by gender.

Raymond Firth was a New Zealander, the son of a carpenter and house-builder. He came to England in 1924 to pursue a career in economics, only to be drawn into social anthropology by the charismatic Bronisław Malinowski.[14] Raymond would go on to develop economic anthropology as a significant discipline within social anthropology.[15] He spent a year on a tiny, remote, almost unknown, largely pagan Pacific island in 1928–29, seventy miles from its nearest neighbour at the far end of the Solomon Islands. The first book he published as a result of his time there, *We, The Tikopia*, was on the verge of publication when he met Rosemary for the first time in 1935. The book rapidly became a classic analysis of a society as yet largely untouched by western colonialism. In time, Raymond Firth would become the almost unchallenged elder statesman of British social anthropology.

Edmund Leach was an outsider within his own family. With twenty-seven first cousins, he was the youngest of his generation in this large, extended family. Most of the male Leaches who had attended school at Marlborough became ardent members of cricket teams; Edmund, however, hated both cricket and his years at Marlborough, which were, he said, the worst years of his life, worse even than the time he spent in Burma during the Second World War. An engineer by training (both Rosemary and Raymond were economists), he spent four years in commerce in China.[16] He returned to England with an interest in anthropology and asked Rosemary to introduce him to Raymond. All three became part of a generation of anthropologists who completed their key pieces of fieldwork in the first half of the twentieth century. Along with Celia, they remained firm friends for the rest of Edmund's life. Edmund's uncompromising approach and formidable intelligence soon propelled him into notoriety: first, as a rebel within the profession and then as a public intellectual whose 1967 BBC Reith Lectures caused a small uproar.

Rosemary, in common with all bright women of her time, was handicapped on account of her gender. Like Edmund, she had been born into the English upper middle class. Like Raymond, she graduated with first-class honours in Economics. Rosemary wanted to use her education and initially expected to follow her aunt Janet Upcott into social work, or what is now called social housing management. Sociable, outspoken, but with inner insecurities, she had seen in Edmund an intellectual equal who enjoyed debate and with whom she could develop her ideas. She was hardworking and ambitious to achieve something, to be socially useful, and she was interested in applying ideas to the real world. With Raymond, she saw the opportunity to do collaborative work, to build something together. Her admiration for Raymond's female colleagues Audrey Richards[17] and Lucy Mair[18] greatly influenced her decision to engage in anthropological fieldwork. Returning in 1940 from their first fieldwork expedition to Malaya, she promptly published the results of her own work there during the war years in 1943.

However, she suffered as a result of the patriarchal attitudes, common amongst academics at the time, that both Edmund and Raymond held towards women and their place as 'equals'.[19] Edmund and Raymond were very different in this respect. Edmund was willing to listen to his wife's comments on a draft lecture, but openly dismissive of his daughter's intellectual abilities and Rosemary's intellectual achievements. Raymond was more subtly patronising, kept a tight control over the salary he brought home and was quite comfortable viewing Rosemary as a wife and mother, rather than a genuine colleague, for nearly twenty years while their son was still at home.

Both Rosemary and Raymond wanted children. As a married woman with a young son, however, the culture of post-war Britain dictated that her role as wife and mother came before any career for herself. Rebuilding a career later, when she was in her mid-forties, was difficult and it was not until the 1960s that she realised three equally important achievements: a University of London lectureship, financial independence and membership of the small professional body of the time, the Association of Social Anthropologists (ASA). It was when they met through the ASA, while Raymond was abroad, that the love between Edmund and Rosemary was able to grow once again.

To some extent, all three were, like many other British anthropologists of the first half of the twentieth century, outsiders of one kind or another in their relationships to the establishment of the time. Social anthropology in Britain in the 1930s was a tiny profession, comprising barely a few dozen unusual individuals – most of them foreigners to the country – who spent lengthy periods living alone in other cultures in conditions that were basic in terms of the creature comforts they afforded. Rosemary, Edmund and Raymond had all come from families that viewed travelling abroad or living abroad as natural. Rosemary's maternal grandfather had fled Prussian militarism; her uncle Maurice Upcott and her aunts Katherine and Janet had all spent time in colonial Malaya as part of the apparatus of British Empire. Some of the Leaches, sons and daughters of a Lancashire mill-owner, including Edmund's father, had acquired land and managed and lived on a large sugar plantation in Jujuy in northern Argentina; Edmund's mother expected him to become a missionary abroad. Wesley, Raymond's father, and his family had emigrated to New Zealand from Lancashire in 1886, when Wesley was just thirteen. Raymond in turn went 'home' to England in 1924 to study, before embarking on his renowned expedition to Tikopia.

Travel and connections were an essential and integral part of life amongst the very small community of British social anthropologists in the 1930s. They all knew each other, and most of them had worked together at some point in their careers, either as colleagues or as students and teachers. Thus, Raymond enabled Edmund Leach to join him at Malinowski's seminars in 1937; Edmund worked as research assistant to Raymond from 1938 to 1939, returning to the London School of Economics (LSE) in 1945 to complete his doctorate under Raymond before becoming Raymond's close colleague as a member of the LSE staff in 1948.

There were other international connections. Raymond knew all the New Zealand anthropologists who qualified before his retirement in 1968. He and Rosemary became good friends with a number of them, including Cyril Belshaw,[20] and kept in touch wherever they were, be it in London in the 1940s, Australia in the 1950s or Vancouver in the 1960s.

The women in these networks, whether they were anthropologists or the wives of anthropologists, often developed especially close relationships. Rosemary and Celia developed a close friendship during the Second World War when Edmund was in the army in Burma, while Rosemary and Cyril's wife Betty Belshaw[21] were both in London with very young children in the late 1940s and saw each other frequently then. Subsequently, when Rosemary and Betty were both in Canberra together in 1951, they shared their thoughts and feelings about being tied to prestigious, busy academics. Rosemary later became very close to the anthropologist Judith Freedman,[22] and to Greta Redfield and Marion Benedict, the latter two respectively married to the American anthropologists Robert Redfield and Burton Benedict.[23] (Long-distance and international telephone calls were extremely expensive until the end of the 1950s, so when they were separated by their own or their husband's jobs, as repeatedly happened, these women regularly wrote to each other to keep in touch.)

Early Influences

One of the most intriguing insights arising from reflections on Edmund, Rosemary and Raymond is the influence that upbringing might have had upon each of them. Raymond had a younger sister, Gretta, who died of measles at the age of two and a half. His mother's grief was intense: she may well have been seriously depressed. She also seems to have suggested to the six-year-old Raymond that he was partly responsible for her death, as he had brought the measles home from school. The consequence was that Raymond apparently experienced little warmth and emotional support from his mother as he grew up. Raymond was often reluctant to express his feelings, had a sensitivity to perceived personal criticism and sometimes seemed to need approval or admiration to maintain his self-esteem – which he sought from his career, his colleagues, his students, his occasional affairs and his wife. At times, he could come across as dogmatic and patronising.

Edmund saw very little of his father, whose birthday was on the same day as his son's and who turned fifty-nine the day Edmund was born. To Edmund, his father was more like a grandfather than a father: old, remote and not someone he empathised with or could relate to. His mother, however, cosseted him and fostered in him the idea that he was exceptionally talented. He later commented, 'I was her nearest and dearest. It made it very difficult to grow up. She slaughtered my girlfriends one after another.'[24] His outward self-confidence, however, belied an inner insecurity. He believed he had to succeed to fulfil his parents' expectations.[25] This translated over time into an inability to bear any competition or tolerate rivals. Edmund certainly lacked the role model of a youthful, actively involved father who was in tune with the feelings of his young children, and his own childhood perhaps led him to assume that the mother would provide the close emotional contact and support for children in a family.

Rosemary faced tragedy early in her life. When she was just twelve years old, her uncle Maurice, whom she adored but who suffered intermittent depression, killed himself. Her relationship with her father, Gilbert Upcott, was positive and close for almost all of his life. Her relationship with her mother Blanche, however, was more complex and possibly more profound. Blanche had had a difficult relationship with her own mother: she had witnessed her younger sister being beaten for her poor eyesight and shut in a cupboard for using local dialect in the family home. Much later, by now an intelligent, independent-minded and artistically gifted young woman with a strong sense of humour, Blanche tried to be a warm and supportive mother to her children. But her forthright personality seems to have made this difficult. Gilbert was a remarkably gentle, unobtrusive man, quiet and supportive as a father. Gilbert and Blanche had had a difficult start to their marriage, living for a year or so with both of Gilbert's sisters, during which time, in Blanche's view, 'Gilbert would not stand up for me'.[26] Certainly Gilbert thought his wife too rigid in her approach to, and discipline with, the girls. When, as a young adolescent, Rosemary's elder sister Margaret underwent a religious conversion, she was so scared of her mother's response that she put a letter under her mother's pillow rather than face her directly.

Rosemary never described herself as having been fearful of her mother, whom she characterised as 'a lively, energetic woman, a great organiser' who was very involved with her children.[27] Yet she almost certainly had to work hard for her mother's approval – and well into Rosemary's adulthood, this may have driven a continuing insecurity, a need for visible, constant support, for an anchor.

There thus appears to have been a tension that remained with Rosemary throughout her adult life. On the one hand, she had the confidence that comes from a secure, fairly privileged upbringing. She had received an unconventional education from 'strong' women teachers who provided her with positive role models, attuned her to gender issues and gave her a strong sense of the undervalued contribution that women make to society. On the other hand, her relationship with her freethinking but forceful mother seems to have bequeathed her an enduring emotional uncertainty and vulnerability.

Notes

1. Social anthropology is the study of human social behaviour through the observation of individuals' behaviour in natural settings. Systematic data collection through prolonged participant observation (fieldwork) was pioneered by Bronisław Malinowski and his students in the first decades of the twentieth century.
2. Raymond Firth, 'Chronology' and 'Reflections of a Centenarian', unpublished.
3. Helen Stocks, daughter of the historian, writer and broadcaster Mary Stocks, was some eight years younger than Rosemary. She worked as a research assistant for Raymond in the 1960s.
4. Rosemary to Rhoda Lilley, 1 April 1986.
5. Ann Oakley, 2021, *Forgotten Wives: How Women Get Written Out of History*, Bristol: Policy Press, p. 10.
6. Rosemary, diary entry, 1 July 1985.
7. Rosemary to Rhoda Lilley, 1 April 1986. Rosemary subsequently placed her professional records, including her fieldwork notes, in an archive at the LSE Library.
8. Martha Macintyre (1945–) is an Australian anthropologist who has specialised in the impact of development in Papua New Guinea. At this point in time, Edmund Leach had suggested to her that she should be his biographer.
9. Rosemary, in a letter to Rhoda Lilley, 1 April 1986, paraphrased Edmund's remarks to Rosemary in his letter of 3 September 1984. Edmund's remark was quite untrue.
10. Rosemary, diary entry, 1 December 1966.
11. Rosemary, diary entry, 19 May 1989.

12. Stephen Hugh-Jones, 1989, *Edmund Leach*, Cambridge: King's College, p. 23.
13. Rosemary, diary entry, 29 January 1986.
14. Bronisław (Bronio) Malinowski (1884–1942), Polish-born British anthropologist, was a lecturer (later professor) at the LSE from 1922 and had published his major work on the Trobriand Islanders the same year.
15. Economic anthropology examines the use of resources by societies through the observation and study of individuals' actual behaviour, whether in developed or underdeveloped, monetary or non-monetary societies, in contrast to economics, which examines large-scale economic behaviour, often in the absence of a social and cultural context.
16. Adam Kuper, 1986, 'An Interview with Edmund Leach', *Current Anthropology* 27(4): 375–82, p. 375.
17. Audrey Richards (1899–1984), another pupil of Malinowski, was a pioneer in studying the impact of western cash economy and taxation on the Bemba of Zambia in the 1930s. As well as being a colleague, she became a warm friend of Raymond, Rosemary and Edmund, and godmother to Rosemary and Raymond's son Hugh.
18. Lucy Mair (1901–86) was also a pupil of Malinowski. She studied social change in Uganda in 1931–32 and developed the influence of anthropology in colonial administration. A very private person, she was a formidable personality who remained primarily a colleague to Raymond, Rosemary and Edmund.
19. Edmund's attitudes closely paralleled those of Ann Oakley's father, Richard Titmuss, as she describes them. (See Ann Oakley, 2014, *Father and Daughter: Patriarchy, Gender and Social Science*, Bristol: Policy Press, pp. 34 and 97–98.) Raymond's mindset was more evenly balanced: particularly later in life, he could be equally patronising to his junior male colleagues.
20. Cyril Belshaw (1921–2018) was a prominent New Zealand anthropologist.
21. Betty Belshaw (1920–79) became a respected lecturer in English Literature at the University of British Columbia, Vancouver.
22. Judith Freedman, neé Djamour (1921–2009) and Maurice Freedman (1920–75) trained at the LSE under Raymond, and both became colleagues and very good friends of the Firths.
23. Margaret (Greta) Redfield (1898–1977) worked with her husband Robert Redfield (1897–1958) during his ethnographic studies in Mexico in the late 1920s and early 1930s. Burton Benedict (1923–2010) taught anthropology at the LSE from 1958 to 1968, then served as a professor at the University of California at Berkeley, becoming director of the Hearst Museum of Anthropology.
24. Adam Kuper, 1986, 'An Interview with Edmund Leach', *Current Anthropology* 27(4): 375–82.
25. Stanley Tambiah, 2002, *Edmund Leach: An Anthropological Life*, Cambridge: Cambridge University Press, pp. 19–29.
26. Rosemary Firth, 'Janet Upcott and Blanche', 9 November 1983, unpublished.
27. Rosemary Firth, 'Blanche Lieschen Brodmeier and Her Family', 1 July 1995, unpublished.

Chapter 1

Edmund

1928–1931

It was a month short of her sixteenth birthday. Two events in the next four weeks would change Rosemary's life forever.

She had arrived at Ederyn in North Wales for a month-long holiday with her father and two sisters in early August 1928. It was at the start of the holiday that Rosemary first met Edmund Leach, a tall, seventeen-year-old young man. He was staying nearby with his uncle, a colleague of Rosemary's father. Over the next three weeks, Edmund came to see Rosemary and her two sisters on several further occasions with a friend on his motorbike.

Rosemary was intrigued, but cautious.

Edmund took the initiative and started writing to her after they returned to their respective homes. He sent chocolates at Christmas and, over time, his interest in Rosemary grew.

૮૪૭

Family holidays were important in the Upcott family. The three girls and their parents had been away every summer since Rosemary was ten years old – first to Cornwall, then to Scotland, Brittany and Wales. For the first few years, their uncle Maurice had joined them, until, in 1925, he took his own life.

That year, their mother Blanche developed cancer of the colon. Although Blanche tried to hide much of how she felt, she became somewhat withdrawn from her daughters. Rosemary subsequently talked little of this time, but the memory of her mother's withdrawal, 'which so hurt me', was seared into her memory.[1]

By August 1928, Blanche was too weak to join the family holiday. She continued her treatment at home in London, while the three girls went with their father to Ederyn.

Soon after their arrival in Wales, Rosemary wrote to her mother, complaining of her mother's 'misunderstandings and mockeries'.[2] When Blanche received it, she read Rosemary's letter 'with tears of sympathy . . . for the stings you had borne'. She replied from London to her fifteen-year-old daughter on 16 August, and wrote about how she had thought she had failed as a mother, but with 'tears of gladness too' because 'you had at last trusted me enough to be frank with me. Now you know that I was not laughing at you – but proud of you – you will gradually feel more comfortable when I laugh – knowing that there is no unkindness in it. . . . I send you my love and one real kiss.'[3]

Rosemary never saw her mother alive again.

Her father Gilbert was called back to London on 28 August in response to Blanche's sudden deterioration and the need for another operation.

Blanche died on 31 August 1928 while Rosemary was still in Wales.

The 'bitter irony'[4] that Rosemary and her mother were never able to talk about this tragic misunderstanding stayed with Rosemary. It was a cruel twist that seemingly left Rosemary not only with aching regret but also with much guilt, as well as anxiety, about losing her loved ones for the rest of her life.

ぐぶら

Edmund continued to pursue Rosemary, by means of letters and small gifts, throughout her time at boarding school and the school holidays she spent at home.

In February 1931, after she had left school and as she was preparing to go to Paris for six weeks, Edmund invited – indeed implored – Rosemary to go to some Cambridge University May Balls with him that summer. 'I refused at first, on the ground that I did not really know him well, found him disturbingly "romantic". . . . Not having a mother, I asked advice of my trusted second cousin Elizabeth Downs[5] then at Cambridge with her husband Brian, at one of the colleges. I knew she could "hostess" me during the week if I accepted. She wrote a letter telling me more or less to enjoy myself with this young man while I was young, and no cause to worry when we were each but eighteen and twenty. So I went. There we both fell somewhat in love with each other.'[6]

What was it that drew them together, and would keep drawing them back together over the next sixty years?

Edmund and Rosemary were both extremely bright, from families that discussed major issues of politics, ethics, literature, philosophy and religion. They shared an interest in big ideas, but above all a belief in the virtue of being frank and honest: both had a strong distaste for insincerity or dishonesty of any kind. They also both had a romantic side; Rosemary had already developed a lifelong love of Elizabethan verse, and poetry served as another means of mutual communication and understanding.

Rosemary had been born in London on 24 September 1912 to a rising civil servant and a mother who, before her marriage in 1908, had been a professional artist exhibiting in galleries in Manchester. Blanche was of the generation who, throughout the turn of the century and the First World War, succeeded in widening the realm of possibilities for women through the vote, employment and professional careers. Blanche and Rosemary were similar in certain regards: both were forthright, sometimes critical and even intimidating to others. Later, as an adult, Rosemary's barbed sense of humour often unintentionally (and occasionally intentionally) hurt people. Her nieces, and Loulou as a child, remember her as someone to be wary of, as she was critical or fierce on occasion. Often outspoken, she could sometimes be rude – especially late in life, when she suffered depression arising from old age. She herself once said that she regretted the 'thousands of things I have said which I ought to have left unsaid'.[7]

If Rosemary's relationship with her mother was sometimes beset with tension, her relationship with her father was a stabilising influence on her. From an early age Rosemary developed a close relationship with her father, and this supported her throughout much of her life – apart from a very brief period of anger with him when he remarried after only a year of widowhood while Rosemary was still in her teens.[8]

In matters other than religion and education, Rosemary's parents ran a conventional upper-middle-class household, complete with a maid who resided upstairs. Rosemary's schooling was, however, unusual. Both Byron House, and later The Grove, which Rosemary attended from the age of eleven, were specifically chosen by Rosemary's mother on the basis of their unusual approach to education. Both were run by women along unconventional lines. Miss Lacey, head of The Grove, had read history at Oxford at a time when the university still refused to grant women full degrees. She disapproved of any kind of individual rivalry. Every girl had her personal timetable, based on individual choice, and attended classes according to her ability in each subject rather than her age.[9]

Edmund, born on 7 November 1910, had a close emotional relationship with his mother, who had him privately educated at home until he was thirteen. Moreover, he had adopted as a role model his great-uncle Henry Howorth, who had authored a respected five-volume history of the Mongols and become a fellow of the Royal Society, a trustee of the British Museum and president of the Royal Archaeological Society.

Rosemary and Edmund each had a penchant for being a rebel, together with a conservativism that was rooted in their class background. Edmund subsequently described himself as being, in an odd way, both 'Rebel and High Tory at the same time'.[10] Rosemary was always a champion of the underdog, but retained an apolitical attachment to social and cultural stability: she would remind others that 'politics is the art of the possible'.

They were each, perhaps for different reasons, unable to restrain their impulse to challenge, to question, to play the devil's advocate – and this certainly drew them together when they really got to know each other in June 1931. Both used discussion and debate as a means of clarifying what they actually believed. Edmund wrote to Rosemary that 'You see, my dear, I am quite incorrigible. Whenever you express an opinion, and even sometimes when you don't, I shall ask you "Why?" It's almost automatic.'[11] Edmund was, by his own admission, always forthright and impetuous in dialogue and in his letters – arguing with himself to work out what he really thought.[12] In contrast, Rosemary was more careful and considered in her letter-writing. Both wanted to be fiercely independent – at least intellectually.

Edmund had a mathematician and engineer's approach to problems. He was prone to seeing issues in terms of right or wrong, true or false, black or white. Furthermore, his mother had educated him to believe in clear moral imperatives. He saw compromise as deeply unsatisfactory, almost cowardly.

Religion – and its associated moral codes – was one topic upon which they came from very different perspectives. Edmund, although no longer a Christian when up at Cambridge, nevertheless still held to the Christian moral principles his mother had imbued in him, especially with regard to sexual behaviour. Unusually for the time, however, both Rosemary's father, Gilbert Upcott, and her mother, Blanche, had been professed atheists from an early age, and so Rosemary had grown up an agnostic.

Their differing perspectives on sexual behaviour, and the influence of Edmund's mother's strict moral code, became one of the issues that drove a wedge between Edmund and Rosemary.

They both had the ability to be intellectually independent, but while Edmund appeared on the surface to be supremely self-confident in expressing his point of view, Rosemary was more uncertain in this respect. At times, Rosemary was confident, quick and witty. Yet, on another level, her self-belief was dented by uncertainty. Her mother's critical reactions to her in early adolescence, and possibly the hurt surrounding the exchange of letters between them just before her mother's death, left her with some ambivalence about voicing her opinions at times. She had also been deeply affected by loss in her wider family and was deeply aware of the impermanence of relationships. Three years before the death of her mother, her beloved uncle Maurice Upcott – 'laughing, and talking such beautiful nonsense, such clear foolishness' – had drowned himself during one of his episodes of depression.

So, whilst Edmund thought he was – or should be – emotionally independent, Rosemary welcomed the 'anchor' of emotional dependence.

CELO

After a whirlwind week in the middle of June 1931, involving a dinner, the theatre, a concert, a boat on the river, tennis and two May Balls, Edmund (now at home in Buckinghamshire) and Rosemary (at home in London) wrote to each other several times a week. Their diary entries from the early summer reveal two young people in the midst of their first experience of love. Early letters from Edmund summarising his background and his life to date reveal a lot about this complicated, wilful and astringent character.

There was much poetry and romanticism in their early letters to each other. In late August 1931, Edmund went travelling in Germany, but already he had thoughts of more distant travel in mind. His letters began to express uncertainty and ambivalence. How much of this was a product of his own thinking and how much originated in his mother's ideas? Whatever the answer, the outcome was that, even at this early point in his relationship with Rosemary, he was expressing his wish to hold on to her while simultaneously denying any tie between them.

EDMUND'S DIARY[13]   Clare College, Cambridge

29 May 1931

. . . R. has not written for a fortnight. I think I have offended her. I wish I didn't make such a divinity of her in my imagination.

2 June

. . . I am still baffled as to how we stand. I suspect (conceitedly) that her attitude like mine is rather one of studied casualness. If so, heaven help us when we meet.

12 June [the day Rosemary joined Edmund in Cambridge]

. . . I do *not* like her voice over the telephone. As I like neither her face, nor her figure, nor the way she dresses; it is becoming increasingly difficult to know what I do like about her – presumably just herself – Help!

16 June

. . . * !! * . . . !! . . . She bewitched me absolutely. . . .

17 June

. . . I am just simmering over with sheer joy. . . .

Figure 1.1. Edmund and Rosemary, 1931. Photographer unknown.

22 June

. . . Oh Heaven, she even kissed me in the middle of Piccadilly Tube Station, and I all the while so cold – self-conscious idiot. . . .

9 July

. . . She would be my mate; and yet so clearly our ways lie apart . . . And yet for all that some primitive fatalism urges me 'Hold on to what you have. Chance is more cunning than your petty Reason'!

24 July

. . . She rounds on my religion and my ethics. Oh this is great! . . . I fear sparks, on the other hand I fear I shall shortly be proposing to marry her!

EDMUND TO ROSEMARY

24 July 1931   **Clare College, Cambridge**

Dear love,

Heaven on earth, [you have] begun to argue, this is the best of all possible worlds! Morals, religion, my observation, my lack of grammar! This is simply marvellous

. . . I plead no excuse. I write them [letters] usually late at night and in great haste and often post them without reading them through. So, as ever, impetuous! . . . Your moon infected E.

ROSEMARY'S DIARY
14 August 1931   **Rosthwaite, Cumbria**

The *outside* part of this holiday has been without exception perfect . . . as today: a sheer face of rock and scree to be scrambled over with a wind – that must be felt to know its terrific force – screaming up a gulley and tearing and battering the attackers of its mountain fastness; mists that fall suddenly upon distant crests, and then writhe treacherously down upon you; a lonely tarn, jet black and wind-skimmed, that lies bleakly below the drenching swamps of a fell side. . . .

And all this time, too, I have been secretly drenched in happiness over E.'s letters and love: here also I definitely heard the satisfying news that a room was offered me this October in Masson Hall, Edinburgh University.

EDMUND TO ROSEMARY
[Undated, summer 1931]   **Town Farm, Ivinghoe, Buckinghamshire**

. . . Your investigations into my family relationships read rather like the forbidden marriages list. I assure you the Leach family is *quite* impossible. . . . Both brother and brother-in-law were at one or another time employed by the family firm in the Argentine. Brother now loses money in England, Brother-in-law does the same rather more effectively by growing coffee beans in Kenya, East Africa. . . .

At the age of two I began to manifest that overbearing inquisitiveness that will undoubtedly be my downfall. Firmly and with sombre voice I demanded 'And what, Nanny, do you think of the Almighty?' The Nanny who was new to the job left without further fuss. Such intellect could clearly not go unrewarded and at the age of eight we were considered a likely candidate for the premiership, indeed we almost thought so ourselves and proceeded to take the premier scholarship into Marlborough (age 13). . . . [I] managed to scrape an Exhibition into Clare. . . . The rest you know. . . .

E.

Edmund then transcribed:

> This is what the fiddle said to the bow: 'No! Oh no!
> You should have warned me before the touch
> Of music that it hurt too much,
> You should have warned, you should have told me
> Before you let the music hold me'. . . .[14]

ROSEMARY'S DIARY

30 August 1931   **Bishopswood Road, Highgate, London**

When he had finally sent me away two minutes before his train [to Germany] was due to start, because we couldn't bear the suspense any longer, I had wandered mechanically off Victoria Station, wondering how on earth I could get home without bursting into tears. All the crowd was hostile, unconcerned, busy; so was the family when I got home; they must not see that I had just said goodbye for a world-without-end three weeks to the man I'd only just realised I loved. . . . If this intensity of longing continues, how am I going to get through four years of work at college? And what then? Are we to be actually, if not theoretically, engaged? Can I face the East if he goes out? How much do we really need each other, youth's romanticism apart? Am I just working up a 'situation' and presuming on our emotions and slight mutual attraction? . . .

EDMUND TO ROSEMARY

3 September 1931   **Dusslingen bei Tübingen**

. . . Whatever happens just now I shudder to think what may happen in another 30 years' time when the present youth of Germany holds the helm. There can be no doubt that hatred engendered in the rising generation . . . during the last 10 years is not a flame that may be easily put out. . . .

Au revoir

Your E.

EDMUND TO ROSEMARY

4 September 1931   **Dusslingen bei Tübingen**

Yes, my dear,

. . . It is true, you know, you and I, save by the trickery of cunning fate, can scarce ever hope for more than 'the joy' of sudden passion – lost and gone. How it is I scarcely know, but the very joy your presence gives me, scares me too. . . . and yet I greatly fear that I do love thee more than a little.

. . . Enough, my darling. So. . . .

Your (yes I say it) very loving E.

ROSEMARY'S DIARY

Monday 7 September 1931   **London**

This morning, without a doubt, the most beautiful letter ever. . . . I was intoxicated – is this then what it feels like to be in love? . . . Oh – but it is so strong, it is too good to last. . . . He has talked of 'our dreams', of whether or not he is 'in love' with me. But now – NOW: 'I love thee' – 'I love thee'. . . .

But the joy he has given me must not blind me to the evident questioning anxiety of the letter. I wrote back fully and frankly, begging him not to be afraid for me, to trust me – but to tell me exactly what was worrying him.

'I do love thee, so much, that I can take most of the responsibility onto my own shoulders: and I am quite content to wait, and wait . . . and in the end remain but the merest of friends, if need be' I said.

EDMUND TO ROSEMARY

[Undated, summer 1931]   Ivinghoe, Buckinghamshire

. . . I yesterday declared myself 'wildly in love with you'; or something like that anyway, and so saying was perhaps more accurate than I knew. For my feeling for you, whatever it be, is a wild thing, reckless and, above all, hopelessly irrational.

I am no puritan about sex, but nevertheless I do hold the archaic and to you no doubt ridiculous idea that if two people love each other in the real, full sense, the answer is marriage. Holding these views, and believing myself, apparently, to be in love with you, it is obvious that I should take every step possible to prevent a similar fate overtaking you, that is I should bid thee for ever farewell; for it is equally obvious that for ten thousand reasons, of temperament and career I shall never marry you. . . .

Logic. I cannot be in love with you; the answer would appear probable enough, except that I do in fact *want* you in an all-embracing sort of way that I have never felt before. As usual I don't know. And so forgive me. . . .

You know whatever else besides.

I am *for ever*, your friend E.

ROSEMARY'S DIARY

12 September 1931   London

Now difficulties are coming thick and fast. His letter is full of contradictions. . . .

I do not know how to write down my thoughts on this letter: I went straight out of doors and walked about in the rain for 3 hours and pondered it all over.

It's curious to compare this with February. Our positions are exactly reversed – it is now I who am the more passionate lover and Edmund who fears that I may be hurt by it – instead of my fearing lest *he* should suffer!

. . . Maybe our love will not last, but in some odd way I feel that that will not matter.

28 September 1931   London

At night, after a whole evening with Edmund. We came home together, and sat in the study for a short time after a Wagner Prom. He made love to me as he's never done before . . . for all my boastings I was afraid, afraid of how much I was going to get hurt. . . .

Then he said 'poor darling' . . . and then he let me go, and he fled . . .

I fell upstairs, collapsed onto the sofa and howled! . . .

EDMUND TO ROSEMARY

1 October 1931   **Ivinghoe, Buckinghamshire**

. . . You must know something of my family. . . . They were all 'in cotton'. That is to say, by a process of exploitation that would not be even dreamed of by the most ambitious of present-day industrialists, they proceeded to amass very considerable fortunes at the expense of the unfortunate population of Lancashire.

. . . I and the whole of my generation of the Leach family suffer from 'wanderlust'. Not a single one of them has remained at home . . .[15]

I have inherited another quality from the Leach side of the family, an odd way of being Rebel and High Tory at the same time. I can't quite explain what I mean by this, it's Lancashire ancestry I think; you'll understand it when you know me better.

And now for the other side of my family. . . . My mother is all emotion, almost fantastically idealist in theory, yet withal surprisingly practical. She is one of those people who do about fifteen things at once and get them all finished. But I can't explain my mother, I don't even properly understand her myself. I have inherited from her a temper not too well controlled, an inquisitiveness that wants to know something about everything . . . and that cursed blessedness, imagination.

. . . When next you write, be brutal – tell me what you loathe about me most, and I will say the same – or try to – oh my dear, methinks I love you very much.

Your E.

EDMUND TO ROSEMARY

9 November 1931   **Clare College, Cambridge**

My dear,

. . . The most important thing about my birthday was a long talk I had with my mother. . . . I have much more of the Brierley[16] in me than the Leach, and it is vital for me that I should be 'in harmony' with my mother . . . and yet so often we quarrel . . . And in this respect, you my dear, are a very potent source of trouble – and it has got to stop. You two, who are the most important people in my world, have got to understand each other and like each other – and it's not going to be too easy. My mother . . . thinks that, being a woman, she learnt more about you in five minutes than I could find out in six months. Well, we have got to prove she is wrong, that's all. . . . In short, she thought of you as a modern young rebel, thrown cruelly young into the stream of life, without having the lifebelt of Ideals to cling to. You see my mother . . . finds in the life of Christ the true perfection of human life and nothing less can satisfy her; . . . for my mother there can be no half measures; she believes most firmly that we *can* all attain perfection. . . . For myself, I do not always go quite so far – but my mother is a very inspiring person, and when I have been with her I do indeed feel that I might conquer worlds. Well that's all there is to it – I want you to understand my mother, and I want my mother to understand you. . . .

Goodnight, adored one

thy E.

EDMUND TO ROSEMARY

1 December 1931   **Clare College, Cambridge**

My dear,

You have the elements of genius about you; always on the occasion you are so wise, a strange instinctive wisdom. Yet where did you learn it – that wisdom? . . .

I feel firstly that despite all fears and flickered doubts I am most inordinately fond of you. I *love* you – irrationally out of all proportion to any real acquaintance with you. We are tied by no inimitable bonds YET. I know it – and there is a part of me that is still over fond of telling me the fact. Yet the bonds are there . . .

. . . Despite your protestations – (or almost because of them) – you are in danger of thinking yourself 'bound' to me. That is untrue. You are not bound. There are no bonds. There must be no bonds. For you and I my dear, I twenty-one, and you nineteen, marriage can have no more substance than a dream. . . . No man has a right to marry until he has sufficient money for two (or even three), and until he is ready to settle down and stick to his job . . . and by that time you will be twenty-five or even more. It is not fair to you. Cannot you see, my dear, that in our relationship it is always you that are giving, and I that am taking. But no, you could not see. The half of what you do, you do not know.

. . . strangest of all you have enabled me for the first time in my life to understand my mother.

But why all this? There is one command of yours that I could not obey. Could not bid you goodbye, yet there are no bonds, you understand!? –

. . . A Dieu, Thy E.

Notes

1. Rosemary, diary entry, 14 November 1961.
2. 'My mother tells me she has to go to the dentist to have a decaying tooth filled. I [Rosemary] say something witty to the effect "Why bother to repair a decaying tooth at your

age?" Mother subsequently regales others with this "clever, daughterly reply" and laughs. I, Rosemary, was deeply offended at the re-telling.' Rosemary Firth, 'Blanche Lieschen Brodmeier and Her Family', 1 July 1995, unpublished.

3. Blanche to Rosemary, 16 August 1928.

4. Rosemary's comment, annotated on the letter from Blanche of 16 August 1928.

5. Elizabeth Downs, née Drew (1887–1965) taught English at Girton College, Cambridge University.

6. Rosemary to Martha Macintyre, 23 January 1987.

7. Rosemary to Raymond, 23 June 1958.

8. That working men might remarry soon after being widowed, so that the new wife could look after children, was well understood at that time. Nevertheless, early remarriage could still be controversial. Rosemary subsequently recognised that Gilbert's marriage to Kathryn was a happier marriage than his marriage to Blanche.

9. Rosemary, 1986, 'Highgate as I Have Known It', unpublished.

10. Edmund to Rosemary, 1 October 1931.

11. Edmund to Rosemary, 23 February 1932.

12. Rosemary Firth, 1990, 'A Cambridge Undergraduate: Some Early Letters from Edmund Leach', *Cambridge Anthropology* 13(3): 9–18, p. 9.

13. These extracts were copied by Edmund himself and sent to Rosemary, along with a letter to her of 23–24 October 1931.

14. Humbert Wolfe (1885–1940). This poem became and remained important to both Edmund and Rosemary.

15. This is a major exaggeration.

16. Edmund's mother's maiden name was Brierley.

Chapter 2

I Know He Will Come Back

1931–1932

The complications in the relationship between Rosemary and Edmund now intensified. Rosemary was becoming increasingly frustrated by Edmund's apparent refusal to make any long-term commitment. In October 1931, she went up to university in Edinburgh and threw herself into undergraduate life. She made friends with a wide variety of men and women there.

Rosemary's relationship with her father Gilbert had strengthened considerably since her mother's death. Having initially resented their stepmother Kathryn, Rosemary and her sisters soon became fond of her and their stepbrother Terence, who also joined the family. Rosemary was probably the daughter to whom Gilbert was closest. She was in the habit of writing to him at length whenever she was away – first at boarding school, then at Edinburgh, and later whenever she was away from London. She had initially thought of studying philosophy, but her father, an ardent atheist, thought that philosophy would attract many future clerics and encouraged her to take a four-year degree in Political Economy (economics, political science, history and a little philosophy, sociology and law). She relished the varied class backgrounds of Edinburgh students and, as well as being hardworking, made the most of social opportunities, such as the Cosmopolitan Club, amongst whose members a close circle of friendships developed, which included Rosemary.

Edmund and Rosemary met in London in the autumn and winter of 1931 for lunches, films, plays and walks, and they corresponded about art, films, ethics and philosophy. There is a patronising tone to Edmund's letters from this time: 'And so you want to get to know the *real* me. Reality my dear, is another of our illusions.'[1] Through the winter of 1931 and the spring of 1932, his letters to her became progressively more and more teasing, contradictory, ambiguous and occasionally downright insulting.

Edmund was in his last year of university. He thought he *must* get a first. As he had not worked hard enough in his first two years, he made a priority of working all out in his final year. He was also seeking a job for when he would complete his degree in June: either in England (where jobs were scarce during the depression) or abroad. He expressed some of his ambivalences (and ironies) in a letter to Rosemary in January 1932: 'I spent the whole of yesterday exploring the Fulham Gas Works. Gas Engineering is just about the dirtiest game it is possible to imagine, but it offers most surprising variety and the job would have many attractions, if I am to stay in England. But as I have tried to explain, such choice has to be bereft of emotional considerations! Easy, isn't it!?'

Rosemary also felt pulled in different directions. In the autumn of 1931, she formed a brief attachment to a final-year economics student, Ragnar Nurkse,[2] although she remained committed to Edmund. By the beginning of April 1932, Edmund was becoming distinctly ambivalent – he may have had his head turned by another woman at Cambridge – and he told Rosemary that he had briefly lost interest in her. Yet both Rosemary's family and friends were clearly expecting an engagement. More letters in May and June were also equivocal, bitter and hurtful – so much so that Rosemary destroyed them. Rosemary felt she had no option but to break off the relationship. She did so in a letter that reached Edmund just after his finals.

He wrote back to ask to see her one more time; she agreed, and he subsequently came to meet her at her parents' home in London on 5 August.

Edmund so upset Rosemary on this visit that Rosemary's younger sister Elizabeth wrote to Edmund to say what she thought of him for having rekindled Rosemary's love for him at the very point he was supposed to be saying goodbye. Edmund's self-defensive reply – unfortunately lost or destroyed – so provoked her father Gilbert that he wrote to forbid Edmund from seeing or writing to any of his daughters without his permission. Gilbert was a mild-mannered man 'who rarely interfered with us in any way, or appeared to mind what we read, who we saw, or how late out at night we stayed, so he must have felt exceptionally provoked'.[3]

Rosemary's father arranged for Rosemary to visit her great-uncle Lewis Upcott[4] (aged eighty-one) and his wife, Emily, in Somerset for a few days to recover emotionally. Rosemary decided to stop writing her diary for a while, thinking it unwise 'to put down my tender feelings, regrets, and longings . . . this cherishing of dreams on paper had better not I think be indulged'.[5]

ROSEMARY TO HER FATHER GILBERT

14 November 1931   **Masson Hall, University of Edinburgh**[6]

Dearly beloved Parent!

You know, life is almost too good to be true! I am feeling extremely happy, extremely tired after a successful bout of work and a long walk . . . and correspondingly affectionate – forgive me!

The 'Zoo' [Edinburgh University Cosmopolitan Club] is most thrilling: I've joined a study group on India. There are about nine of us – three Indians, an American, three Scots students – and Rogers. I was the only woman, but am assured another woman is coming next time. . . . We will have a good deal of reading to do for it – and it ought to be worthwhile because we're small enough and unitedly 'earnest' enough . . .

Ragnar Nurkse – the Estonian – is the most glorious person! He is killingly funny and utterly inconsequent. He loves music and has lent me some Bach.[7] He plays the harpsichord, besides the piano, and has a good voice and is a walker. We had a priceless afternoon on Arthur's seat in the rain this afternoon, then I had tea in his digs. I hope he comes to London so you may meet him some day!

Ever your affectionate

Rosemary.

ROSEMARY'S DIARY

29 November 1931   **Masson Hall, Edinburgh**

[. . . Ragnar Nurkse] just took me in his arms, after tea, and devoured me with kisses. And this time I gave back in good measure: I was all awake and on fire, and because I hadn't held Edmund for so long I gave all my body to Rag and I loved him that evening . . . but no, not my body entirely and though almost I think we went so far and yet stopped *then* that it made it worse, for thus we were both left very highly strung up but unrelieved, unfulfilled.

. . . But it's dreadful, being as highly sexual as I am: I *don't* know how I'm going to remain [a] virgin for five or six years at the least . . . waiting for Edmund! . . .

16 December 1931   **Edinburgh**

Something must be radically wrong with me – this is all a dreadful mess now, and *I* don't know whether I'm being a horrible hypocrite – a vamp all the way thro'. . . . It is a mess – life is a muddle! – Oh, God . . .

Edmund after all has always been so anxious – I was thinking quite affectionately, he hardly *deserves* to be happy because he *is* so afraid to take a step which *may* lead to unhappiness. . . . Then Rag came: he does not say more than is essential –

he towers in his own effortless strength and restful self-confidence – yet he is utterly without vanity, or fuss, or worry. He has the most infectious and beautiful smile that I know, in fact in all things Edmund's opposite – or complement, I don't know? And he wooed me forcibly, gently, but wordlessly, and I was swept off my feet, and I just let myself go to him . . .

This evening I loved Rag as I've not done before. He was marvellous – and I felt a warm spring of love that was much more than physical spring up for him. He came very close tonight – so that I suddenly knew I must tell him. And I told him, and he was even more marvellous. . . . 'What a situation to be in!' . . . he said. 'Who'd have thought, a respectable girl from Highgate . . .'

'Oh Rag – it is a mess. . . .' And there's no denying it, I loved him more than ever when he kissed me gently goodnight, and left me . . .

12 January 1932   **Bishopswood Road, London**

How quickly the scene shifts! It seems only yesterday I left Edinburgh in a panic and a muddle . . .

A week's interval, and then Edmund home [to visit Rosemary in London], and to a dance with the family. Here I can't distinctly remember what happened except that we behaved as if we loved passionately, which we did; but I know he took me away and told me definitely that I must realise he could never marry me – we were both too egoistic – it would be a wreck . . .

And then some more about it being awful to have to hurt me . . .

And I went out into the night, and gazed with horror at the prospect of a repetition of the weary search for the well-worn path . . . and then gazed in despair at Mother's miniature . . .

EDMUND TO ROSEMARY

15 January 1932   **Clare College, Cambridge**

My dear,

. . . I see that it would be very easy now to be very unkind. I will be serious. The trouble I suppose breeds in that unfortunate remark of mine that 'I shall never be able to marry you' . . .

I want to be able to say quite honestly that I am ready to sacrifice my own desires and intentions for your good; at the moment I am not.

Four to one was the chance I set against the likelihood of our ever getting married. Perhaps a little optimistic, yet there is at this moment nothing in the whole world that I desire more. Let us reckon it up. If I go abroad, whether you willed it or not I should have no right to let you follow. . . . You are of course 'quite content to wait', nevertheless it remains a fact that it is extremely improbable (if I stay in

England) that I shall be earning a 'marriageable' income much before I am thirty. . . . Besides, the Male is fickle too. – But enough of the odds. On the other side I need only remark that I have not the slightest intention of letting you go just yet. Besides I *am* just a bit of a fatalist. When I left you on Saturday I thought we had given ourselves six months in which to allow that status quo to develop, if that is not an impossible mixture of metaphor. Anyway why not? Six months can do neither of us any harm, and it may do both of us a lot of good. And so why not be happy?

. . . And now, beloved, write to me again. Not in a fury of rage and anger at my stupidity but in calmness and quiet, tell me why it is that you find it so hard to be quite simply happy.

. . . E.

ROSEMARY'S DIARY

19 January 1932   Edinburgh

I came back bewildered, and tired out by emotional storms – when Edmund wrote it was a happy 'live to the present', and teasing letter. It felt to my ragged nerves like cruelty of the most selfish and thoughtless kind – and I wrote back in a fury of rage . . .

4 February 1932   Edinburgh

. . . How *can* I get . . . outside myself – get anchored, not to personalities – I want to rely on something. At first I relied on Mother, then on loved ones such as Constance, Dodo and Terence.[8] Now it may be Edmund – now chiefly my own damn self . . .

. . . Rag is behaving splendidly this term – he started teasing and being friendly directly I met him, and he asked me to have tea with him at Martin's! He jokes about 'history repeating itself' – and if I'm 'shy about coming to his rooms again' – and then he suddenly asked – 'Well, Madame and are you engaged to be married? I followed *The Times* most carefully during the term for a notice about you.'

. . . We were far more united passionately than Edmund and I have ever been, and yet when the need arises, Rag can sever the lovers' tie and carry on triumphantly with the perfect 'friendship' – it's incredible! E. [Edmund] and I would have been dramatic, and parted 'never to meet again'. I am glad – I must see a lot of Rag, for his unbounded sense of humour is just what I need to assimilate, and his strength! Undoubtedly, if I'd not met Edmund – well, Rag is far more suited for me if one reasons it out, so if there's another in this world I'd better not be in too much of a hurry about marrying Edmund. . . . Oh dear, I must be careful not to get caught in the net again – he's absolutely fascinating.

. . . I asked him [Rag] why he wasn't selfish, and rude, and dishonest, and so on and he said 'It's inartistic' –

That's it! Artistic to the finger tips . . .[9]

12 March 1932   Edinburgh

. . . I got a terrible shock the other day. In reply to a letter of mine congratulating her on her engagement, cousin Dora[10] wrote to me: 'I have a sort of idea that you are in a position to be able to sympathise – if so I do so very much hope you will be happy . . . If my guess is right, my many best wishes' . . .

Good God! But really – this is serious! It's one thing for the family to tease me about Edmund – nobody would mind that. But Dora has never seen us, and if rumour can reach her ears, it must mean that it is circulating amongst the family that I'm shortly going to announce an engagement. My immediate reaction was fury – fury that E. should be put into such a position after all the care he's taken to show me there are no bonds, and I wrote a letter at once to Dora vehemently denying it, and one to Daddy telling him frankly the position of Edmund and me and begging him to stop this malicious rumour . . .

Unfortunately, later in the day I had a letter from Edmund that was in curious contrast to the very beautiful, very tenderly loving one before: it was cold and cynical and a little unkind. I remembered that this was, after all, *not* the first time I'd been asked if I was engaged – in fact everyone expected it. E. was putting me in a most unfair position, making love to me, treating me in every way as if he wanted to marry me – and then saying it mustn't be – he preferred the tropics – we could enjoy ourselves now, but soon he'd leave me . . . *he* could enjoy *me* now, rather: perhaps he doesn't realise how much of my feelings for him brings pain and not joy: and when he's 'used me up', he will have finished with me. If he feels like that, he ought to know he should say goodbye to me at once – he's no right to get the best of both worlds like that . . .

23 April 1932   Edinburgh

This is the end. I had thought I *could not* be hurt any *more* than I have been, but it is so. And this has GOT to be the end. He writes in the same sentence: 'At the moment I think you are the most adorable, lovely and desirable young lady in the world, but only a fortnight ago I could write in my diary "I wonder why I have suddenly lost all interest in her. Was the whole thing just a wild fantasy of autosuggestion?"' . . .

Oh Hell! *Hell!! Hell!!!* He should have been so beautiful inside and out! And I *can't* work . . .

But whatever he says, I don't regret it. I *have* touched the bedrock, I *have* been entirely true to my highest when I've loved him. I've known genuine happiness – it's brought genuine grief too, but I have been genuine, I couldn't have behaved otherwise . . .

EDMUND TO ROSEMARY

[Undated, late April 1932]   **Ivinghoe, Buckinghamshire**

Best Beloved,

When the reaction is so charming I am sorely tempted to continue being unpleasant! But no. . . . My dear, I admit it. My last letter was unmentionably vile. I do apologise. But then – you asked for the real me, and that was unwise, for just at the moment the real me happened to be unmentionably vile as well – never mind, forget it.

I send this to Highgate, lest it might miss you . . .

Auf Wiedersehen, thy E.

Figure 2.1. Edmund, 1931. Photographer unknown.

ROSEMARY'S DIARY

April 1932   **[A Break in the Relationship]**   **London**

I wrote a letter to E.R.L. [Edmund] to break off all future relationship, but did not *post* it till 6 June after his Final exam [was] over with the intent not to upset him at that time.[11]

EDMUND TO ROSEMARY

24 July 1932   **Hetton-le-Hole, County Durham**

Dear Rosemary

. . . These last two months, and more particularly since the receipt of that last letter of yours I have had plenty of time for thinking. . . . Surely we two, who have taken so much trouble to get to know one another, should not put ourselves so out of reach that we cannot help one another. . . . Rosemary dear, can't we be friends – true friends. Heaven knows, we've hurt each other in the past; perhaps we've wronged each other. For my part certainly for all my caution I was more careless than I knew. But surely there remains something else beside the kisses; something worth retaining. Rosemary *trust* me, just once more. I think I can help you, and I think you can help me, and I don't think we need suffer pain in the doing of it.

But that decision rests with you. . . . Certainly I would give the world to see you once again. May we then meet when I get home again? Say yes, and don't be fretful.

Your friend Edmund

ROSEMARY'S DIARY

6 August 1932   **London**

Edmund came to see me yesterday. We said goodbye to each other . . .

O Gott im Himmel! He's brought me to life again – he's set the life wind of love swaying in my sails and I'm no longer drifting at sea like a ship without anchor. What with him writing to me rudely in a rather unbalanced state of mind during [his] finals, what with Uncle Arthur,[12] the parents and family, and Ruth and Betsy[13] all telling me he was a cad, and with the superb Rag up in Edinburgh to offer such an unhappy contrast, I'd really persuaded myself almost to hate – at any rate despise – my Edmund.

But the gods didn't mean us to hate each other: they didn't bring us together as if by chance for a week in north Wales [in 1928] and held us together through such difficulties for four years, for us to hate each other at the end. . . . They did not mean that all my patient efforts to understand one weak, loving Edmund should be frustrated by the outcry of my outraged family and friends at the very end . . .

'I want to be that anchor for your ship, but I cannot bear to see you being hurt and I shall hurt you now as I have done before. I am conscious that I have thrown away something immeasurably precious and that I shall always regret it – but it cannot now be helped.' . . .

I couldn't look at him. . . . I was crying . . .

He kissed me and got up still holding my hand – I daren't watch him go – he opened the door – Then suddenly he was back, kneeling in front of me holding my hands and saying all sorts of dear last things. And I suddenly remembered we oughtn't to be so sad, solemn – were we not closing the sweetest phase of our lives so far . . .?

'And when we're grown up I think we shall come back again' – he said suddenly laughing, and I felt wildly happy . . .

10 August 1932   [Staying with great-uncle Lewis]   'Hillside', Somerset

. . . Good heavens – Edmund could not have behaved in a more idiotic fashion! . . . I know he didn't mean to hurt me again by writing such an abominably rude letter to E. [Elizabeth] just after he'd made me elatedly happy, but this letter crushed me so, that Daddy suddenly went mad. He wrote to Edmund on his own accord and forbade him to see or write to 'any of his daughters without his permission!'

So! Now comes the absurd melodrama of family feud! Forbidden by my father to write to me or see me – my own Edmund, my very self, who would not break the cords that tied us entirely, who left me with such memories to hold . . . and my father cuts the tie.

. . . No! You must come back to me, sooner . . . *or later*.

12 August 1932   Somerset

. . . Just sleeping and eating, breathing the fresh air, taking a morning stroll with Uncle Lewis to watch the sea and doing some quiet work for next term, I gain immense relief. No bright hard, uncompassionate young people – no need to be sociable, to strive against other animals for the mastery of the sex . . . For the moment, no false attempts to be happy – to hide from all, my wounded and wounding heart . . .

I *know* he will come back . . .

Notes

1. Edmund to Rosemary, 10 February 1932.
2. Ragnar Nurkse (1907–1959), born in Estonia, graduated with a first-class degree in 1932 and pursued a career as an economist, particularly as a professor at Columbia University

from 1949. He emphasised the role of savings and capital formation in economic development, and the lack of saving in poor nations as perpetuating a vicious cycle of poverty.

3. Rosemary to Martha Macintyre, 23 January 1987.

4. Lewis Upcott (1851–1947) was one of her grandfather Charles Upcott's younger brothers, a brilliant and dedicated sixth-form master at Marlborough, as well as a painter and a pianist. Rosemary was very fond of him.

5. Rosemary, diary entry, 31 August 1932.

6. Masson Hall, then at 31 George Square, Edinburgh.

7. Rosemary added the following annotation in 1994: 'for my gramophone I think – No piano in my rooms'.

8. Rosemary had a crush on Constance West at school when she was aged fourteen or fifteen. Dodo was Margaret Bagnall, a good friend; Terence was Rosemary's stepbrother.

9. The authors have retained Rosemary's original usage of language wherever possible. This includes her use of words that would normally be hyphenated in contemporary writing. Incorrect spelling, unless clearly deliberate, has however been corrected.

10. Dora Weightman, the adopted daughter of Rosemary's mother Blanche's younger sister Lily.

11. Rosemary added this comment some years later as a marginal note to her diary entry for 23 April 1932.

12. Arthur Waugh (1866–1943), author, literary critic, father of Alec and Evelyn Waugh, managing director and chairman of Chapman and Hall. He was a close friend of the family, known as 'Uncle Arthur', and he wrote regularly to Rosemary for over twenty years.

13. 'Ruth' might be Ruth Hart, who was a good friend, probably a fellow undergraduate, with whom Rosemary went on a walking holiday in Skye and the Highlands for a week in June 1932. Betsy's identity is not known.

Chapter 3

A Proposal

1932–1934

After Rosemary called a halt to her relationship with Edmund, she developed a deep attachment to a young man called James Livingstone,[1] a history student who had, since early 1932, been part of the circle that formed through the Cosmopolitan Club and Economics Society, a circle that also included Ragnar Nurkse. Rosemary started seeing James for tea, coffee, then dinner, in early October. The relationship soon became serious.

However, the following summer, in June 1933, James went home to Bo'ness in Scotland and Rosemary returned home to London.

On 30 November 1932, barely four months after Rosemary's father had issued his uncharacteristic instruction forbidding Edmund from contacting Rosemary, Edmund's father died. Rosemary's father would have seen the notice in *The Times* or heard the news from his colleagues; Rosemary, having experienced the deaths of both her uncle and her mother, wrote to Edmund and to his mother. Edmund replied in a letter that was appropriate to the occasion.

Edmund wrote again in February 1933 – a letter that Rosemary described as 'quite mad' and did not keep. But he suggested they meet again and they duly did so for lunch on 1 April. This was followed by dinner two weeks later. Rosemary continued to see James frequently in May, and the two of them went walking together in the Highlands of Scotland for two weeks in June 1933. But, on 1 July, Rosemary's engagement diary recorded a 'ghastly parting from James' when she left Edinburgh for home – possibly because she had told him she might see Edmund again. A second courtship with Edmund

Figure 3.1. James Livingstone, Edinburgh, 1932. Photographer unknown.

began (if there were letters from this period, they are missing): Rosemary saw Edmund every week in July for either lunch, dinner, the ballet, theatre or a film. For much of August, she was away in Devon. Something of the emotional tug of war Rosemary was experiencing can be sensed both from the fact that when James was briefly in London, she had dinner with both James and

Edmund together on 5 September, before going to the cinema with James, and from terse entries in her engagement diary: '29 August: Sad letter from James. 30 August: Wrote long letter to James. 5 September: James in London! Dinner with Edmund (and James).'

But this second phase of the romance with Edmund developed into the same odd paradoxical tangle as the previous one. Edmund had taken a job in January with Butterfield and Swire, a merchant trading company, and was preparing to leave England in October to go to China for nearly four years.

The strength of Edmund's intent to spend such a lengthy period so far away can be judged from a comment in his diary that January: 'The great and obvious snag is that it is so far away. . . . To me this is an asset. . . . Rightly speaking I suppose I am acting very selfishly in going abroad at all, but I feel very strongly that I could completely waste my life if I stayed at home. [Mother] for all her good intentions treats me like a baby and accordingly I act like one.'[2]

Nevertheless, Rosemary interpreted his renewed desire to spend time with her, and his heightened physical passion, as a sign that he understood her expectations better this time. He had even come to meet Rosemary's father again for tea on 21 July. She was certainly expecting something like a long-term engagement for an eventual marriage, although she was also much more prepared for loss this time.

They spent a passionate afternoon together on Nabury Common in the Surrey hills on Saturday, 9 September. Rosemary found herself head over heels in love with Edmund again and hoped for a letter offering an engagement or a promise of marriage on Edmund's return from China.

Instead, Edmund wrote a long letter jilting Rosemary: 'My love, do try to understand; we were not meant for one another. Take it then thus and set it in your bosom, the full flushed rose in all her ecstasy. I beg you do not wait until the petals curl and fall away.'[3] Rosemary was left torn and, in part, unbelieving.

On 12 October 1933, Edmund Leach sailed to China, from whence he did not return until 1937.

ဃ

Before he left for China, Edmund wrote Rosemary two farewell letters. The first was sent for her twenty-first birthday (24 September 1933) and he enclosed a copy of Karel Čapek's *Letters from Spain*[4] as a present; the second was sent from Rochdale just before he left. From his ship somewhere off Marseilles, he wrote about his mother, with a clarity he had not shown previously in his writing. It seems likely that there had been two corrosive factors at work throughout their relationship. One was the tension between Edmund's real and passionate love for Rosemary and his desire to be free to explore the world. The other was his mother's disparaging view of Rosemary as a bad influence on him.

EDMUND TO ROSEMARY

6 December 1932   **Ivinghoe, Buckinghamshire**

Dear Rosemary

It was kind of you to write; I was so glad. Thank you very much. Death is a strange mystery; very frightening when it comes, but often far kinder than it would seem. We at least have much to be thankful for. My father has had a very tired and aching body these last six months and has always been in pain, and the end when it came was sudden and decisive without any of the prolonged suffering of illness. Two days and it was over. It has been a great shock to us, even though we have known for years that it would come that way. It is not easy to realise how much the structure of our lives may depend upon one corner stone, until it be removed. My father was a great gentleman. He had two ideals – loyalty and courage; they are not such bad ones even in these days.

My mother greatly appreciated the fact that you should have written to her. She poor darling has had a terrible autumn . . .

It seems strange to be writing to you once more. . . . I wonder if you have altered. I have – there is little of the rebel left in these days; I fancy you would like me less, and dislike me much less. Probably I am very dull.

I have no job, though on this farm there is always plenty to do. I still want to go abroad though these present happenings make the going very difficult. But I have not yet sunk so low that I am contented. I live, love and laugh, but only by halves as it were. Apart from making the utter stupidity of losing you, I have made very few discoveries among the major problems of this life.

I think of you so much, and often wonder whether you might not just now and again tell me how you do.

But there, I am trespassing on forbidden territory . . .

Thank you again very sincerely for your sympathy, and I beg you if you think of me, think not too hardly. I have been foolish, clumsy, and often ill-tempered but I never wished you anything but well.

Thank you. Yours Edmund.

ROSEMARY'S DIARY

24 August 1933   **Bishopswood Road, London**

Good. That was the real thing. I shall not have a better 21st birthday present than that.[5] Edmund gave me sufficiency tonight. A kiss that was as if the bow touched the fiddle strings again, taut, and firm, and tender and true and the note that was given out was perfect. And in gratitude to that I can be 'friendly' only, and calm to him, because he goes to China for 3 years on Oct. 9.[6] And because of that I *can* wait for the real thing to come again . . .

I don't think he'd ever kissed me before like that. I'm sure I've never kissed anyone but him so, except perhaps Rag. Though we are not now in love with each other, for half an hour we permitted ourselves to be. And now after that half hour of reality I realise that nothing else has been real – James [Livingstone] isn't real to me; the others – William [MacKenzie], Arthur,[7] . . . aren't real. But I'm capable of touching reality again, that I've learnt, and I shall wait for it once more.

EDMUND TO ROSEMARY

10 September 1933   **Ivinghoe, Buckinghamshire**

I wonder what you are expecting me to write. It would be pleasant to know because then I could be perverse and write the other thing . . .

The facts indeed are odd enough. The me that you love is that raw elemental person that eats blackberries and is fond of buttercups, and yet that is the facet of me of which you know least of all. That other person, slightly cynical and always critical, you cordially despise not because he thinks, but because you think otherwise, and it is not ultimately possible to admire that which you disbelieve. Besides you have that sterling vanity which makes your rightness obvious – to you . . .

Have you ever realised that to the outside observer your behaviour has been that of the designing feminine out to enthral me at any cost quite regardless of the resultant happiness of either. Mind you, *I* do not judge you so. You are an egoist, and being such it is impossible for you to conceive that what is good to you, may not be good to me. . . . Oh I know you think yourself a realist; that by gazing at the sunset you have got back to the root of things; that life must be taken as it is. Exactly – but what is it? A suburban villadom of Tudor Villarettes, or the grey solitude of a Scottish highland? Don't deceive yourself, it is more likely to be the former than the latter.

What after all are your ideas? You have a grand obsession that you cannot stand alone, and proceed to act the limpet to a quicksand. . . . Yet you are content, and bow down saying 'Anchor I must have, or else I die.' But in fact, you would not die, or need not do so. . . . Out of your own enthusiasm must you forge your anchor, not from the fickle fancies of another's love . . .

You little realised all that you were doing, when yesterday you made me kiss you. True there was no compulsion in it, but it was your will, not mine. I had no such felt intention. You have taught me to drink deep into the passionate, to reach orgasmic completion and to lie exhausted. The sheer exultant happiness of powerlessness. . . . But like Pirandello's characters we cannot go forever naked and unashamed. Adam and Eve were driven from their garden and became civilised beings. I fancy that from that time forth they quarrelled constantly.

You find sufficiency in love, but I do not for I find no permanency in life nor in affection either. You are ready enough with willing sacrifice, ready if need be to bind your soul into eternity. But for your good I *beg* you do not seek to anchor here. Sail on, steer your own course alone until you come to safer harbourage. I can act convoy if you will, but nothing more.

Oh my dear, don't judge me as cruel and heartless. You cannot know how difficult it is to play deserter.

This last memory of ours has been so perfect. Unsullied and apart; somehow it has wiped out all the long past of striving and misunderstanding. For that I thank you, more I love you for it; and so I have perceived the whole insincerity of this my other self. My love, do try to understand; we were not meant for one another . . .

I do not think I shall see you again; fate has decided that this week it is impossible and thereafter it will be easier.

If you can bear it write to me just once, of all you feel. I think I shall understand . . .

So to our memory, I drink success.

Your Edmund

7 October 1933   **Rochdale, Lancashire**

You must be thinking, I fancy, that I must have gone off into the blue [to China] without so much as a by your leave . . .

I wish I could have seen you again, but it was better not. Such an uprooting is bad for the temper, and I should only have spoilt happy memories.

At the moment my mind is strangely blank, one life has finished and the other has not yet begun . . .

Write to me sometimes and tell me how you fare. C/o Butterfield and Swire Hong Kong[8] will always find me but I will give you a better address later.

Live, love and laugh and tell me all about it, and I will try and do the same.

Oh dear, I cannot write after all, the heart is still too sore.

My love to you, God bless you

Be happy

Edmund

13 October 1933   **S.S. *Hector*, Mediterranean**

Dear Rosemary

I got your letter when I reached Marseilles, having come overland from London . . .

Now to your letter: Yes, as regards myself, I am quite at ease about my setting forth. As a matter of fact I am looking forward to it all in quite indecent fashion. For me the fascination of new experience is irresistible quite apart from the quality of the experience itself. – But, as you say, there is my mother.

Poor dear, she will be very lonely now . . . I confess at times I am very anxious.

You ask if I would like you to see my mother, and I answer yes, and for this express purpose – to draw her out and force her to enjoy herself. My mother *loves* a theatre or a concert; if you can lure her into attending one you have my everlasting gratitude. But mind you it will be difficult. She is jealous, and where you are concerned that jealousy sometimes comes near to hate. You see at the height of our first pristine affair, I was just beginning to formulate ideas of my own, and in so far as they took a form which she did not admire, she laid the blame at your door. And remember too, she does not know you at first hand but only as she sees you mirrored in me or in your letters. Her resultant opinion of you is instructive. She credits you with a vast intelligence which perhaps is only partly your due; and she laments that, that being so, you have no positive ideals to control your life.

. . . My mother would regard you as shallow and artificial, a poseur with designs on the defenceless male. How much she could or does comprehend our odd sympathetic relationship I do not know. Certainly, I have no doubt that she understands it a great deal better than I do myself!

So, there you are, if you feel like attempting a difficult task, go to it. . . . But do impress upon her that it was your idea and not mine; and I gently suggest that you do not make the opening move until a month or so has passed from my departure . . .[9]

. . . For you *au revoir* . . .

A dieu, Edmund.

21 November 1933   **Shanghai, China**

Dear Rosemary,

. . . Now that I have received two letters from you and sent none in return I feel you seriously on my conscience. . . . It was grand to feel a slice of the old atmosphere again and to know that you were enjoying your beloved Scotland. For me just now there is just too much happening for me to have time to think of being homesick. . . . No, my dear, I have as yet found no almond-eyed charmer to wipe my tears away, but you never know, they are very charming and I have only been here a week . . .

Yours,

Edmund.

〰

When Edmund sailed to China after having jilted her so firmly, Rosemary was left in a quandary about her relationship with James Livingstone – she had, after all, been much in love with him for some nine months since they got together the previous autumn. She explained her conflicted feelings to James when they went for a long walk on 12 October. Her engagement diary states: 'Edmund leaves for Hong Kong. Walk with J. Important talk.' James's diary recorded: 'There was a red, eerie, fateful sunset over the glen. Rosemary turned serious and told me that we couldn't continue in our relationship of the previous year. Another day we went for a long walk at Cramond. Edmund Leach has now gone to work in China. . . . Rosemary remarked that she could never bring herself to live out of England: I probably pointed out that this was Scotland!'[10]

Nevertheless, Rosemary and James gradually became more deeply involved again during the autumn of 1933 and during 1934. They saw a great deal of each other while in Edinburgh and made trips together to the Lakes, the Borders and Carradale in Kintyre. While Rosemary and Edmund were, in some respects, very similar – both from the English upper middle class, inclined towards romanticism in their own ways, impatient, forceful and even stubborn in their beliefs and attitudes – Rosemary and James were very different in terms of both their backgrounds and their outlooks. James's origins and affiliations were working class, unlike Rosemary's. He was quiet and patient. But they shared a sense of humour. James used to tease her that they differed in two 'important' ways: a policeman is regarded by Rosemary as a friend, by James as a potential enemy; Rosemary, at a restaurant, looks first at the left-hand column of the menu, then to the right (prices); James looks first at the prices.

Rosemary recalled: 'We walked all over Scotland together, ate innumerable inexpensive meals in a Chinese restaurant in Edinburgh, went to concerts, stayed in a country cottage with my sisters in Prince's Risborough and several other young men – went to theatres, meetings, political and other.'[11]

James was clearly much attached to her. She wrote: 'I remember at the end of a long 27-mile walk between youth hostels, packs on back, we had a final 5 mile stretch of hard road and I was almost beaten by tiredness. He just lifted my rucksack off my shoulders and carried it over his own. The feeling of physical relief and emotional gratitude, coupled with some shame,' remained vivid in Rosemary's memory.[12]

Despite Rosemary's continued relationship with James Livingstone (she later said they were 'deeply in love with each other'),[13] the evidence both from her behaviour at the time, and from her reflections much later, unequivocally suggests that, during Edmund's first year in China at least, she was still waiting in the hope that he would write suggesting marriage on his return. She continued to correspond regularly, albeit not frequently, with Edmund over the four years he was in China. 'We wrote to each other in restricted friendship style, as he requested . . . but I was still attached to him.'[14]

Edmund had sent a brief letter a week after he reached Shanghai in November; he appears not to have written again for seven months, until June 1934 – although it is possible that some letters have not survived. He was confronted by the contrast between two alien cultures: the European culture of Shanghai, with its many western buildings and facilities, and the largely agricultural (pre-communist) Chinese hinterland, with its traditional culture, art and music. When not at work at his desk job, he endeavoured to understand a civilisation that he admired and learn some Chinese. But he was 'almost desperately lonely'[15] – he did not find his fellow expatriates' company congenial – and perhaps this reinforced his somewhat alienated way of thinking about his fellow human beings, encapsulated in his comment: 'We have no entity outside the words we write.'[16]

Rosemary no doubt felt very torn by this letter. He upbraided her for being 'still too fond of me; you must forget me'. He emphasised the point: 'the Edmund that loved you and, that you loved, died somewhere upon the Surrey hills.'[17] This can only have served as a painful reminder that, although what he had written might be true, the Rosemary that loved Edmund had in no sense died. She was in no mood to forget him; rather, hope triumphing over reason, she in all likelihood believed it was still possible that he might change his mind when he did eventually return from China.

∽

In August 1934, Rosemary invited James to join her for four weeks in a simple cottage she had rented at Prince's Risborough in the Chilterns (there was an outside chemical toilet, no electricity and water had to be hand-pumped into the kitchen). Her sisters Margaret and Elizabeth came for part of the time, and they invited a variety of friends for shorter or longer stays. There were three bedrooms and 'we had a "dormitory" for each sex. This plan appealed less to some than to others!'[18] James stayed for virtually the entire month.

On 21 August, James Livingstone proposed to Rosemary. His pocket diary simply notes:[19] '*Walk to Kimble. My refusal!*'

Rosemary's diaries do not record James's proposal. Her response was almost certainly more ambiguous than a straight refusal; James perhaps felt that, for his own sake at least, he should end the relationship if Rosemary was still awaiting Edmund's return and hoped-for proposal. They parted at the end of the four-week holiday 'with affectionate farewells'. When they met again in October, it was on a handshaking basis: there was an awkward period, but by the end of the year they were meeting on an easy footing again as good friends. They remained close friends throughout James's life.[20]

EDMUND TO ROSEMARY

17 June 1934   **Shanghai, China**

Dear Rosemary

I have started this letter so many times that parts of it I seem almost to know off by heart. . . .

I find you in these days a very difficult person to write to. Odd that; for there was a time when writing to you was as much a part of the day's work as breathing, but now it's difficult. Don't think me ungrateful, I loved having your letters, if you can continue to write to so uncivil a correspondent please continue to do so. I am afraid that it is a thankless task.

Let us begin at the end. In China everything begins at the end, including books, and meals which end with the soup; children are the immortality of old men, and you leave the room backwards. Since we parted so long ago in somewhat ecstatic fashion, I have returned a long way towards childhood and simplicity. . . . I am grown younger in my added age; your mind still seems much tortured by long words. That seems an unkind thing to say; but are you not at times too conscious of yourself, too anxious to force your own image into the words you write? You distort yourself, my dear, you are a much more genuine person than your letters would suggest. You are still too fond of me; you must forget me quite, save as a myth to write your letters to.

But under such conditions no one but a fool would write at all, and I should hate that, for I like to have your letters. You see I am really very selfish, which makes it difficult to write this letter; unlike you I hold no brief for selfishness. . . . Your sympathy is welcome, but I am too far, too fond of dreaming. In all my life I have never really treated you as a human being, you can hardly expect me to begin now. You are a voice, and I am a voice without sentiment and without soul. We have no entity outside the words we write. My name is, if you will, Edmund, yours Rosemary; but the Edmund that loved you and, that you loved, died somewhere upon the Surrey hills. I have said much the same before now, but this time it is nearer to the truth. I have begun you see at the end.

. . . Here I am enjoying life even though at times I feel almost desperately lonely. . . Just at the moment I am alarmingly out of touch with all my family . . .

Shanghai of course is a European city, or rather an American one, complete with skyscrapers, racketeers, or what you will. The [European] population is of every breed and not enormously attractive at that; their insularity of mind is positively staggering. It is a world in which sex and commerce fill the whole of existence. After a while such a society might become tedious to the point of desperation, but for the moment the varieties of type afford me almost endless interest and ever widening experience. In the autumn I expect to be moved far inland up to Chungking. There I shall be high among the mountains in a country governed by gentlemen who are little less than bandits; a world where revolvers afford as frequent argument as pens and where I shall be very much in the middle of China. I think I shall enjoy myself not a little. . . . Perhaps if I devote my stay in China to collecting jade I shall one day understand just a little of the Chinese . . .

I suppose you will ask if we are going to have a war out here.[21] Ultimately yes; but not this year, nor the year after. When it comes it will be serious, and Russia will win. But wars as usual will start in petulant Europe.

I am too sleepy to write more. This must be a dull letter. Maybe I shall write again. I hope that you will. I know that I am uncivil, but I don't want to lose touch.

Yours, Edmund

12 October 1934   **Chungking, Szechwan, China**

Dear Rosemary

I can't remember whether when last I wrote to you, I was pleasant or unpleasant. Most probably the latter . . .

My last letter from home relates that you had visited the farm. Good work. My mother . . . was delighted to see you so call again if you are anywhere around . . .

Figure 3.2. Edmund's letter to Rosemary, 12 October 1934: 'Pleasant or unpleasant?' Photograph by Hugh Firth.

Chungking! . . . Scenically it's very lovely; mountains everywhere, not very high but very steep and steps, steps, steps everywhere. . . . Its mineral resources alone are stupendous . . . in fact I'm afraid the real fate of this lovely countryside is to become a second Tyneside or Rhondda Valley . . .

What of your lovers English, Scots and Esthonians [sic]? I suppose you'll be seriously considering marrying one before too long. How odd. Anyway stick to the proletariat; kings and dictators get assassinated much too quickly these days. . . . To be candid I'm still scared stiff of those eyes of yours –

. . . yours ever Edmund

Notes

1. James Livingstone (1912–91), born in Bo'ness, had a long and successful career as an administrator within the British Council, receiving an OBE in 1951. He married Mair Livingstone (1920–2015), epidemiologist, sculptor and close friend of Rosalind Franklin, co-discoverer of the structure of DNA. Rosemary remained close friends with them throughout their lives.
2. Edmund, diary entry, 15 January 1933, quoted in Stanley Tambiah, 2002, *Edmund Leach: An Anthropological Life*, Cambridge: Cambridge University Press, p. 23.
3. Edmund to Rosemary, 10 September 1933.
4. Karel Čapek (1890–1938), Czech journalist and science fiction author, nominated for the Nobel Prize in Literature, was a fierce anti-fascist and anti-communist. He featured on the Gestapo's wanted list as 'public enemy number two'.
5. Rosemary's twenty-first birthday was one month later on 24 September.
6. Edmund's plans changed: he eventually left for China on 12 October.
7. William MacKenzie was a fellow student who became a doctor and remained a good friend of Rosemary's for many years. Arthur's identity is unknown.
8. Butterfield and Swire was a merchant trading company established in Shanghai and Hong Kong in 1866. It now trades in China under the name Taikoo.
9. Rosemary visited Edmund's mother, Mildred, at Town Farm while on holiday in Buckinghamshire in the summer of 1934 and had lunch with her in January 1935.
10. James Livingstone: notes compiled in 1989, sent to Rosemary as part of their correspondence at that time. Courtesy Anna Livingstone.
11. Rosemary to Anna Livingstone, 2 January 1992.
12. Rosemary to Anna Livingstone, 2 January 1992.
13. Rosemary to Anna Livingstone, 2 January 1992.
14. Rosemary to Martha Macintyre, 23 January 1987.
15. Edmund to Rosemary, 17 June 1934.
16. Edmund to Rosemary, 17 June 1934.
17. Edmund to Rosemary, 17 June 1934.
18. Rosemary, Prince's Risborough diary entry, undated, July 1934.
19. James Livingstone, 'Sketch of 1932–1934', compiled by James, 1988 (unpublished), and sent to Rosemary. Courtesy Anna Livingstone.
20. James Livingstone, 'Extracts from Engagement Books: 1934', 1989 (unpublished). Courtesy Anna Livingstone.
21. Japan had conquered Manchuria in 1931.

Chapter 4

Raymond

1934–1935

By the end of 1934, Edmund had been gone for nearly fifteen months. From the tone of his letters, it was probably clear to Rosemary by then that even if there was still love between them, Edmund was not going to propose marriage on his return from China. Rosemary had turned down one proposal of marriage from someone to whom she was deeply attached. Then, early in 1935, she became attracted to a vivacious and unusual Hungarian geneticist: Pio Koller,[1] a lapsed Benedictine priest trying to forge an academic career in genetics in Britain. He had found the institutional politics of his Hungarian research colleagues too constraining, and the Church's influence too suffocating. At times torn by intense guilt, Pio wrestled to assimilate his Catholic training with his scientific frame of mind, his understanding of genetics and his love for women. In correspondence with his colleague, mentor and friend Cyril Darlington[2] on the subject of how to protect women from unwanted pregnancies, he commented: 'Do you know that to prevent fertilisation we can offer a dozen entirely effective devices?'[3] In the course of her relationship with Pio, in March 1935, Rosemary lost her virginity.[4]

Rosemary was due to take her finals at Edinburgh in May 1935. The spring term ended on 15 March, and that afternoon she took the train from Scotland back to London to spend the first two weeks of the vacation in England. On the last day of March, Rosemary's older cousin Elizabeth Downs (who had accommodated Rosemary when she first spent a week with Edmund in Cambridge in May 1931) held a dinner-dance at the Gargoyle in London.[5] One of Elizabeth's guests had been Eileen Power,[6] a major economic historian at a time when very few women entered academia. Rosemary had briefly met her in Edinburgh in 1933. Eileen fell ill and Elizabeth invited Rosemary to take her place at the last minute.

At the dinner-dance, Rosemary met an anthropologist who was a close friend of Eileen Power's historian colleague and future husband Munia Postan.[7] The anthropologist was Raymond Firth, a striking, self-assured New Zealander who had spent a year on a remote Pacific Island.[8]

The following night, Rosemary returned to Edinburgh by sleeper train for the remainder of the vacation and her final term at Edinburgh. In the succeeding weeks, she saw much of Pio, who sent her flowers almost every week. At the end of May, James Livingstone, with whom Rosemary had had such a deep relationship the previous year, drove her up to a cottage on Loch Long, where she spent a week on her own, revising for her finals. Her finals finished in the first week of June. A few days later, she and Pio went on a three-week walking holiday together in Skye and the Highlands. Her tutor had arranged to telegram Rosemary with her results: 'I asked my walking companion, Dr. P. Koller . . . to collect the telegram and inform me of my class silently by kisses – I being shy and anxious. Perhaps the only time in my younger life when I was pleased to receive only one kiss!'[9] Rosemary returned to Edinburgh for barely a week for her graduation, after which she went home to London.

What were Rosemary's ideas and intentions now that she had graduated? She hoped to follow in the footsteps of her aunt, Janet Upcott, managing what we would now describe as social housing, and attended a job interview in London before she went abroad that summer. Edmund commented in a letter to her in May that 'it ought to be decidedly interesting if you can stand the "climate" as it were, and you should be able to learn a lot about slum conditions at first hand'.[10]

Rosemary ended the relationship with Pio sometime in the summer of that year, probably in mid-July, at about the time she met Raymond for the second time at another Gargoyle party. Pio was devastated: to his friend Cyril, he later confided, 'I have no feelings! I cannot love! I am unable to love! R.U. [Rosemary] killed everything in me. . . . Seems to me I lost my soul! If I had any – and now I cannot trust women at all!'[11]

Shortly after their second meeting, Raymond invited Rosemary to a drinks party at his flat at 32 Great Ormond Street. Realising that Rosemary was about to spend five months travelling on the Continent and would be visiting Salzburg and Vienna, and as he was also about to travel to Austria for a climbing holiday, Raymond suggested meeting up in Austria.

The idea must have appealed to Rosemary: they made arrangements to meet during the Salzburg Festival in August.

Figure 4.1. Raymond, Sydney, 1932. Photograph by Sarah Chinnery.

Much later, she wrote to their son Hugh that 'I remember myself being very lonely after I'd taken my finals in 1935 and was touring Europe. . . . Perhaps that was why I fell so easily for Raymond Firth who turned up in Vienna at that time!!'[12]

Yet there was more to this relationship than that comment might imply. Raymond was a dashing young man, eleven years older than Rosemary, and he was sophisticated, experienced and cosmopolitan as neither Edmund nor James had been. Raymond had neither the romanticism nor the flowery language of Edmund; he was down-to-earth and politically aware like James, but he also had an allure that stemmed from his extensive travelling. Most significant of all, he had been entranced by Rosemary from their first meeting. He had the confidence and enthusiasm to captivate her, and the zeal not to be put off by the knowledge that her heart was still, at least in part, in China with Edmund.

Rosemary was swept off her feet.

Who was this self-assured New Zealander who was so attractive to Rosemary?

Raymond Firth was just a little too young to be conscripted into the New Zealand Expeditionary Force in the 1914–18 war. Born near Auckland on 25 March 1901, he had been riding to school on 'Darky', a small black gelding when Rosemary was still an infant. For his first five years at school, he had walked the three miles each way to and from Mauku primary school, barefoot. Shoes were only worn on Sundays.

Raymond's father, Wesley, was a housebuilder, a carpenter from a family of carpenters who had emigrated from Lancashire in 1886 to escape the Great Depression. Wesley was just thirteen years old when he sailed from Liverpool with his family aboard the *Kaikoura*, a ship powered both by steam and sail. Wesley's housebuilding was successful but stressful – supervising by day, accounting and planning by night. He retired aged thirty-seven as a result of stress and bought a farm. Nine-year-old Raymond took readily to the outdoor life that this entailed.

Wesley was a thoughtful parent whose relationship with Raymond remained strong throughout his life: 'My father was . . . rightly thought of as a wise man, especially as he grew older . . . essentially a thinker-through of problems, and relatively unconventional in his own private approach to them.'[13] It was soon clear to Wesley that although Raymond liked growing up on the farm, farming was not the activity for him. Moreover, Raymond was bright: as a schoolboy, he had developed an interest in Māori customs and culture, and won a scholarship to Auckland Grammar School in 1915.

Raymond's relationship with his mother was more complex: 'My mother, more emotional, less intellectual . . . was more sensitive to public opinion – or to what she judged to be such – more apt to prejudiced views . . . more anxious.'[14] The death of his baby sister Gretta from measles greatly affected his mother and her relationship with Raymond. It seems likely that this contributed to some emotional reserve and defensiveness that surfaced periodically in his adult life.

In 1919, he went to Auckland University College. He graduated in 1921 in Economics; the papers were marked by an overseas examiner – John Maynard Keynes.[15] For his master's on the Kauri gum (tree resin) industry, Raymond did something very unusual for an economist: he interviewed Māori diggers where they worked.

The Firths had been Methodists for several generations (and teetotallers). Raymond taught at Auckland Grammar School for two years and became superintendent of the local Sunday school for a while. Just before he left for England in 1924, he became engaged to a fellow Sunday schoolteacher, Dorothy Joynt. While in London, Raymond disavowed his Methodism and espoused humanism, although quite when is unclear. He had his first taste of wine soon after arriving in England and was undoubtedly agnostic by the time he returned to see his parents in December 1927.

It had become clear to Raymond that he wanted to pursue a more academic career. This involved making the six-week-long sea journey to England to undertake a PhD at the London School of Economics. When he arrived, he met the energetic and charismatic Polish anthropologist Bronio (Bronisław) Malinowski, who was about to start a weekly research seminar in social anthropology, which soon became famous for its vigorous debate, intellectual challenge, inclusivity and sheer duration. Raymond chose to register his PhD – in Economics – under Malinowski. Raymond's distinctive topic – the economics of the New Zealand Māori before the arrival of money – demonstrated his deep commitment to the idea that economics is about the management of scarcity, not just the operation of money. In the tiny discipline of social anthropology, Raymond was one of only a very few postgraduate students at that time: he was the first of Malinowski's students to complete his doctorate.

Malinowski taught in London during term time but returned during the vacations to the home he had made with his wife and children in the foothills of the Dolomites at Oberbozen in the German-speaking Tyrol in northern Italy. Raymond spent lengthy periods on the Continent each summer; these trips centred around visits to the Malinowskis, during which he and Bronio had lengthy discussions about Raymond's thesis and Malinowski's publications (Raymond was also working as Malinowski's research assistant).

Although Raymond was quite capable of being content while living or working alone, he found it easy to make a connection with people of almost any culture or social rank. He had made good friends in London. He was closest to Munia Postan, a medieval historian at the LSE, but he socialised and travelled abroad with his colleagues and friends from Malinowski's seminar, including all three of his postgraduate colleagues: Isaac Schapera, Edward Evans-Pritchard and Hortense Powdermaker.[16]

The personal impression he made on Malinowski and his wife Elsie Masson[17] is illustrated by their letters when Raymond sailed for Australia and

New Zealand early in November 1927, a few days after being awarded his doctorate. 'I had my own personal problems to face in New Zealand, particularly the dissolution of my engagement to Dorothy Joynt, and the pain that this caused my parents as well as her. In this I had some support from Elsie', who wrote, 'be true to yourself and sincere *with* yourself in all you do and say. But it's not so easy, is it?'[18] Bronio wrote from London to Elsie in Oberbozen: 'He is evidently very attached to you and a great admirer and said you are among the four people he really minds leaving behind. . . . I like him very much and have become very attached to him.'[19] Elsie replied to Bronio: 'I wanted to write or telegraph to the boat, but *no one* told me the name of the boat. . . . Please send me his N.Z. address . . .'[20] A week later, Elsie wrote to Raymond that 'Bronio was awfully cut up at your having left and told me he was "devoted" to you, a phrase I don't believe he has ever used in his life before about anyone. I believe it is mutual and I also believe it will be lasting.'[21] Elsie was diagnosed with multiple sclerosis just a year later; she died in 1935. Malinowski married Valetta Swann[22] in 1940.

Almost immediately after Raymond arrived in Sydney, where he had a teaching post in anthropology, he began preparing, at the age of twenty-seven, for what proved to be the most significant fieldwork of his life: his expedition to the remote Polynesian island of Tikopia at the far eastern end of the Solomon Islands. In the 1920s, anthropological fieldwork expeditions were potentially risky. The aim was to study, and live within, a society as untouched by western influences as possible. They entailed long journeys by sea with many cases of provisions, almost no communication with the outside world, living for a year in extremely primitive physical conditions, and reappearance usually only after a long time – or never. A young Sydney anthropologist, Bernard Deacon, had recently died of Blackwater fever on a Pacific Island. Fieldwork of this kind had anxiety mixed in at least equal measure with excitement.

The year 1928 thus became an important one for Raymond, and for anthropology. Raymond spent a year alone on the island of Tikopia, immersing himself in the language, culture and pagan religious rituals of the people there. His account, *We, The Tikopia*, was published in 1936 and remains in print; it has become not only a classic for anthropologists but also a reference work for the Tikopia themselves today.

Raymond's first priority in December 1927, however, was a visit to New Zealand to see his parents and Dorothy Joynt, and explain his change of heart about his engagement. He 'valued, [the engagement, although it] later seemed to offer too much difference of interests and temperament, and which on my initiative was ended, amid some bitterness and my mother's disapproval. This was a distressing period. I had written from London breaking my engagement, and Dorothy and my mother did not understand, since there was no-one else.'[23] Raymond now lived in a different world from that of his early Sunday school days – the cosmopolitan, free-thinking, sexually permissive, artistic and intellectual worlds of Bloomsbury, London, and Kings Cross, Sydney. His father, although still Methodist in outlook, understood. His mother and erstwhile fiancée did not.

Raymond was on Tikopia from July 1928 until July 1929. The three years in Sydney that followed were amongst the best in his life – he was carefree, with a secure job in a pleasant climate, surrounded by a circle of friends, anthropologists, writers, and musicians.

(In contrast to Raymond, Edmund seems not to have had a period of his life quite like this, moving as he did to China soon after university – which, while fascinating, engrossing and formative, was a lonely experience.)

Yet Raymond was drawn back to London to work with Malinowski, now a professor. In January 1933, Raymond returned to a lectureship at the LSE. By 1935, he had been promoted to a readership on the princely salary of £600 per annum and was working hard on finishing *We, The Tikopia*. He was socialising with his close friends Munia Postan, Eileen Power and Rosemary's cousin Elizabeth Downs. Through Munia, Raymond joined the fringes of the Bloomsbury set and associated with a variety of left-wing intellectuals such as R.H. Tawney and William Beveridge (then director of the LSE).[24]

His social life was busy: badminton, teas, weekends at Beveridge's cottage in Avebury, or with Elizabeth and Brian Downs in Cambridge, walking Britain with Munia Postan, or climbing in the Tyrol with colleagues and friends, both male and female.

Eight years had passed since he had broken off his earlier engagement. He had been attracted to other women during his time in Sydney and probably also during his time in London. Yet it seems that when, in March 1935, Raymond met Rosemary, a young economics student about to graduate from Edinburgh, he took an especial interest in her. She returned to Scotland, where she remained until early July. But, on 12 July, they again met at another Gargoyle dinner-dance. So – as we know – when Rosemary came to his drinks party two weeks later, and Raymond realised they would both be in Austria shortly, he suggested they meet up in Salzburg.

Rosemary took up his offer with alacrity: they spent a week together in Salzburg at the end of August and another week together in Vienna at the end of September.

Rosemary first spent a fortnight near Innsbruck in Austria. Germany had been fashionable because of the political and sexual freedom in the country in the 1920s, but it had been under Nazi rule since 1933, as a result of which Austria had instead become the favourite destination abroad for young people who could afford to travel. Rosemary met Stephen Spender,[25] author and poet, and his friends from a nearby village on several occasions, but commented to her father, 'I haven't done as much climbing as I should have liked to though – partly for lack of company . . . I didn't find them very interesting.'[26] In Salzburg, she enjoyed the festival enormously – 'a fortnight of Mozart operas and music, Schubert, Strauss and a little Bach'.[27]

Rosemary had been in Salzburg for ten days when Raymond arrived. They spent most of the next week together, climbing local peaks, talking, dining, going to concerts and sharing much about themselves and their lives to date. Rosemary was already sufficiently enamoured of Raymond that she arranged to spend another week with him a month later in Vienna.

When Raymond joined her there in mid-September, they spent a glorious week going to Wagner operas, walking in the Vienna woods, visiting the Schönbrunn Palace and in the Kunsthistorisches Museum looking at the Breughels, Vermeers and Holbeins.[28] Raymond then returned to his teaching post at the London School of Economics for the autumn. Rosemary stayed on in Vienna, returning to London shortly before Christmas 1935.

As soon as Raymond left Vienna for London in late September, Rosemary started writing to him. They had first met six months ago. But the intensity of the two weeks they spent together in Austria – one in August, then another a month later – had quickly drawn them very close: so much so, that in Rosemary's first letter to Raymond, she is already wondering whether this might be a relationship for life and not just another false start.

ROSEMARY TO RAYMOND

30 September 1935   **Lichtenstein Straße, Vienna, Austria**

My dear

. . . Do you remember how you came over to ask me, just as I was leaving your flat after your sherry party, five days before I left England, just exactly when I expected to be in Salzburg? . . . And still, you've only known me for a little *under* a fortnight . . . ridiculous, isn't it! . . . I adore London in the autumn – there will be that intoxicating damp, leafy, yet essentially street and not country smell, about the place in the late afternoon and evening. A London autumn smell is one of the few smells that are nicer than country smells – do you think so too, or not? One has to go away from London, in order properly to enjoy the pleasure of coming back to it! . . . Give my love to London.

Never the less, I don't mind telling you, I am far from being miserable in Vienna or anxious to return home – yet! I am still tingling with excitement at the prospect of another ten weeks or so wandering where-so-e'er I will all over the Continent.

Your cyclamens are still full of life; it may interest your metaphorical mind (or heart?) to know that they have lasted much longer than any other of the flowers in my room . . .

My dear, it seems to me that you are going to be such a serious element in my life, that I daren't go too fast. I am putting all the brakes on and have constantly to check my wilder flights of fancy. I have made so many false starts before, if this is to be the right one, I must make really sure of it.

. . . Dearest, you have not yet had 'all of me'. But perhaps, someday, you will have . . .

Rosemary.

5 October 1935   **Lichtenstein Straße, Vienna**

My dear

I wish you wouldn't write me letters that make me feel almost that I want to return to London tomorrow! Do you realise, my dear Dr Firth, that I have still eight more weeks at least in which to enjoy wandering freely about on the Continent, unfettered and at leisure; and could you therefore consider *pretending* that I am still unfettered, instead of continually rubbing it in to me, how [much] stronger the fetters are daily growing? I just ask, politely, if this altruistic alternative had occurred to you? . . . but I suppose not! . . .

There is one part of your letter, which makes me a little doubting. . . . Yes, my dear, I want you to think critically of me, you must do so, if you are to be any help to me in life. But the criticism must be mutual. Now there are one or two things which you have said, and this sentence . . . which made me wonder, momentarily, whether you aren't rather asking me only to accept not to criticise: 'I wonder,' you say, 'how you will react to certain bits of *my* life or *my* surroundings.' Doesn't this sound just a bit as if I was to walk into your already made life, and take it or leave it? You have implied this before, when talking about your friends, for instance – I am to take them at *your* valuation. As a basis, perhaps. But not necessarily. I cannot live in a house which *you* have built and furnished, and adjust myself quite simply to it. There *must* be a building together, a mutual adventuring, a reciprocal elasticity. My dear, I know that this is partly where that hated subject of these twelve years crop up again [Raymond was then thirty-four; Rosemary had only just turned twenty-three]: but even if your house is further advanced in structure than mine is, there must still be room for a mutual discussion and decision of much of its form and superstructure. If there is not, there can be no earthly value to either of us in an alliance. If I am to accept you, readymade, and accept or at least not criticise your standards, then I might as well forfeit your companionship . . .

That is one of [the] things I am frightened for you about – that you are primarily perhaps too much attracted by my intelligence (please, forgive me!) and my passionateness. There is a third element in me, not divorced of course from these – a longing for sight of the *stars*, which is quite as important. You . . . always looked at me alone when you kissed me: I looked at you and the stars above you. I think

I loved Edmund so much because he saw his stars so clearly; and I don't want to lose my star gazing habit!

. . . Thank you again, my dear, for your letter – your precious letter

Your Rosemary

Figure 4.2. Rosemary, 1935. Photograph by Stuart Hamilton.

18 October 1935   **Lichtenstein Straße, Vienna**

My Dearest

. . . Dearest I don't really expect all to be yet known and understood between us – in fact God forbid! – and I was a fool to have expected even subconsciously, that fine intimacy which comes with long practice and which, alone, really breaks a wreft [sic] in the clouds to reveal the stars one is always seeking. Don't think I am really setting too high a standard for you – love doesn't have standards, of attainment at any rate, only of striving . . .

I love you, not for what you are, but what you want to be – better still, for what we both together want to be, together . . .

I felt suddenly, on reading your first letter . . . how marvellous at last to feel anchored somewhere. Selfishly enough, I don't feel particularly like writing to you – but I just feel, there is my Raymond in London enjoying the same things as I enjoy, as in Vienna, and understanding and loving me a little – and what more can one want from life? To know that between two people, a real sympathy and affection exists:

'. . . that alters not when it alteration finds

Or bends with the remover to remove . . .

That looks on tempests and is never shaken.'[29]

Perhaps I am too cocksure – am I, Raymond? . . . I had, with yours, a long sad letter from my sister Elizabeth who is in the middle of a great muddle of breaking hearts and breaking her own – and I thought, one is tired of broken hearts – one wants at last something that will grow, that is positive, peaceful and sure of its foundations. That there is the chance for such a thing, in this present world of ruin and negation, to grow strong and beautiful, I can only hope to God.

. . . Don't be angry with me – or disappointed.

You are very precious in my thoughts.

Your Rosemary.

ROSEMARY TO HER FATHER

20 October 1935   **Lichtenstein Straße, Vienna**

Dear Daddy,

. . . Life continues to be as strange and thrilling as possible, but my air-excursion to Budapest was certainly one of the most fantastic things I have yet done! . . .

The old town of Buda on the right bank of the Danube is charming. . . . I found a little restaurant, and drinking coffee there by myself one morning, as I was exploring Buda, made excellent friends with the proprietor – in German of course. . . . One evening, I had been wearing a bunch of violets, which I left on the table for dead as we left. The next evening, when we came back, the beaming host brought the violets in a vase, quite revived, and smilingly said he had been keeping them for me! . . . Before I left Budapest, I sent him some more violets with the message only 'von der Engländerin' [from the English woman]! ...

Contrary to general hearsay, Budapest struck *me* as much poorer than Vienna – but that may be because there is less 'middle class' there. It is extraordinary how conscious they are of the injustices of the [1920] Peace Treaty and their lost territory.[30] In every tram, shop and public place is a notice – 'I believe in one God – one Hungary – etc. which was and shall be again'. On every ashtray and receipt stamp and bill is a diagram of Hungary as she was and shall be – translated it means 'She was – she shall be! . . .' With the young people to whom I talked there is a terrible feeling of poverty and powerlessness – both individually and as a nation they feel helpless, friendless, and lost. I didn't feel that resigned *bitterness* and helplessness, in either Germany or Austria so much . . .

Rosemary.

ROSEMARY TO RAYMOND

21 October 1935   Monday evening – in bed   Lichtenstein Straße, Vienna

My dear

It was so lovely to hear your voice from London, coming to me right over the Channel, half Europe and to imagine you sitting by your huge fire on a lovely quiet misty London evening – talking to me! . . . You really are an angel to telephone to me – I tremble when I think of the cost!

. . . Dearest, you were mad, ringing me up from London – and calmly announcing 'Raymond speaking!' I expected it to be my father saying 'War on, come home at once' or my step mother telling me Daddy had died or gone bankrupt at least! But all that, just for the . . . just for the love . . . of me? Dare I say so? Sweetheart, you are so care-full of me – so protective. It gives me a delicious, warm, contented, calm feeling – Like drinking a hot toddy with rum in it!!! Forgive me!

. . . Goodnight, my dear.

Your R.

November 1935 undated   Lichtenstein Straße, Vienna

. . . It is curious, this psychology of letter writing. You say, that for the first time in your life, you write to me everything that comes into your head, and for the first time in *my* life, *I* feel that I don't want to write to the beloved one! It is partly, that I was made rather afraid of letters, once before. It is so easy to build up an ideal friend or lover from letters, who has no real existence outside one's own mind and the blue ink and paper. I am so anxious that you shall be *real* for me . . . of flesh and blood, loveable and fightable, protecting and scolding, and criticising, disagreeing and arguing, but liking the same things, or many of them, still.

. . . I love your letters in spite of their lack of variety of subject matter! It *still* interests me – I'll tell you when it doesn't any longer!

Your Rosemary.

RAYMOND TO ROSEMARY

13 November 1935   **Gt. Ormond St., Bloomsbury, London**

My dearest Rosemary

Just a note which I hope will greet you on your arrival in Dresden . . .

I should like to have been with you in Vienna during these last days and see the change of the seasons – your descriptions were marvellous, and I feel that I can visualise so well the city as it begins to take on winter dress.

London has definitely gone in for winter clothes – the leaves have mostly gone, and the sun too; there is a blue haze over everything under a perpetually grey sky, and one's breath goes out in little frosty puffs. At the moment I sit before a glowing fire, and make pictures in which you are the chief figure.

. . . A little while ago, just as I was beginning to write, there was a ring on my bell – a man with a letter, wanting a job. I should say quite honest, with a pitiful tale, torn coat and thin shoe soles. He appealed to my Christianity, and seemed flummoxed when I told him I wasn't a Christian. He went off with a couple of shillings, promising to spend it properly – but I told him I didn't mind what he did with it. Poor devil – I felt that to have more money than someone else in such cases puts one in a cursedly moral position; I could be rude to him, and he would swallow it; I could question his story and he had to swallow that; I could give him advice and he would have to take it thankfully. . . . 'Charity' is such an ugly word nowadays – full of self-righteousness – and I can't believe all these myths about beggars who have large bank accounts. Modern civilisation is really pitiless in some ways.

To turn to a more cheerful subject – your homecoming. Darling, of course I shall meet you at Victoria. . . . If you said 'come' I'd go over the world to meet you, and you know it.

I have decided that another name for you which I shall hold in reserve for you will be 'Gentian' – a flower with a lovely pure colour, starry eyed, which loves the cool air of high mountains, and is difficult to climb up to, and therefore highly prized, but not altogether out of reach!

. . . The memory of your last letter is with me, so powerfully, and I thank the stars for you, nightly.

. . . Ever your Raymond.

ROSEMARY TO RAYMOND

22 November 1935   **Lichtenstein Straße, Vienna**

My dearest

. . . I keep saying to myself – 'And does he love me like that! – does he really love me like that?' and all the while I feel rather a pig, because I know I won't yet let myself go – you are still such a stranger, and so far away in space. But one day, quite soon, I shall have to open the sluice gates of my heart to you – and then – and then, if it is as I really and tremblingly think that it may be, you will have all the love I lavished on Edmund and more, because it will not be one-sided. . . . If you will give me your complete companionship, a certain amount of passion, a good deal of bossing and criticising in the important things of life, but a fairly free hand in the little things, especially the things which appertain particularly to a woman, that is, the house and the family, the sick bed and the things of the instinct. If we can make this exchange, then we ought to be able to build something really great and lasting, something worthwhile to show to a faithless and distracted world – '*This* we have made out of the ruin we found.'

I wonder, my Raymond – can it really be done? But leave me my own sphere! – There was a man in Edinburgh [James] whom I was in love with on the rebound from Edmund – a really nice sensitive Scotsman – but he made me hate him, by insisting, for instance that he could *cook* better than I (which may be was quite true but he should have concealed it!) while in other matters of perhaps minor importance but still, wherein a man should lead, such as where we should go and what we should do he always made me decide in the last resort.

. . . We went on a walking tour in Scotland once, but on a disastrous basis of purity, which was certainly one of the reasons we quarrelled so much between our lovemaking. It's from that experience I learnt bitterly that one must go the *whole hog*, or not at all, where physical affection is concerned – to put it vulgarly.

. . . *Leb' wohl, mein Kind* [Goodbye, my loved one]

Rosemary.

25 November 1935   **Lichtenstein Straße, Vienna**

My dear

. . . I've just been reading the *Manchester Guardian* weekly, [an] article on prison conditions in Germany. The *M/G* is marvellous – it keeps up these articles (presumably fairly reliable) on conditions in Germany, Jew persecution etc. etc. regularly, while papers like *The Times*, which made much of such barbarities immediately the Nazis came into power, have now completely dropped the subject; and apparently have decided that Nazi Germany has now been in existence long enough to be relegated to the venerable place of 'respectability' – along with Russia, fox hunting, the Tory party, French friendship, and other things which simply by age have acquired virtue in their eyes. These *M/G* articles make me so angry that I am on the point of refusing to stay in Germany at all – some demonstration urged 'civilised people' to refuse to be guests of such a barbaric country: if I hadn't relatives in Dresden,[31] I'd certainly be more likely to cut my stay at least to a day or two of lingering. It all makes me simply furious inside . . . this exasperating docility before mass propaganda and newspaper lies and deceit . . .

That such things as Nazism in Germany and Fascism in Italy exist, and in such terrible forms of oppression, both of art and of liberty, makes me sometimes so depressed that I wonder what on earth is the point, in a world which is rapidly following in their mad footsteps, of trying to make a beautiful thing of life, and above all, of hoping to bring other beings into it . . .

Did you ever read *A Handful of Dust* by Evelyn Waugh?[32] A most brilliant and depressing book. I think it incorporates so brilliantly the absolutely baffled, hopeless, bitter and yet even a little detachedly sad as well as cynical modern attitude. . . . Humanity has decked the sky with so many ugly clouds it is difficult to believe any longer in the existence of stars behind the clouds. One must remember I suppose that clouds can only hide the stars – not touch their real existence. But it is difficult . . .

Your Rosemary.

10 December 1935   **Canaletto Straße, Dresden, Germany**

Raymond darling –

Now when I think of you I feel quite sick inside – do you know that feeling? It's rather like warming frozen fingers before a warm fire.

Last night I couldn't sleep for thinking of you – your eyes, your mouth – and longing to cherish you. I want you so much, now, that I almost can't write, because it hurts to think of you . . .

. . . I have enjoyed this fortnight in Dresden very much – but I must say, I shall really be heartily glad to get out of Germany. I don't write, because of course most letters are opened, and I must take care of this family even if not of myself. I've learnt a great deal, though, since I've been here; all of which has only deepened my feelings of disgust. I'll tell you about it in England. It is extraordinary, the different atmosphere here, from in Vienna. In Vienna there were enough armed policemen about, it is true, but not these eternal bands of marching singing S.A.[33] youths! And all the rest of it . . . poor Germany, she is not what she was . . .

I am so afraid, that all this which we are both hoping for, is too good to be true – I am afraid, so afraid, that something will happen between now . . . [and] Victoria 4.20 pm Wednesday 18 December 1935 – so please Dr Firth, don't forget!

. . . Sweetheart, I can't write any more just now, but that I love you. And I pray to God that our dream will come true . . .

Your Rosemary

Notes

1. Károly Pius Koller (1901–79), an early cytogeneticist, born in Nagykanizsa, Hungary. He left Hungary in 1931 to pursue his research career, working primarily at Edinburgh University and the John Innes Horticultural Institute. In 1935, he broke with the Benedictine Order and the Catholic Church (Karin Koller, personal communication). His work focused particularly on the crossing of genetic material between chromosomes as a source of genetic variation and cancer.
2. Cyril Darlington (1903–81), a geneticist who elucidated the mechanics of chromosomal crossover. He worked at the John Innes Horticultural Institution from 1923 until 1953. As Professor of Botany at Oxford until 1971, his views on genetics and race were highly controversial.
3. Cyril Darlington archive, Bodleian Library, 21 May 1934, courtesy Karin Koller.
4. Rosemary, engagement diary entry, 18 March 1935.
5. The Gargoyle was a private members' club in Soho, founded in the late 1920s, with designs by Henri Matisse. It was an upmarket example of the dance halls that were popular all over England in the 1930s.
6. Eileen Power (1889–1940) was a distinguished economic historian of the medieval period. She married Raymond's closest male friend, Munia Postan, in 1937; Raymond was a witness at their wedding. Eileen tragically died of a heart attack three years later.
7. Munia (Michael) Postan (1899–1981) had been one of Raymond's closest friends since 1924, when they met at the London School of Economics, where they were both working. Munia Postan was Professor of Economic History at Cambridge from 1937. In 1937, he married Eileen Power. Five years after her death in 1940, Munia married Cynthia Keppell (1918–2017).
8. Raymond landed on Tikopia a month before Rosemary met Edmund in 1928.
9. Rosemary to Peter Freshwater, deputy librarian, Edinburgh University, 3 July 1994.
10. Edmund to Rosemary, 16 May 1935, from Chungking.
11. Pio Koller to Rosemary's future brother-in-law Cyril Darlington. Cyril Darlington archive, Bodleian Library, 28 May 1936, courtesy Karin Koller.
12. Rosemary to Hugh, 24 October 1968.
13. Raymond Firth, 2001, 'Reflections of a Centenarian', unpublished.
14. Raymond Firth, 2001, 'Reflections', unpublished.
15. John Maynard Keynes (1883–1946), one of the most important economists of the twentieth century. He published his key work *The General Theory of Employment, Interest and Money* in 1936, advocating government spending in recessions to stimulate demand and reduce unemployment.
16. Isaac (Schap) Schapera (1905–2003) was a South African anthropologist who spent most of his career as a professor at the LSE. He was a good friend of Raymond and Rosemary. E.E. Evans-Pritchard (1902–73) was Professor of Social Anthropology at Oxford University from 1946 to 1970. Hortense Powdermaker (1900–70) was an American anthropologist who went on to study African-American communities in Mississippi, and the Hollywood film industry (see Hortense Powdermaker, 1950, *Hollywood, The Dream Factory*, Boston, MA: Little, Brown).
17. Elsie Masson (1890–1935), an Australian photographer and journalist, married Bronisław Malinowski in 1919.
18. Raymond Firth, 2001, 'Reflections', unpublished. Raymond quotes from Elsie Masson to Raymond, 17 October 1927.

19. Helena Wayne (ed.), 1995, *The Story of a Marriage: The Letters of Bronisław Malinowski and Elsie Masson*, Volume 2, London: Routledge. Bronio Malinowski to Elsie, 1 November 1927.

20. Wayne, *The Story of a Marriage*. Elsie Masson to Bronio, 10 November 1927.

21. Wayne, *The Story of a Marriage*. Elsie Masson to Raymond, 18 November 1927.

22. Valetta Swann (née Hayman-Joyce) (1904–73) was an artist who lived and worked in Mexico for much of her career.

23. Raymond Firth, 'Chronology', unpublished.

24. Richard Tawney (1880–1962) was an economic historian and Professor of Economic History at the LSE from 1931 to 1949. William Beveridge (1879–1963) was an economist and author of the 1942 'Beveridge Report', entitled *Social Insurance and Allied Services*, which was the basis for the post-war welfare state.

25. Stephen Spender (1909–95), author and poet, spent long periods first in Germany, and then Austria, between 1929 and 1936. He was living in Vienna at this time.

26. Rosemary to her father, 14 August 1935.

27. Rosemary to her father, 4 September 1935.

28. Kunsthistorisches Museum (The Museum of Art History), Vienna, exhibits works that Rosemary particularly appreciated, including works by Hans Holbein, Pieter Breughel the Elder, Pieter Breughel the Younger and Johannes Vermeer.

29. William Shakespeare, Sonnet 116.

30. The sense of national injustice felt by ethnic Hungarians in relation to their treatment by the Treaty of Trianon (4 June 1920) remains active today. The treaty between the victorious allies in the First World War and the Kingdom of Hungary transferred some two-thirds of Hungary's territory and population to other nations, including Romania and Czechoslovakia. Hungary also lost its access to the Adriatic Sea, and thus its navy.

31. Rosemary returned from Vienna in Austria via Dresden in Germany, where she stayed with the Gerlachs. Her mother's sister, Hetty Brodmeier, had married Frans Gerlach, a cousin, and gone to live in Germany with him.

32. Evelyn Waugh (1903–66), novelist and journalist, was the son of Arthur Waugh, author, critic and publisher. Rosemary and her father were close friends of Arthur and his wife Kate.

33. Brownshirts or *Sturmabteilung* (Storm detachment) were the Nazi's first paramilitary organisation.

Chapter 5

Except by the Trickery of Cunning Fate

1936–1938

It had been a whirlwind courtship.

Rosemary was met by Raymond on her return to London on 18 December 1935. They had only spent some two weeks together physically in each other's company. Yet when she saw Raymond for lunch and supper on Thursday, 19 December, and he proposed, she accepted.

Rosemary never directly spoke about why she declined James Livingstone's proposal in August 1934, but accepted Raymond Firth in December 1935. It seems probable that in 1934 she had still been hoping that Edmund might write or return from China with an offer of marriage, but that a year later she had come to realise that he would not do so. She had also said that she 'was tired of broken hearts'.[1]

Nonetheless, she did write much later that 'When Edmund was in China . . . I was still attached to him beneath a number of other . . . sexual encounters. In fact, when Raymond . . . first met and courted me, in Summer 1935, I solemnly warned him that I would give no engagement to any man until a certain chap returned from three years in China!' And yet she did not wait until Edmund returned: she said 'yes' to Raymond a year before Edmund was due to return. Her own perspective, looking back, was that when she told Raymond about Edmund, 'R. just smiled, as it were, and said "We'll see about that". He was committed to me from the very first, and this was something so unusual after the years of confusion with E., that I did not take very long . . . to make up my mind to our marriage.'[2]

Rosemary and Raymond's engagement was announced in *The Times* on Monday, 6 January 1936. Raymond was probably surprised that it attracted press attention: *The Evening Standard* declared 'Wanted Easier Divorce – Now He Is to Wed: Dr Raymond Firth . . . who has often expressed pronounced views on marriage and divorce, is engaged to Miss Rosemary Upcott, daughter of Sir Gilbert Upcott. . . . One typical utterance of Dr Firth's was "Since we have no recognised system of trial marriage, it seems to me a greater freedom of divorce would allow escape from those 'difficult' marriages which arise through no fault of the couples concerned."'[3] (Divorce was a contentious issue, with a Bill brought before Parliament the following year.)[4]

What Raymond's – or Rosemary's – views were, at this time, about extra-marital sexual behaviour is less clear. Many years later, Raymond told Hugh that, in the 1930s, he and Rosemary were both influenced to some degree by the Bloomsbury culture of which they were on the fringe, a culture that rejected traditional 'Victorian' values and in which extramarital sexual relationships were not uncommon.

Rosemary and Raymond were married in London on 24 June 1936, in a registry office ceremony. This was followed by a dinner-dance at the Gargoyle Club. They had a honeymoon walking in the Lake District and, in August, a walking and climbing holiday in Austria; sadly, Rosemary lost her engagement ring on the train in Germany, which greatly upset her.

The following year, Rosemary took an important life step: with a small inheritance, she purchased Holway, a cottage in Dorset, for the princely sum of £300, partly as a bolt-hole for the likely impending war. The cottage had an outside toilet, oil lamps for reading, and no electricity or running water, but it was an investment that gave them both immense pleasure throughout their lives.

Rosemary threw herself into their new life together in Raymond's flat in Great Ormond Street, London. Their social life was busy and featured friends from Rosemary's university days, as well as Raymond's anthropology colleagues and his close friends Munia Postan and Eileen Power. Meeting Raymond's colleagues – especially the female anthropologists Audrey Richards and Lucy Mair – soon persuaded Rosemary that she should get involved in anthropology rather than social work. 'The obvious thing to do seemed to be to learn the language and habits of the group into which I was marrying.'[5] She attended Malinowski's seminars, read voraciously and began planning a new future for herself involving joint fieldwork with Raymond on the economic aspects of rural village life, with China as their likely destination.

In the 1930s, China exerted a fascination for those interested in foreign cultures, whether individuals like Edmund, missionaries or historians and

Figure 5.1. Rosemary and Raymond, 24 June 1936. Photograph by Kensington Press Agency.

social scientists. With beautiful scenery, buildings and artwork from two thousand years of history and culture, it constituted an exotic society that was utterly different from that of any European country, while still being based on a highly developed civilisation with distinct religious and social roots and values. Though still suffering from the aftermath of civil wars, it was nominally a democratic republic. (Japan, by contrast, was in the grip of expansionist right-wing nationalism.)

Anthropologists were particularly attracted to the study of Chinese family kinship and religious belief systems. However, Raymond and Rosemary had a different focus: the economics of small-scale peasant agriculture, which was still ubiquitous in China. The hardships of an expedition to China were small in comparison to those experienced on Tikopia; although they would have lived in primitive rural housing, China had health services and postal and transport systems that could be used if the need arose. In early 1937, Rosemary and Raymond began learning Chinese and working with Raymond's colleague Fei Hsaio-tung[6] in preparation for an expedition to Shandong province in north China in 1938. However, in July 1937, skirmishes escalated between the Chinese and the Japanese (who had occupied Manchuria in 1931), leading to a full-scale Japanese invasion across China. Raymond and Rosemary had to change their plans. After an initial preference for Yunnan in south China, towards the end of 1938 they were forced to take the decision to undertake their fieldwork instead amongst the fishing communities of Kelantan on the north-east coast of Malaya.

Anthropology was just developing as a profession. Bronio Malinowski in Britain and Franz Boas[7] in the United States had both been establishing a scientific approach to the study of other cultures. Both, in different ways, were emphasising the importance of understanding other societies on their own terms: understanding other cultures' behaviour in terms of those cultures' own belief systems. In the United States, Franz Boas had established a dedicated following, which included the controversial anthropologist Margaret Mead.[8] In Britain, Malinowski championed the collection of objective information through mastery of the local language and immersion in the society being studied. He built on the work of Charles Seligman, Maria Czaplicka, Katherine Routledge and others,[9] who had lived amongst their informants in New Guinea, Siberia or on Easter Island, in contrast to the previous approach taken by people such as Edward Tylor and James Frazer,[10] who had gathered information from brief visits and second-hand reports.

Rosemary learnt to be an anthropologist by way of self-directed learning and apprenticeship, through the process Malinowski advocated of immersion in the community to be studied, learning the local dialect and the systematic gathering of data whilst living amongst the community. Although she attended Malinowski's seminars, she did not undertake a university doctorate.

Rosemary entered the field of anthropology through Raymond. It was also through Raymond that Edmund became an anthropologist, although his first contact with anthropology came about through the American psychiatrist and amateur anthropologist Kilton Stewart, who, from Beijing, organised a brief expedition to Botel Tobago (Orchid Island, off Taiwan) in early 1937, then part of the Japanese empire. Edmund, just twenty-six, joined Kilton Stewart 'with no idea what I was up to, made ethnographic notes . . . and drew accurate scale drawings of the boats and houses'.[11] Edmund wrote to Rosemary around this time: 'We may yet be exchanging learned papers on the Sexual Aberrations of Melanesian Primitives!!'[12] Edmund had kept in touch with Rosemary throughout his time in China; on his return in May 1937, he promptly wrote to ask for her advice about a career in anthropology.

Rosemary encouraged Edmund in his desire to meet Raymond; the three of them met over tea and again over dinner at the end of May. Early on in their discussions, Raymond apparently remarked to Edmund, 'You have asked all the wrong questions but you had better meet Malinowski'.[13] Edmund enrolled for a doctorate at the LSE with Raymond as his supervisor, started attending Malinowski's seminars and began making preparations to do field-work amongst the Kurds in Iraq the following year. Edmund not only saw quite a bit of Raymond that summer; he also invited Rosemary to tea with his mother at her home in Finchley and took her to dinner and the ballet in early July. Over the next twelve months, both socially and in anthropological contexts, Rosemary and Edmund saw each other quite frequently (often with Raymond).

C33O

But there was more chemistry to the relationship between Edmund and Rosemary than just friendship: their previous love was rekindled.

In the early summer of 1938, Edmund was admitted briefly into a nursing home. Rosemary went to visit him there a couple of times.[14] Shortly thereafter, on 1 July, when Raymond was away in Oxford for a couple of days, Edmund took Rosemary out to dinner at a Hungarian restaurant. It was clearly an emotionally charged night, during which they again expressed their love openly; they almost certainly spent the night together.[15] Rosemary later wrote of this time when Edmund again 'became attached to me in rebound against a love affair of his that had gone wrong' and 'regretted his jilting me in 1933'.[16] Although Rosemary occasionally flirted with other men in this early period of their marriage, this was no mere flirtation with Edmund. It is likely that the issue of their longer-term attachment was addressed again that night or in the succeeding few days. It seems most probable that Rosemary was ready to embark on a serious and extended affair with Edmund. At the time, Rosemary made only the briefest of entries in her diary for 1 July 1938. Later, she wrote that Edmund's 'overweening ambition and vanity made him [again] find excuses to throw me off, in 1938'.[17] Indeed, Edmund might well have regretted his rejection of Rosemary five years earlier – but, contemplating an ongoing relationship with his supervisor's wife, he might have chosen to safeguard his new-found career.

Moreover, Edmund was also still attached to his love of a year earlier, Leslie Scott,[18] and still had hopes for that relationship.

At the time, Leslie was working in Iraq as an archaeologist and Edmund hoped to meet her there. He arrived in Baghdad on 27 July 1938. By mid-September, he had spent three weeks with the Kurds, amassing three hundred pages of notes, but he decided to pull the plug on his fieldwork. He was ill, disorientated, depressed and – perhaps as a result – had not settled in with his Kurdish hosts. He told Rosemary that he had three reasons for coming home. He had mild but persistent dysentery. Hitler's demands for Czech territory threatened war (Neville Chamberlain's appeasement at Munich was still weeks away). But his most pressing motivation for returning was emotional. And although he had, just two months earlier, treated Rosemary as his sweetheart and sexual partner, he now sought her sympathy, assistance, suggestions and support as if she were a sister.

EDMUND TO ROSEMARY

28 February 1936   **Tsingtao, China**

Dear Rosemary

I should apologise I suppose for not writing sooner to offer you congratulation (or should it be commiseration?) [on your engagement] – but as a matter of fact I have quite purposely delayed writing to you, persuading myself . . . that I should only do so when finally I had the leisure time to think out carefully what I was going to say . . .

First let me tell you how glad I am that you have found your harbour and your happiness. You deserve it; you've hardly had your share till now. [Rosemary annotated in pencil 'What nonsense! Little did he know what Rosemary was up to!'] You know, you weren't designed to be solitary, loneliness made you too self-conscious and introspective [Rosemary annotated, 'Nor was I, ever, socially or sexually!']. But now – you don't have to tell me you are happy; you are quite exultantly outside yourself; the beginnings of laughter bubble gayly through your letter like the froth of muscatel – I haven't heard you shout at the wind like that for five years at least! I *am* so glad; and I am sure you will make a tremendous success of your new life but I hope you won't altogether forget your companions in the old one. Maybe we shall meet sometime – I hope so anyway.

Anthropology ought to be great fun – though I should like to know whether its adherents claim it as a science or a religion. Not that it matters much; personally I should revel in anything that gave me an excuse for travelling to improbable places and making resolutely dogmatic assertions on the basis of the slenderest impossibilities . . .

. . . You'll be wondering perhaps, with yourself so matrimonially engrossed, whether I too am likely to abandon the blessed single state. Hardly, I think. True I fall in love and out again with most precipitate abandon but never with any great intensity – I am afraid I sadly lack a sense of serious responsibility. When I achieve years of discretion, perhaps I shall think again.

This letter seems after all to have been almost exclusively about myself. Perhaps that's appropriate enough for after [all] I *am* a complete egoist, and it is that which is the kernel of your exasperation.

Even so I hope that in the intervals of your excitement you will find time to write to me sometimes.

God bless you and give you lasting happiness.

With love Edmund

EDMUND TO ROSEMARY – In anticipation of her marriage
2 June 1936   **Tsingtao, China**

Dear Rosemary

This with luck should reach you a day or so before Miss Upcott's happy demise.

It is not meant as a letter but just to assure you that I shall be thinking of you on June 24th.

My very best wishes to both of you.

With love Edmund

෴

Rosemary and Raymond were married on 24 June 1936, while Edmund was still in China. Shortly after, in early 1937, he joined Kilton Stewart's expedition to Botel Tobago.

EDMUND TO ROSEMARY
11 March 1937   **Peiping [Beijing]**

Dear Rosemary,

. . . I had a marvellous time on Botel Tobago. I was only there six weeks which wasn't anything like long enough . . . so we'll have to do the best we can with the material. I shall want Raymond's advice on the subject . . .

. . . What comes next after I get home depends on a lot of things both inside the family and out; but there's no need to make a hurried decision. If I may resume an ancient habit, I may even consider your advice on the subject! It would simplify things a good deal if I got married, all this emotional bumping about is too distracting. I agree with you that the odds are pretty heavy against a perfect marriage but if two people can recognise that each possesses a separate individual personality with its own private right to existence the problem should not be utterly impossible even for normal erring humanity. . . . I'll be seeing you sometime in May or June, till then the very best of everything.

With love

Edmund

Whitsun [16 May] 1937   **Kingsley Way, London**

Dear Rosemary

. . . I got back last Thursday dishevelled and weary . . .

Anyway here I am, and I hope you won't object if I set about forthwith to exploit our past acquaintance. Strictly speaking, having just been firmly jilted by the girl I had intended to marry,[19] I am not entirely in the most cheerful countenance; but all that . . . must be discussed, if at all, strictly *entre nous* . . .

I tend to agree with you that live men are more interesting than dead ones, and I am looking to you to give me honest advice about the prospects, advantages and disadvantages of tackling some aspect of Anthropology. . . . I have been dilettante long enough, and am determined that whatever I start on now, I really stick to. So naturally I'm feeling a bit cautious. Are you still planning to go to China? . . .

With love

Edmund.

ROSEMARY'S DIARY

(A year after Edmund's return, following their dinner together at a Hungarian restaurant)

1 July 1938   **Bloomsbury, London**

'Except by the trickery of cunning fate, ours will only be the sudden joy of passion, lost and gone'.[20]

ೞೞ

By 27 July, Edmund was in Iraq and writing to Rosemary. He had hoped or believed that Leslie Scott would be in Iraq on an archaeological expedition at the same time that he was there amongst the Kurds. On 3 September, he wrote to Rosemary that 'I had a vague hope at one point that Leslie would come out and join me here, but it doesn't look much like it at the moment'.

EDMUND TO ROSEMARY

14 September 1938   **Maude Hotel, Baghdad, Iraq**

Dear Rosemary,

This is a very personal and private letter; I hope you will forgive me writing it but you seem to be the natural person to write to when I'm in trouble and I feel I must write to somebody.

Yesterday I had a cable from Leslie saying 'marrying Peter suddenly'. . . . I have no idea who Peter is – unless he's an aimless sentimental American for whom she had always expressed the greatest contempt, he must be somebody she's met during the last six weeks!! . . . I shouldn't like to have to get up in a court of ethics and defend her behaviour but I can sympathise more or less. But it's a terrible shock for me – she had finally convinced me before I left England that she was going to marry me. . . . Until this telegram there had been nothing to indicate any change of feeling – indeed on the contrary. No, it beats me.

Anyway I'm numb and completely winded so hence this letter. For one thing I don't know what to do next.

As you know I came to Kurdistan largely in deference to Leslie's Archaeological interests . . . everything about this country is saturated with associations that I want to get away from. To go into solitary confinement among the Kurdish snows at this point would I think put me too near the mad house.

The sensible advice of the outsider of course is – 'Good riddance, a lucky escape – keep away from England till you see things in that light.' But –

. . . If I turn up home again before long don't be too surprised. Let Raymond have the gist of this – he'll doubtless think I've been a fool of the first water – in theory I know one shouldn't let a woman's temperamental peculiarities interfere with the whole plan of one's life . . .

Psychologically I suppose time is a great healer – I mean presumably by this time she's already married so that the first source of mental agony, uncertainty, is finally removed. Still it's interesting to notice the immediate effects – I'm flooded with two entirely contrary emotions; firstly an utter horror at the thought of having to start all over again to build up mental and emotional intimacy with a woman . . . the Entire Ego having received a sharp slap in the face recoils from ever showing himself in public again!! And then quite contrary to all that is the emotion that produces this letter – that without some woman whom I can trust and to whom I can speak intimately I am lost altogether. With no Leslie I shall be so desperately lonely I feel more like a widower than a bachelor.

I do apologise for pouring all this on your shoulder, but somehow it helps, and somehow I don't think you'll mind. If you do, please forgive me.

I don't seem to be very good at choosing a wife, I think you'd better find one for me.

Au revoir

Much love Edmund

16 September 1938   **Maude Hotel, Baghdad, Iraq**

Dear Rosemary

I got your letter of the 10th [September] this morning and it has crossed with my rather nerve shattered moan of two days ago. You are very shrewd. . . . 'It is obvious that your heart refuses your mind the logical explanation that the lady doesn't love you.' And because I write letters with my mind I could[n't] tell you what I did not know myself!? Though of course I did know it all the time, only I hadn't the guts to face the implications of what I knew; but even so to be brought up against reality with a crash in a moment of complete solitude when one is [already] on the horns of a dilemma is pretty shattering . . .

The point is, I've decided to come home and I can't decide if I'm being eminently sensible or a complete fool.

. . . Anyway, I'm coming home . . . my supreme desire is to have someone to talk to, preferably a female! I hope you don't object to my writing like this; in such a crisis you are marvellously useful!

Underneath too I've got other problems. . . . What am I doing? Why am I doing it? This last year of anthropology has in many ways been an absolute revelation to me – the complexities and interactions of human behaviour are perceived with an entirely new clarity and fascination – but what does it all mean for me? I'm not designed as a university professor, but what else?

Strictly speaking, I'm a colossal failure – I've got an enormous amount of ability at almost anything (except apparently making love to women!) and yet so far I've made absolutely no use of it. It makes me think a bit. . . . I am a highly organised piece of mental apparatus for which nobody has any use.

Let's hope I'm just about to turn over a new leaf.

. . . My love to Raymond. Tell him I hope to attend his seminars.

Au revoir

With love E.

Notes

1. Rosemary to Raymond, 18 October 1935.
2. Rosemary to Martha Macintyre, 23 January 1987.
3. *Evening Standard*, 6 January 1936.
4. The Matrimonial Causes Act 1937 for the first time allowed the 'matrimonial offences' of cruelty, desertion or incurable insanity as grounds for divorce.

5. Rosemary Firth, 1972, 'From Wife to Anthropologist', in S.T. Kimball and J.B. Watson (eds), *Crossing Cultural Boundaries: The Anthropological Experience*, San Francisco, CA: Chandler, pp. 10–32, p. 10.

6. Fei Hsaio-tung (Fei Xiaotong, 1910–2005) was a distinguished Chinese anthropologist and sociologist. Unable to teach or research from the 'Hundred Flowers' of 1956–57 until his rehabilitation after Mao Tse-tung's death in 1976, he became a prominent Chinese public intellectual.

7. Franz Boas (1858–1942) was a German-born Professor of Anthropology at Columbia University. He was an ardent proponent of the idea, subsequently termed 'cultural relativity', that different cultures were not better or worse, more or less advanced; their values were each equally valid in their own terms. He was a vigorous opponent of the racially discriminating theories of the 1920s and 1930s.

8. Charles King's 2019 *The Reinvention of Humanity* is a biography focusing on the circle of unusual women who worked with Boas. Margaret Mead (1901–78) was an American anthropologist who became well known for *Coming of Age in Samoa*, published in 1928. For a rounded biography, see Paul Shankman, 2021, *Margaret Mead*, Oxford: Berghahn.

9. See Frances Larson, 2021, *Undreamed Shores: The Hidden Heroines of British Anthropology*, London: Granta.

10. Edward Tylor (1832–1917) and James Frazer (1854–1941) are regarded as the precursors of modern social anthropology in Britain. Both derived almost all their material from extensive reading of missionaries' and travellers' reports, not through fieldwork.

11. Adam Kuper, 1986, 'An Interview with Edmund Leach', *Current Anthropology* 27: 375–82.

12. Edmund to Rosemary, 30 November 1936.

13. Edmund reported this anecdote from 1937 in a letter to Rosemary of 3 September 1984. Edmund enrolled for a doctorate but only completed an MA at this point.

14. Why Edmund was admitted to a nursing home is unclear.

15. The entries in Rosemary's pocket engagement diaries from both 1938 and 1969, although cryptic, indicate almost certainly that she slept with Edmund on both occasions: on 10 April 1969, she transcribed the date '1 July 1938', with a poetry quote about herself completing 'my circle just, and makes me end where I begun'.

16. Rosemary, note attached to a file of Edmund's letters, dated 1 December 1966, found after her death; Rosemary to Rhoda Lilley, 1 April 1986.

17. Rosemary, diary entry, 29 January 1986.

18. Leslie Scott, archaeologist, worked with Mortimer Wheeler. It is not known how or when she met Edmund Leach.

19. It is presumed that this was Leslie Scott.

20. A reference to Edmund's letter to Rosemary of 4 September 1931, see p. 22.

Chapter 6

Have You Been Bombed?

1938–1940

Edmund returned from Kurdistan at the end of September 1938 and immediately went to see Rosemary. He was dispirited and needed a good deal of encouragement from Raymond to be persuaded that he could rescue an MA thesis from the salvaged material from his short field visit. Raymond employed him as a research assistant, and throughout the next nine months the three of them saw a great deal of each other professionally as well as socially. Edmund recovered a more balanced state of mind.

Rosemary and Raymond were now actively preparing to spend a year amongst the fishing villages of Kelantan in north-east Malaya. Raymond, as Edmund's supervisor, worked with him, planning for him to spend a year in the hills of Burma (now Myanmar). The intention was that each of them would focus on the economics of village life and its associated social structures. This was to be Edmund's doctoral research.

As Edmund returned from Iraq, Neville Chamberlain was returning triumphant from Munich after his 'Peace for our time' agreement with Nazi Germany, which allowed the partition of the Sudetenland from Czechoslovakia. Six months later, in March 1939, Germany overran the rest of Czechoslovakia and escalated its demands for a slice of Poland and the annexation of Danzig.[1] Britain pledged support if Poland were attacked and war with Germany was therefore now a very real possibility. Moreover, tensions with Japan were slowly escalating: Japan had conquered Manchuria in 1931, invaded the rest of China in 1937 and was threatening south-east Asia in its militaristic search for oil supplies.

Nevertheless, Raymond and Rosemary persisted with their plans for field-work. In the 1930s, any travel abroad was still a major event, whether for colonial administrators and their families or for anthropologists studying less developed economies. The journey itself, largely by boat, from London to a village on the north-east coast of the Malay Peninsula took six whole weeks. When Rosemary (still only twenty-six years old) set sail on 7 July 1939 from Plymouth bound for Penang, she, like most of her generation in the 1930s, had never travelled outside Europe. When she arrived, she wrote to her step-brother Terence: 'At the moment, the memory of that sherry party in our flat before we left is very vivid. It did seem then as if we were saying goodbye to something much more than a few friends for a year. That we were saying goodbye to an epoch.'[2] Their eventual destination was Bacho'k,[3] then a small fishing village within the state of Kelantan, an 'independent' state under British protection – effectively a British colony. Considerable puzzlement and consternation was caused amongst the local Malay – as well as the Europe-ans – by Rosemary and Raymond's decision to live in the midst of this small fishing village, some miles from the nearest Europeans, with a young Malay and his wife from the village employed to attend to their housekeeping. The British Advisor was hospitable and helpful, but most local Europeans, who had little close contact with the Malay community, regarded them with sus-picion. Raymond and Rosemary did not share the common expatriate preju-dices against the Malays; championing them to the extent of living amongst them in some tiny village must have seemed strange or even perverse to many European colonials.

Just a couple of weeks later, Edmund set out from Birkenhead, also sailing via Penang, although his final destination was the hills above Mandalay in Burma (a British colony at the time), close to the border with Yunnan in the lush mountains of south-western China. Mao Tse-tung and large portions of the Red Army had passed through Yunnan just four years earlier on their 'Long March' in retreat from Chinese nationalist forces; it would be another ten years before the communists would be victorious in China.

On 1 September 1939, Germany invaded Poland, bombing and shelling all its towns and cities. On 3 September, in response to its obligations to Poland, Great Britain declared war on Germany. Edmund, just beginning his fieldwork, joined the army as a Reservist, with some ambivalence. But little happened in the first months of war with Germany. Edmund was initially allowed to go into the mountains to do fieldwork amongst the Kachin.

Edmund in Burma and Rosemary in Malaya corresponded frequently and in some detail over the following year, relaying to each other their progress with their fieldwork (or the lack of progress). Edmund's first, lengthy letters recount his preliminary enquiries: 'a detailed census of the inhabitants and their kinship affiliations, their land holdings, and their livestock'; the prices

Figure 6.1. Rosemary and Raymond in Kelantan, 1939. Photographer unknown.

of chickens, pigs, cattle and buffaloes; the workings of rice growing and markets; sacrifices to the ancestor spirits; funerals and life stories. Later letters convey his observations and developing ideas, particularly his interest in social change as a result of outside influences. The demands of the army made it difficult for Edmund to gather the kind of economic data that Raymond had hoped he would, but Edmund's fascination with the politics of marriage and the changing influence of different social groups on each other soon far outweighed the economic focus of his supervisor.

Recalled for officer training in November 1939, Edmund chafed at almost every aspect of the British presence in Burma, especially the amateur and misguided attempts of the British to reorganise local villages into hill country 'Chiefdoms' in complete ignorance of the complex social hierarchies to which the Kachin adhered. He was irritated by the lack of policy and poor communication in the Burma army, and the arrogant and outdated attitudes of the British expatriates. Sheer boredom and frustration with his officer training alternated with periods of more positive reflection. In early December, he was commenting in his letters to Rosemary on ways in which Kachin marriage arrangements differed from the neat models described by previous observers of the region, foreshadowing the controversial analysis of changing patterns of political organisation that he would eventually publish fifteen years later.

Before leaving England, Edmund had met Celia Buckmaster, a poet and artist. When they first met in 1938, Celia was living a somewhat bohemian life in London, writing poetry and working as a florist, buying and arranging flowers for wealthy people. She had recently suffered a great deal. Her father had died in 1937, when she was twenty-two, and she had married Robert Gibson-Fleming[4] in August of that year. The marriage proved disastrous and the couple had very quickly separated. She then lived with Lynette Roberts,[5] who became an established poet in the 1940s. Celia's first marriage remained a very well-kept secret; it is certain that neither Edmund's mother nor any other member of Edmund's family at that time *ever* learnt that she had been married before she met Edmund. (Loulou herself dramatically discovered that her mother had previously been married when she was aged twenty-one and, until 2020, knew little about her mother's life in the 1930s before she met Edmund.)

Edmund had originally hoped to marry Celia when home on leave from the British army in Burma, but cancellation of his leave spurred him to ask her to come out to marry him there. As soon as she had obtained her divorce from her first husband, she travelled out to Burma to be with Edmund. Despite efforts by Edmund's mother to frustrate their plan, she started her long sea journey to Burma in late 1939 and arrived in Rangoon on 16 February 1940. They married the following day. Edmund, who, in 1933, had so roundly castigated Rosemary for her desire for an anchor, remarked, 'I'm hopeful that with Celia here things will be rather different. On the purely material plane it will be much more difficult to bounce around like a squib, but on the mental [side] too I think she'll provide the sort of anchor I need.'[6]

The army released Edmund back into the Reserve on his marriage and he took the opportunity to return to Hpalang in the Kachin highlands with Celia, although the vicissitudes of bureaucracy and housebuilding delayed them until May. After his marriage, Edmund continued to write to Rosemary every few weeks until their correspondence became increasingly disrupted, first by Edmund's army duties and then by the war with the Japanese. He bemoaned the attempts of the British colonial administration to 'improve the lot of the unfortunate native [with] western agriculture and missions and reading and writing and wages and all the rest . . . policy is controlled by a set of dyed in the wool *pukkah* colonial service commissioners who know all about administering natives and are quite satisfied that the benefits of our marvellous culture should be pushed down people's throats like castor oil.'[7]

Edmund later noted that had it not been for the war – which, through the interruption to his fieldwork, had prevented him gathering consistent economic data – he and Raymond would have built parallel careers around the economics of less developed societies.[8] However, even in 1940, he was already beginning to move away from Raymond's influence, becoming 'more and more tied up in the problem of trying to unravel the Kinship tangle, while economics of any sort becomes more and more remote'.[9] By September 1940, he was recalled back into the army again, only this time to travel throughout the Kachin highlands as a recruiting officer. In the process, he encountered a variety of types of political organisation amongst Kachin hill villages and Shans from the plains. Observing this diversity was to be crucial in driving Edmund's thinking towards a radical rejection of the traditional concept of 'tribes' as essentially closed systems. This was to become a distinctive but controversial feature of his thinking.

ༀༀ

On the coast in Kelantan, Raymond and Rosemary were adopting a numerical approach; Raymond gathered information on the fishing economy from the men, going down to the beach every afternoon to see the catches and hear the price of fish. Rosemary studied the domestic life and position of women. As was the case for Edmund, this was slow work that first required developing trust amongst the locals as well as a real fluency in the local dialect, which took many weeks (they worked without an interpreter; Edmund employed an interpreter initially). Fluency and flexibility paid dividends: when they undertook a short comparative study further south, their 'knowledge of fishing and knowledge of the dialect . . . enabled us to make quick and direct contact with fishermen at first [either] hostile, silent or shy. [The British colonial administrator] was frankly amazed he said when he came with us one day to see how we worked, to see me squatting cross legged . . . exchanging banter with the women, whom he swore had never seen a white woman out of a car – much less spoken to one!'[10]

Data gathering meant hours of conversation, day in, day out, and assiduous note-taking and cross-checking. They administered simple medicines and attended births, weddings, exorcisms and funerals. Rosemary noted how 'Many of the women are in fact more literate than their husbands, and there are several who have schools to teach the Koran to small boys, while their husbands cannot read or write!'[11] She also made some striking observations on the interrelationships of the three main ethnic groups: 'The position of the Chinese and of the Indians is . . . the perfect proof that the Jewish question is entirely sociological and not physical or religious. The Chinese . . . do not, ever, in Malaya, cultivate the soil. The Chinese and Indians who come and live here, come as . . . traders and money lenders. Consequently they have acquired exactly the same reputation as the Jews . . . cunning, generally rich, plausible and polite and ingratiating, heartless and financially minded, levying interest forbidden to all good Muhammedans. – This is the general attitude! Yet in China, the peasant is as hard working [an] agriculturalist as any, who is exploited, in his turn, by the wily Japanese. But [in Malaya] he is the outsider, the bourgeois, the shylock, the infidel. . . . It is a striking parallel.'[12]

Her focus was on the economics of housekeeping, which, in 1939, had 'only recently been thought fit for scientific study',[13] and on the social context, including divorce and polygamy. In this, Rosemary consciously modelled herself on Raymond's colleague Audrey Richards, deciding that: 'Without having any ambition to match her theoretical competence, after attending some of her lectures . . . and reading her Bemba monograph, . . . her approach to anthropology was the only sensible one for a woman to adopt. I made her my role model from the first and hoped to match the simplicity and polish of her writing in my own work.'[14] She also sought out Audrey's *Land, Labour and Diet* when it was published, just before her Malay expedition. Audrey, a self-confident woman forging an academic career for herself, with a keen sense of the extent to which women were often 'invisible' in British society, had completed two major periods of fieldwork on women and the production of food and nutrition amongst the Bemba in East Africa.[15]

For Rosemary, as a woman in a Muslim society, learning appropriate behaviour was particularly important; she later said, 'you have got to make yourself . . . temporarily into a Malay woman. But . . . to make yourself into a Malay woman is not what you are paid to go out there and do. You have also . . . to be the scientist watching and looking at what is going on.'[16]

The most challenging aspects of anthropology for Edmund, with his engineering background, were developing and testing general principles, and understanding the impact of the observer. For Rosemary however (as for Malinowski) a key attainment was to fully understand not just the behaviour, but the culture and perspective of the society studied: 'To me, the experience of becoming an anthropologist includes that of learning to play a part so well that one may occasionally forget whether it is a natural one or not . . .'[17] She also commented later that 'if there is one experience in my life which has changed my whole attitude to other things, it is the field experience . . . it is having been forced in the field to gain a new way of looking at things, a new perspective, and then to come back to the ordinary life and see one's own life in [a different] way.'[18]

Rosemary and Raymond worked together closely, sharing and discussing their insights into their hosts' lives. The skills and insights Rosemary acquired while living with the Malay villagers were to prove indispensable, not only for her professional career but also for her subsequent work during the Second World War.

Although Rosemary, her family and friends had anticipated for at least a couple of years that a war with Hitler's Germany was increasingly likely, when war came it was nevertheless a great shock. Raymond and Rosemary had to consider the consequences for their livelihood: the LSE was evacuated to Cambridge, retaining only a skeleton staff. Malinowski, the head of the anthropology department at the LSE, had been teaching in the United States. Upon the outbreak of war, he chose to remain there. There was some doubt as to whether the department would survive the war at all. Raymond and Rosemary had funds for less than a year, and anyone leaving Malaya required a special emigration licence.[19] Despite this, for a brief period Rosemary and Raymond apparently seriously considered travelling north through Burma into Yunnan in south-west China (their preferred fieldwork area at one point in 1938). Edmund hoped they could then meet up in Burma, but Raymond and Rosemary decided against the idea, presumably because of the escalation of the war in Europe.[20]

When war was declared, Rosemary naturally became anxious about her family back in England. Letters could take up to five weeks to arrive, so Rosemary was always in a state of uncertainty as she never had up-to-date news. Yet, between September 1939 and May 1940, hostilities hardly touched most British civilians. Rosemary's father anxiously followed news of the German occupation of Denmark and Norway, and the Soviet invasion of Finland: 'I was . . . much depressed by a broadcast from a British correspondent, arrived in Viipuri from Helsinki yesterday afternoon just in time to enjoy the worst Russian air raid they have yet had. The first bomb turned his hotel into a cascade of glass but he got safely to the nearest shelter which was full of Finns behaving as if they were just sheltering from a heavy shower of rain. . . . The constant interruption of life and nervous strain must be very hard to bear. I hope that we shall have as much courage if the storm bursts upon us this spring.'[21]

The situation did change dramatically when, on 10 May 1940, Germany invaded France, the Netherlands and Belgium, and swept through to the Channel coast, necessitating the evacuation of over three hundred thousand troops from Dunkirk by 4 June and threatening an imminent invasion of Britain. Rosemary and Raymond were nearing completion of their study of the Kelantan village at this moment, with a census of 1,300 villagers. Although both Rosemary and Raymond would have wished to stay longer to complete their fieldwork, they were anxious not to be stranded abroad in the event of a German invasion of England.

They left Kelantan at the very end of June 1940. Rosemary concluded that 'On the whole I think I have been more consistently and deeply contented here in our Malay village than I've ever been anywhere in my life before.'[22]

ROSEMARY TO HER FATHER

22 July 1939   **S.S. *Perseus*: Just left Port Sudan**

My dear Daddy,

After yesterday and especially after last night I really feel I know what heat is. I suppose you can hardly imagine a temperature of 108° [42°C] . . . The most surprising thing . . . was the wind which blew off the desert: it was hot, as hot as the air which comes out of an oven.

[. . . Suez] was a lovely sight, big rocky mountains, purple on one side . . . people walking indiscriminately on footpath or road, women squatting in groups on the kerbs chatting; veiled women with children – charming children, very dirty, galore. Piles of eastern fruit and vegetables for sale. Flies. Smells. A man selling iced water out of a kind of machine he carried on his back which looked like a cross between a geyser and bagpipes! . . .

And then we came into the sandstorm. . . . [putting] an unearthly veil over sight so that you can see a fair distance out to sea but through this queer coloured haze, a ghastly blue green light which makes the waters look like the waters of death. . . . In addition to this there is the peculiar smell of the sand – an acrid unpleasant smell, which at first I thought was burning paint. . . . Meanwhile the ship slips silently and slowly through these steel waves, there is a bit of wind but not much, and the fog horn booms every five minutes. . . . A most peculiar experience . . .

The next day we left the Red Sea and came into the Indian Ocean where we met the Monsoon. . . . Suddenly a flash of spray came on deck. . . . Conversation lapsed noticeably. A few passengers disappeared. . . . Then I realised that the ship was rolling and squirming like a worm, – crash after crash of water coming over the starboard side, and I was enjoying it, hilariously! . . . The decks were drenched, and half the passengers beneath. It lasted only about two days and I never felt fitter in my life – I would have liked it rougher – it exhilarated me like rain and wind on a mountain. . . .

Circulate this letter will you, and keep for reference? My best love to you.

Rosemary.

EDMUND TO ROSEMARY

22 July 1939   **M.V. *Menestheus*, Birkenhead**

Dear Rosemary

This is to greet you in Terengganu [Malaya] [23] and to let you know that I too have really started . . .

So far as personal matters are concerned – Celia – 'onions' to you! – has got her divorce and if nothing startling happens in the interval I shall probably marry her when I get back, but her fancies are as flexible as mine and nobody is really committed to anything. There's only one thing that could be said in favour of such a marriage but it's definitely a bull point – we've more or less lived together for the last month or so and both liked it; but love of the all-consuming passionate kind – well that's another matter, if you understand me! . . .

With love. Edmund.

17 August 1939   **Penang, Malaya [en route to Burma]**

Dear Rosemary

. . . In my own person I think I am more at peace than for a long time. Certainly there's none of the appalling emotional tension of a year ago or of the horrified and distracted numbness of last November – you 'talked' me out of that as much as anyone and I'm very grateful. That and the job with Raymond were the things that really 'saved my soul' from a really bad crumpling and there's an enormous lot that I owe to both of you.

The future's still a bit vague. . . . I've said I will marry Celia and she's said she will marry me, but I wouldn't be really surprised if she didn't wait for me. She means to of course, but a year's a long time to sleep alone. . . . Meanwhile good luck to you both; and don't forget my address –

Love! Edmund.

☙❧

On 1 September 1939, Germany invaded Poland. On 3 September, Great Britain declared war on Germany. At this point, Rosemary and Raymond had not yet found accommodation in a local fishing village. They therefore heard the news while staying temporarily with British colonial administrators in Kelantan.

ROSEMARY TO HONOR TRACEY[24]

September 1939   **Bacho'k, near Kota Bharu, Kelantan**

Dear Honor,

. . . It was funny how we heard the news of war. These things are always so different from what one imagines. . . . The day that Poland was attacked, we were sitting on the beach at dusk . . . midday in Europe. The telephone went, just as someone had made some particularly good joke, and amid a roar of laughter, one man got up to answer it. He came back while we were still laughing and announced in the voice of one telling a very tall story which he hardly expects to be believed, 'The Germans are attacking Poland on all sides.' Someone said: 'Are you joking or serious?' Someone else 'Well, at last! Now we're for it' . . . 'I don't believe it!' I said. And I didn't then, we'd heard so many rumours that the Nazis had marched. But as we broke up, the other Europeans to go back to Kota Bharu for dinner in their cars . . . the [telephone] bell went again. I answered it, just as they left, and someone said, a different person this time: 'I rang up to tell Captain Greaves, Poland is being bombed on all sides'. 'I see' I said stupidly. 'All right, I'll tell him. Thank you'. And then I *knew*, and understood, and felt perfectly awful. I remember R. and I walked back to our bungalow for dinner hardly saying a word, but all the time I kept repeating to myself – 'Poland being bombed, my

God, Poland being bombed. They're bombing Poland now.' . . . We hardly spoke during dinner. It felt awful, ghastly. It did not seem to be of more than secondary importance that England hadn't yet declared war.

. . . Let me know how you are, and poor old misty musty London in war time in winter!

My love to you and write to me – Rosemary

ROSEMARY TO HER FATHER

5 September 1939   Bacho'k, Kelantan

My dearest Daddy

. . . So far all our news, which has been of the very scantiest, has come from the occasional visitors, and their telephone calls when war was actually declared. . . .

I feel very cut off and ignorant of many details at home which we are dying to know. I don't know where your address will be, or indeed the address of any of our friends, as I suppose nearly everyone has left London? We do not know if you have been bombed, if Terence [Rosemary's stepbrother] has been conscripted or anything. All we know is, there is war and it is difficult to apprehend all that will mean to us and to you. . . .

It makes it very difficult for us to make any plans at all – or to get on with our work. For instance, is it worth building a house as we intended, if we may not be able to stay in it more than a few months, and so on. I feel very, very, sorry for Raymond who has been looking forward to this bout of field work for so long, and now it seems he won't be able to finish it properly. . . .

At any rate we are both here *together* which is a lot. . . .

Look after yourselves and don't worry about us and send us all the news you can.

Your very loving Rosemary.

HER FATHER TO ROSEMARY[25]

9 September 1939   Bishopswood Road, Highgate, London

My dearest Rosemary,

Here in London we sit and wait: even the innumerable A.R.P. [Air Raid Precautions][26] people have little else to do at the moment. We can only be thankful for the quiet interlude, but that is no reason for thinking that we shall not get horrors enough soon. The Germans obviously intend to finish Poland before attending to the war in the West, and that they are doing effectively and very quickly. . . .

. . . We are finding your gramophone a solace as the B.B.C. only gives us one programme now of utter trash. I hope your property deposited here will survive.[27] The Govt. does not promise us any compensation for destruction – only as much as they can afford when the war is over, and that may not be much.

Terence is driving an ambulance for Westminster Hospital until his turn for conscription comes.

Our best love to you both. I have been thinking of last Christmas and wondering when we shall all be together again, if ever.

Your affect. Daddy.

 လၢၤ

In September 1939, Celia was still in London and Edmund was on his way into the Burmese mountains, about to start work among the Kachin.

EDMUND TO ROSEMARY

8 September 1939   **Bhamo, Burma**

Dear Rosemary

. . . Since I arrived in Rangoon my plans have been more or less . . . in crisis. . . . Then while I was on the way up river, the war started. . . . Still, the easy-going attitude of the tiny European community here was very calming to the nerves, and the war began to seem a long way off after all, and with the mountains so invitingly near. . . .

. . . In due course I reached Sinlum and found Wilkie the D.C. [District Commissioner] dressed in grey flannels and a sports coat sitting in front of a roaring fire. . . . It was wildly exciting . . . it was like being back in [China], the same jungle, the same flowers and butterflies, the same views, indeed very nearly the same mountains. . . . Wilkie is an entirely marvellous person, entirely unperturbed by the war. . . .

And the place is an anthropological zoo. . . . There was a bazaar in Sinlum the day I was there, and there were present Shans from the plains. . . . Chinese from Yunnan; Jingpaws, Atsis, Hkauris (three varieties of Kachin); Yawyins . . . and then just a few odd individual Burmese, Indians, and Karens. Could anything be simpler?

Until a few years ago the administration didn't bother about the Kachins. . . . Then the authorities got bitten with the bug of 'indirect rule' and it was decided to 're-establish the power of the Chiefs'. . . . Whether the consequences will be as intended is another matter. . . . Still what a chance for sociological comparisons. You see just across the border there are Kachins who are not Christian and not administered at all. . . .

Thank you for your very kind and sensitive letter about me and matrimony and Celia. . . . I feel that for the first time I have really begun to understand and sympathise with the inner feelings of other people – I've become more 'human'. . . . Almost for the first time in my life I really feel that I know what I am doing. . . .

Celia for instance . . . she is a personality who becomes more and more interesting the deeper one gets, she is an extraordinarily 'onion-like' person. . . . That's all

Figure 6.2. Edmund in the Burma hills, possibly at the district commissioner's house at Sinlum. Photographer unknown.

very well you may say, but are you in love? But there is no answer to that, love is no simple counter, black or white. . . . A year ago Celia and I were both of us being butchered for love's sake. . . . Can you blame us if we are love-shy? . . . It seems to me the argument should not be 'if you love one another then you will be able to live together happily' but rather 'if you can live together happily . . . then indeed you have found true love.' You've good cause to be suspicious I know! But as I say . . . I know what I'm doing. . . . Are you satisfied? . . . And now to work. I start off on Monday with a caravan of fourteen mules – can you imagine!!

Love to you both . . .

Love E.

16 September 1939   **Hpalang, Kachin Hills, Burma**

Dear Rosemary

Goodness only knows when this will reach you. . . . I'm in Heaven, an entirely unbelievable spot 5000 feet up in the air on a hill-crest looking down into China, and 45 miles from the nearest motor-car, and at least 20 from the nearest radio. The Kachins are just glorious; the most fantastic crowd of ragamuffins you ever saw, but real aristocrats – they treat you as an equal without any cringing sycophancy.

At the moment I have no interpreter, and nobody understands a word I say and we are all having a whale of a time, but everyone thinks it's a terrific joke and we are all great friends. They are not unlike my Kurds in some ways, blood feuds and all the rest, but I'm enjoying this far more – last year I was at heart scared stiff – here at least there is no danger of anyone bumping me off and that does make a difference! . . . Anthropologically the thing is just a glorious muddle. . . .

Life is complete bedlam: I've landed in the middle of a harvest festival without grasping what was happening. . . . Anyway tomorrow we slaughter a buffalo – and I have got invited to that! . . .

Love to you both, Edmund.

ROSEMARY TO HER FATHER

21 October 1939   **Bacho'k, Kelantan**

My dearest Daddy

. . . I cannot imagine anything more gloomy than living in London just now. . . .

I do wish by some stroke of magic you could be transported out here! It is so lovely, and so peaceful, it is almost incredible to think of a war taking place any-where. . . . We have an ideal spot [for] our own house which stands in the middle of the village, facing the sea which is a few hundred yards away only, and yet we are just a little on our own, no native houses absolutely near. The reason for this is delicious. There is a black brackish pool of water rather dark and mysterious to the side of our house. It transpired after a bit that a '*Hantu*' (a Spirit) lives there. We were told this by a delightful old man of 70 in just the same tone of voice as he tells us where his son lives. He also told us the name of the spirit. 'No Malay', he said, 'would dare to live where the *Tuan*[28] lives.'

I think it must have been due to the machinations of the said *Hantu* that our house was so long in building too. The District Officer, an educated and charming Malay, originally told us it would only take a week to put up a house; but it dragged on and on until after five weeks we arrived, having been promised it was ready, to find no roof on half the house, no doors, windows not made and the place absolutely swarming with workmen. . . . We had arrived with eight large packing cases, two army sacks with our camp beds, eight trunks, four chairs and a table, a bath, a crate of kitchen equipment, several braziers, a roll of mats, two copper vases bought as specimens, not to mention two servants and *their* luggage. Also a sack of rice! . . . And we surveyed our roofless house in despair. . . .

Next morning our [housekeeper] Marmo't, walked down the beach to meet us. His face was long. He said they had been driven nearly mad with mosquitoes, they had no fire, and had to eat bananas for supper, the house couldn't be finished for three more days, and in short he really didn't think we could stand it.

We walked back along the beach with him in the most profound gloom. Finding the roof at least finished, we firmly announced our intention to sleep there, and the men must finish the house round us. We demanded a fire at once.

Our presence . . . galvanised the builders into activity, and to tell the truth, I think if we had not turned up, the house could have taken another month! . . .

If only it keeps out the rain during the monsoon it will be perfect. It is built raised on stakes about 3 ft. off the ground, entirely of bamboo. Bamboo stakes and the walls are plaited bamboo like very thick raffia, in strips an inch and a half wide. These are lashed to the stakes by bamboo thread, no nails anywhere, as bamboo won't hold a nail. The floor is wooden boards, laid loosely together so that you can often see the chickens running under the house. . . .

We have discovered Marmo't's wife is a superb cook. Every evening we have a big bowl of rice and the most delectable fishes of all kinds, straight out of the sea, and spiced and grilled, or cooked in coconut milk and curry. Local vegetables such as pumpkin, a native string bean, aubergines (or egg plants), ladies' fingers, cooked native cucumbers – all cooked in coconut milk and coconut oil, with freshly ground spices every day – it makes mouth-watering meals, not hot as an Indian curry, but just spiced and deliciously flavoured. . . .

. . . All our water is carried from the well, boiled and filtered. Our house is kept clean, all our washing is done daily and ironing (with a charcoal filled iron!). Our shopping is done by Marmo't (and he decides what to buy). . . . They have both turned out very efficient, and having, I think, come to the conclusion that we are crazy to want to live here, have managed all our affairs for us, ordering the workmen about, keeping off unwanted strangers, bargaining over the price of a cupboard or vegetables as we could never do.

. . . Take care of yourself – and love to K. [Kathryn, Rosemary's stepmother] also.

Your loving Rosemary.

11 November 1939   **Bacho'k, Kelantan**

Dear, dearest Daddy

. . . Fortifications are now going up in preparation for the monsoon weather which is now beginning. . . . The other day we had a terrific storm which got up in a few minutes. I was reading your letter on the veranda, it was a heavy grey cloudy day, all colour drained out of both sea and sky, which were a kind of sickly lifeless yellow white. Just as the fishing fleet was returning, about three o'clock or a little earlier, there came a rustle and a hustle over the sea, and the wind approached, and like a man entering the house, suddenly turned all the palm leaves upside down, seized papers, books and scattered them, lifted the rush mats bodily off the floor and then with a roar, brought the rain. And it *rained*! Like a blanket of water it fell out of the sky, pouring into the house through every crack and cranny, blowing up through the floor and running down in pools into the middle of the room. The noise was deafening, it was like a bombardment! We sprung up to lower the shutters, struggling to tie down the windows against that terrific wind – you could see almost nothing out to sea but a curtain of ugly black rain, and all the poor little boats hastily taking down their sails and struggling home, limping, against the storm. You could hardly hear yourself speak for the noise and roar of the wind and rain! . . .

My best love to you.

Rosemary.

EDMUND TO ROSEMARY

13 November 1939   **Officers Training School, Maymyo, Burma**

Dear Rosemary

Oh God, Oh Montreal, this is the world's end. I have just got your letter of 29th October and it makes me wildly jealous – I have been torn from my Kachins and made an officer in H.M. Forces. Of course I can't tell you anything about it – the Official Secrets Act and all that – but it wouldn't make any difference if I could, no one knows what we are being trained to do, or where we are supposed to do it. Anyway my fieldwork is effectively wrecked. . . . Oh damn, oh blast. But I hope anyway that you people manage to keep out of it; the only way I can keep cheerful is to plan for an entirely imaginary future! . . . I feel desperately lonely – I am far more alone here than ever I was in Hpalang. . . .

Love to you both, E.

ROSEMARY TO HER FATHER

22 January 1940   **Bacho'k, Kelantan**

My dearest Daddy

. . . I have been very much busier in the last month than ever before, [. . . making] detailed daily enquiries into household budgets. Every morning and every evening

I go my round, and take the daily expenses of seven families. I now have accurate records for nearly a month of everything eaten and every cent spent on rice, betel for chewing, fish and vegetables, oil and matches. . . . It takes considerable tact and patience to elicit from a woman in precise and accurate detail an account of what she is not accustomed to accounting for, in the way we are, half an hour a day was by [no] means long for such an interview. . . . At first, my enquiries, what do you eat, were greeted with moans about the poverty of the family, there was no money, they had hardly anything to eat, and so on. . . . And even now, after two months of visiting one woman, she never tells me off her own bat what she's spent; I always have to go through the list, item by item; 'Rice – did you buy any today, – how much – what price?' 'Oil – did you buy that?' And of course, since this is very boring for them, I have to intersperse my questionnaire with general conversation about their children, the fishing season, and local gossip. . . . They like my visiting them, and a white woman in a Malay village is apparently so unusual that my visits have apparently given a certain prestige to the recipients. . . .

. . . Love to all the family from us both. Rosemary.

EDMUND TO ROSEMARY
4 February 1940   **Maymyo, Burma**
Dear Rosemary

I have your letter of 21 January which for once has come through uncensored.

. . . Celia is due out here on the 16th but there seems to have been some hitch in the air mails this last week. . . . If she does turn up we shall of course get married straight away . . . I think you can understand well enough why we want to get married . . . one must have some stable nucleus in one's life in which one can attach faith and confidence. After all you seem to have reached almost the same conclusion yourself . . . as it is, it's obviously all a bit of a gamble for both of us but I believe it will work and so does she, and what more can one say of any marriage at the beginning. . . .

. . . The world of tomorrow will be different from the world of today but not necessarily more difficult to live in. The period of the liberal ideal has been an episode in history and we who have been brought up as liberals find it difficult to be sympathetic with any other idealism. But there have been other ideals in the past and the world has survived them, so don't be too gloomy. . . .

My love to you both. Wish me luck. E.

ROSEMARY TO HER FATHER
13 February 1940   **Bacho'k, Kelantan**
My dearest Daddy

. . . Edmund was caught on his way to the Burmese Hills to do fieldwork by a since regretted wave of patriotism, and for the last 3 months has been training as an officer in the Burmese Reserve. He was very sick, as he had just been getting on good terms with his people, and now he can go back, the rains are due to arrive in a month's time, and are pretty bad up there. He last wrote to me that he expects a certain young woman to fly out in the middle of February to marry him.[29] I hope he gets happily married, he has had a very tortured and unhappy time with one thing and another ever since I knew him, largely due I think to a very jealous and possessive mother who he tells me was really responsible for wrecking all his affairs with young women, beginning from [with] me, whom she persuaded E. was not really worthy of him! It has taken him a long time to shake himself free of that unhealthy emotional relationship with his mother, and to grow up spiritually, but I think he has done it at last, though with a great deal of suffering to himself and to others. It has been very lucky that E. [Edmund] should have made such immediate friends with Raymond, and R. [Raymond] with him, so that in the last year when he was working for R., and I was rescuing him from an emotional breakdown over that other girl, all the misunderstandings and ugliness of our earlier relations have been wiped out. I don't know his new wife, I only met her twice, as E. was not sure if he was going to marry her when we left England; but she seems a nice person, with her eyes open. . . .

We still thoroughly expect to go to New Zealand [to see Raymond's parents] on our way back to England. . . .

My best love and birthday wishes. R.

EDMUND TO ROSEMARY

16 February 1940   **Strand Hotel, Rangoon, Burma**

My dear

This is a mad world and few things could be madder than that I should be married by this time tomorrow – but there you are. Celia is due in this afternoon. . . . Please wish us well; we'll both need all we've got in the way of a sense of humour . . . this is such a perfectly God damned awful spot that I'm overwhelmed with guilt for poor Celia. . . . The Englishman in Burma is mediaeval; all the worst features of caste and racial prejudice . . . a man can get sacked from his firm for associating in public with an Anglo-Indian girl!! . . .

Don't worry about Celia and self it will work out all right, though I'm afraid she's in for a poor sort of time for the first few months. . . .

Love to you both. E.

11 March 1940   **Sinlumkaba, Bhamo, Burma**

Dear Rosemary

. . . At the moment we are still stuck in Bhamo [with] various minor obstructions. . . .

Marriage is an interesting experience isn't it?! I think this one will work out pretty well in time; at the moment I haven't at all got used to thinking in terms of 'us' instead of 'I'. Obviously one gains enormously in emotional stability, but one loses to some extent one's personal freedom of action . . . but if you are living with someone, you must in self-defence become considerate, and at the moment I'm not awfully good at that! . . .

My love to you both. E.

ᙏᘔᙐ

On 10 May 1940, Germany invaded France, the Netherlands and Belgium, leading to the evacuation of the British and many French forces from Dunkirk.

Rosemary and Raymond curtailed their fieldwork slightly before travelling home to England by ship, going via Auckland to spend some time with Raymond's parents. They were only able to get passage on a slow boat, which took two weeks to reach Freemantle, Western Australia. From there, they travelled by train across Australia to Sydney and thence by boat to Auckland. They would return to England via the Panama Canal and across the Atlantic.

ROSEMARY TO HER FATHER

13 May 1940   **Bacho'k, Kelantan**

My dearest Daddy

The latest news of the war has really cast a gloom over us. . . . We feel we want to come home; if dreadful things are going to happen to our friends and one's country, not to be there is a mixed blessing – it is better to be really *in* it. . . . I suppose we shall beat the Germans in the end, but at the moment it looks at least as unlikely as likely. I don't know how you feel about the gov.t or our new P.M.[30] but it seems to me that really Chamberlain[31] had to go. Whatever his other qualifications I think he had not the daring and the imagination which we absolutely must have if we are to match Hitler. . . .

We never for *one* instant contemplated missing out New Zealand . . . In the present state of the world, not to visit Raymond's parents would be absolutely unpardonable. . . .

I am trying to write this letter in the intervals of watching two enormous rat eating snakes which are curling about the rafters of the house. They are quite harmless, they are useful in fact – they strangle (not bite) rats and then swallow them whole - an incredible sight to watch. But they are enormous things, six feet long and as thick as my wrist. There are two that keep wandering about looking for rats and give me the shivers! . . .

We sail the first week in July – I won't give the date *in case* there is any danger – though we have not specifically been asked to be secretive. . . .

Your loving

Rosemary.

6 June 1940   **Bacho'k, Kelantan**

My dearest Daddy

. . . The situation in Europe is so critical that we live from day to day regarding plans. . . . Raymond may decide to leave all our notes in N.Z. till the end of the war – if England is invaded and the very worse happens to us through defeat, we may of course not sail for home at all. . . . We have attained a sort of stoical resignation, ready but not terrified for the loss of everything. . . .

You see we are thoroughly seized for the gravity of the situation. . . .

I think this year in Malaya has been one of the happiest of my life, and if it is to be [my] last happiness – well, we are ready for it. At least we are two together, and only two, and I think we can adapt ourselves to almost any kind of life as well and perhaps better than most people. . . .

My dearest to you, and courage in the next months!

Yours Rosemary.

EDMUND TO ROSEMARY

15 July 1940   **Hpalang, Kachin Hills, Burma**

Dear Rosemary

. . . The last I heard from you was on May 25th, and as the censor had made right merry with their black ink it wasn't all that intelligible. . . .

. . . I imagine that at the moment this is about as unwarlike a spot as anywhere in Asia, but still the Japs are only about 300 miles away [in Indo-China] and [. . . cut by censor . . .] of course there's the fact that I may at any minute be called back into the army. Considering all of which it seems to me that my fieldwork has made not bad progress! . . . The Kachin kinship system seems to include about 250,000 people in an area about the size of Britain, the local variations are palpably simply enormous and yet there does remain some sort of cultural unity right through the whole group – how on earth to define it I can't imagine.

With love, Edmund.

ROSEMARY TO HER FATHER

10 August 1940   **Otara, Otahuhu, Auckland, New Zealand**

My dearest Daddy

. . . We arrived at [Freemantle] Perth, Australia, instead of Sydney, and had to travel overland to Sydney. . . . As each state in Australia has a different railway and gauge we had to change five times! The first lap was the Tuesday evening. . . . Neither of us could sleep, we were so cold in the night, even with 3 big rugs on us. . . . [At Kalgoorlie] it was killingly cold while we waited for half an hour on a bitter frosty morning in a completely unheated stationary train . . . thought I should never be warm again in my life. . . . For these [next] two days we travelled in a practically straight line . . . across . . . a tree-less, house-less, shrub-less, river-less, hill-less eternity of earth, earth, earth; red earth, rolling earth, rolling away on all sides as far as the eye could see, nothing, so that you could see the curvature of the earth's surface, as you can on the ocean, rolling out past the flying train under the great unblinking heat of the sun by day, and the huge starlit dome of the sky by night, bitterly cold under the shining face of the stars . . . the whole expanse of the Nullarbor Plain. . . . It was like the surface of the moon or some planet where life has never flickered. . . .

Towards the end of the journey . . . a sudden mob of sheep, startled by the train, scurried off into the wilderness, a reminder that here were sheep stations and some life, at last, buried in so much of death – or rather not death, for here life was in complete negation and seemed never to have been thought of. . . .

In Sydney we had a glorious week; met by a little crowd of Raymond's old friends. . . .[32]

Here in N.Z. [New Zealand] everything looks tiny compared to Australia, there are no smart women, the houses are heartbreakingly ugly of wood and corrugated iron but the sheep are fatter than ever. . . .We are in the country here and the weather is mild and warm in the sun. It is very quiet and domestic and the F. [Firth] parents are being frightfully nice to me. Mrs F. had bought me delicious woolly nightgowns which I wear with joy and I've been made to have breakfast in bed every morning! I think we shall both enjoy a quiet month here, though petrol restrictions cut down possible touring of the country. . . .

Love R.

9 September 1940   **Otahuhu, Auckland**

Dearest Daddy

. . . N.Z. is a funny country . . . everything is imitation English, suitably watered down to fit the most bourgeois population on earth. . . . There are no restaurants open after 6.0 except hotels, and no alcohol sold after 6.0 p.m. and none in restaurants anyway. Food is the eternal but very good 'roast and 2 veg'. . . . Life seems well off, but oh, so barren!

The position of the Māori makes the picture even more barren, I think. There is no colour bar of course and Māori have held prominent positions in exceptional cases in public life. But the majority of Māori, their own culture entirely disrupted, live on the fringes of poverty in the most hideous European clothes, in unsavoury little corrugated iron huts, doing wood work, or minding a few pigs and growing potatoes. In some places, they have deliberately resurrected a kind of museum piece of their own culture. . . . I thought it was awful and tragic. A kind of grotesque pantomime or fancy-dress ball to see these sophisticated people aping and caricaturing their own customs for the delight of strangers. Inevitable perhaps. But pathetic. . . . A bogus native life and art are worse than any product of culture contact.

. . . The intellectual life of N.Z. is being slowly killed by the policy of the present government. . . . It is the 'communist' scare again of course, and the war has provided a golden opportunity for the government, but their policy was well on this path long before the war. . . . Books are censored on arrival in this country and anything slightly left wing refused as 'subversive'. Recently some books (unspecified!) were removed from a public library for the same reason. Letters to England criticising the [N.Z.] gov.t domestic policy were censored, until such an outcry arose, the P.M. apologised and said it would be stopped and it was due to 'misunderstanding on part of Censors'. A W.E.A.[33] man, on the university staff was sacked at Cabinet instigation because of 'subversion' – I think left wing and liberal views privately expressed. Worst of all, all government servants were circularised, [inviting them] to notify the authorities, (*anonymously* if liked) of any persons they knew in their dept. suspected of 'subversion'. A great friend of R.'s of left wing and pacifist views, but not more so than say Terence, and not a public speaker or agitator (I'll tell you who when I get back)[34] was interviewed by the police, 'quite privately and friendly' they said, and he was asked to keep it secret, and the answers to a list of questions as follows were written down: 'Are you loyal?' 'What do you think of Russia?' 'Do you approve of the war?' 'What friends do you discuss these things with?' etc. No charge was brought. It was merely 'to clear up matters and make sure all was OK' this British Gestapo agent remarked! . . .

It will be nice to see you all again at home – until then, au revoir

and my love to you all.

Rosemary.

EDMUND TO ROSEMARY

2 November 1940 [arrived 18 January 1941]   **as from Maymyo, Burma**

Dear Rosemary

I have just got your letter of 30th August from NZ – I myself haven't written to you for months as . . . I knew you were supposed to be heading home. . . . However assuming that you have got home I hope you are having no difficulty in keeping alive. . . . Your description of political conditions in Australia and NZ was very interesting showing up how essentially fascist in outlook we are all becoming. . . .

Of course I am back in the army, it was really too much to hope that I should be allowed to carry on with my Kachin idyll indefinitely, but it nearly broke my heart to come away. At the moment things could be worse – I'm a recruiting officer and spend my time running around the Kachin hills collecting candidates for the army (a beautifully ironic occupation for an anthropologist . . .). Celia meanwhile is in Maymyo. . . .

Write again soon and tell us something of wartime England

– And is London in ruins or isn't it?

Good luck to you both, with love, Edmund.

Notes

1. Danzig (now Gdansk in Poland) was a free city with a substantial German population, geographically surrounded by Polish territory.
2. Rosemary to Terence, 26 August 1939.
3. In the local Kelantan dialect, pronounced Bacho' (ending with a glottal stop).
4. Little is known about Robert Gibson-Fleming after he and Celia parted. He married again, had children and distinguished himself in battle during the Second World War. He was killed sometime in the 1950s in a railway accident.
5. Lynette Roberts (1909–95) was a Welsh writer and poet, admired by T.S. Eliot and Dylan Thomas.
6. Edmund to Rosemary, 25 January 1940.
7. Edmund to Rosemary, 11 April 1940.
8. Adam Kuper, 1986, 'An Interview with Edmund Leach', *Current Anthropology* 27: 375–82, p. 376.
9. Edmund to Rosemary, 4 May 1940.
10. Rosemary to her father, Gilbert, 26 May 1940.
11. Rosemary to her father, 26 February 1940.
12. Rosemary to her father, 23 December 1939.
13. Rosemary Firth, 1943, *Housekeeping among Malay Peasants*, London: Percy Lund Humphries (2nd edn: London: Athlone Press, 1966).
14. Rosemary Firth, 1986, 'An Unusual Friendship', *Cambridge Anthropology* 10(1): 29–31, p. 29. She first emphasised this point when interviewed by Alan Macfarlane, 1983, retrieved 26 April 2022 from https://www.youtube.com/watch?v=P1jc3VOTiBE.
15. Audrey Richards, 1932, *Hunger and Work in a Savage Tribe: A Functional Study of Nutrition Among the Southern Bantu*, London: Routledge and Kegan Paul; and Audrey Richards, 1939, *Land, Labour and Diet in Northern Rhodesia: An Economic Study of the Bemba Tribe*, Oxford: Oxford University Press. For Audrey's sense of gender inequity, we are grateful to Andrew Bank (personal communication).
16. Rosemary Firth, 1983, interview by Alan Macfarlane.
17. Rosemary Firth, 1972, 'From Wife to Anthropologist', in S.T. Kimball, and J.B. Watson (eds). *Crossing Cultural Boundaries*, pp. 10–32, San Francisco, CA: Chandler.
18. Raymond and Rosemary Firth, 1982, interview by Anthony Forge, retrieved 26 April 2022 from https://www.youtube.com/watch?v=IRgFtuAsAyI.
19. Rosemary to her father, 12 September 1939.
20. Edmund to Rosemary, 11 April 1940.
21. Rosemary's father, Gilbert, to Rosemary, 16 February 1940, courtesy Oliver Darlington. The Finns defended themselves efficiently and valiantly but were forced to cede Viipuri

(now Vyborg) in a peace treaty in March 1940: see John Langdon-Davies, 1940, *Finland: The First Total War*, London: Routledge.

22. Rosemary to her father, 26 January 1940.
23. Rosemary and Raymond originally planned to work in Terengganu, just south of Kelantan.
24. An old friend from Rosemary's schooldays.
25. Courtesy Oliver Darlington.
26. Air Raid Precautions: the ARP service was established in 1937 to protect civilians in the event of war.
27. Raymond and Rosemary had given up their flat in Great Ormond Street, so they had to leave all their furniture and belongings with Rosemary's family in Highgate.
28. *Tuan*: literally 'Sir' or 'Mister', a term of respect applied particularly to Europeans at that time. '*Tuans*' might refer to Europeans of both sexes.
29. In fact, she made much of the journey by sea.
30. Winston Churchill (1874–1965), British prime minister from May 1940 until 1945.
31. Neville Chamberlain (1867–1940), British prime minister from May 1937 until he resigned in May 1940, to make way for the national government led by Winston Churchill. Chamberlain had negotiated the surrender of the Sudetenland by Czechoslovakia to Germany in 1938. His conduct of the war was fiercely criticised after the fall of Norway in April 1940.
32. From Raymond's time living in Sydney, 1929–32.
33. Workers' Educational Association.
34. Robert Falla, a friend of Raymond's from primary school who became a celebrated ornithologist and museum administrator.

Chapter 7

Under Attack

1940

Rosemary and Raymond left New Zealand at the end of September 1940. They made their six-week journey back to England by merchant ship: the RMS *Rangitiki*, laden with meat, butter and wool. They sailed across the Pacific and through the Panama Canal, interrupting their journey briefly at Halifax, Nova Scotia, in Canada. Wartime censorship meant that their family and friends knew only of their intended return to England and approximately when they departed – the name of their ship and dates of its movements were to be kept secret.

But Rosemary had written to her father Gilbert in a letter shortly after they set sail: 'We are a tiny family party on this enormous ship. . . . There is *one* first class passenger, who spends most of his time with us – we nicknamed him the Admiral, but really, he is a young man in his twenties just entered the Navy; he is officering about ten young petty officers in the 3rd class . . .'[1]

Rosemary, it would transpire, had let slip more information in this letter than she would have intended.

Shortly after leaving Halifax, on 28 October, the *Rangitiki* joined some three dozen other ships to form convoy HX 84. Just over halfway between Newfoundland and Ireland, at around midday on 5 November 1940, the convoy was spotted by a reconnaissance plane from the German pocket battleship *Admiral Scheer*. The battleship was ninety miles from the convoy, so it was not until nearly dusk that it got within sight and range. Shortly before 5 PM, the *Admiral Scheer* opened fire, aiming at the minimally armed merchant ship *Jervis Bay*, which was the escort for the other thirty-eight ships.

Figure 7.1. Raymond and Rosemary on the *Rangitiki*, 1940. Photographer unknown.

The *Jervis Bay* fought off the *Admiral Scheer* in an act of self-sacrifice by Captain Fegen that saved most of the ships in the convoy and earned him the Victoria Cross. For a precious twenty or so minutes, the battleship was prevented from targeting the convoy, which was able to begin spreading a smokescreen.

The battleship then directed its fire at the largest freighter in the convoy, the *Rangitiki*. The first salvo of 3,000-pound, 11-inch shells fell short; the second straddled either side of the *Rangitiki* amidships, but luckily did not hit the ship itself. The third exploded only yards away, scattering shrapnel into the *Rangitiki*. Rosemary and Raymond felt a terrific bang and a thud that shook the whole vessel.

They both expected the next salvo to hit and sink the *Rangitiki*. From the *Admiral Scheer*, Captain Krancke saw a flash and reported a hit on the *Rangitiki*. Other ships in the convoy also observed the *Rangitiki* light up. As the *Rangitiki* turned and disappeared into the smoke, Captain Krancke fired a couple more salvoes at the disappearing vessel and then turned his fire on the other ships.

German radio reported the *Rangitiki* as sunk, based on Captain Krancke's record of the *Rangitiki* as one of fourteen ships he had sunk or damaged. The attack on the convoy and the German claims were widely reported in the British press the following morning. Rosemary's father Gilbert, in some anxiety, immediately made enquiries of the New Zealand Shipping Company. The shipping clerk, assuming that Sir Gilbert Upcott's daughter and her husband would be travelling first-class, tried to reassure him that they could not be on the *Rangitiki* 'as there was only one first-class passenger on board'. Gilbert then realised – because of what Rosemary had let slip in her letter – that they had indeed been aboard the *Rangitiki*. He was left fearing his daughter had been lost at sea.

But apparently one of the *Rangitiki*'s smokescreen canisters had flared on hitting the water. Obscured by the smokescreen, the *Rangitiki* and many of her sister ships were able to scatter in the gathering night and head for safety.[2] Rosemary's only records – terse in the extreme – are from her tiny engagement diary, 5 November: 'Convoy attacked by German Battleship'; 6 November: 'Proceeding alone un-convoyed. 2nd scare of raider – did not materialise'; 8 November: 'Aeroplane and torpedo scare – Captain decided not to go to *rendez-vous*'.

They reached Milford Haven on 12 November, but the passengers became increasingly perplexed and frustrated as they were not allowed to disembark until 17 November (for reasons that remain unclear), greatly adding to the anxiety of their relatives. Only over the following two weeks as individual convoy ships, including the stricken tanker *San Demetrio*,[3] reached British shores did it become clear which ships had in fact survived. The *Jervis Bay* and five of the other thirty-eight ships in the convoy had been sunk. One hundred and ninety-one seamen lost their lives.

The battle received widespread publicity as a result of a statement made by Churchill on 13 November in praise of the 'forlorn and heroic action fought by the captain, officers and ship's company of the *Jervis Bay* in giving battle against overwhelming odds in order to protect the merchant convoy which they were escorting, and thus securing the escape of by far the greater part of that convoy'.[4]

Although friends did not know they were on board the *Rangitiki*, or even whether they were in the Atlantic at that moment, all knew that Rosemary and Raymond were on their way home.

EDMUND TO ROSEMARY

23 December 1940   **Maymyo, Burma**

Dear Rosemary,

I have heard nothing of you since you left New Zealand and I'm getting a bit anxious. Letters take such a fantastic time to get through that no news alone should not be cause for alarm; but ships in the Atlantic lately seem to have been going down about five a night so I hope you have written to say you are alive . . .

Much love to you both, Edmund.

WILLIAM STANNER[5] TO ROSEMARY

1 March 1941   **Sydney, Australia**

Rosemary, Rosemary, what a lovely letter, and what a relief to hear that you are both safe (safe!) in England. Ian [Hogbin][6] and I had worked it out one morning in his room at the University that Raymond and you had a very good chance of being in that convoy. . . . Of course, we did not *know* when you had gone, but the general times seemed to coincide rather terribly . . . and I must say that my heart contracted when I finally realised that you both had an excellent chance of being in the very thick of it . . .

William

Notes

1. Rosemary to her father, undated, October 1940. The letter would have gone by air from their first port of call.
2. Two excellent – although differing – accounts of the battle have been published: Gerald L. Duskin and Ralph Segman, 2005, *If the Gods Are Good: The Sacrifice of the Jervis Bay*, Manchester: Crécy Publishing (see especially pp. 104–8, 139–41, 178), and Theodor Krancke and H.J. Brennecke, 1975, *Pocket Battleship*, London: Tandem, pp. 43–64.
3. F. Tennyson Jesse, 1942, *The Saga of San Demetrio*, London: Her Majesty's Stationery Office; Calum MacNeil, 1957, *San Demetrio*, Sydney: Angus and Robertson.
4. Duskin and Segman, *If the Gods Are Good*, p. 211.
5. William Stanner (1905–81) was an Australian anthropologist who had worked with Raymond in 1937–38, stayed at Holway Cottage in Dorset and become a close friend of Rosemary's. They met up with him on their way through Sydney in 1940.
6. Ian Hogbin (1904–1989) was an anthropologist who had gone to work in Australia, knew Raymond well from Sydney in 1930, and had got to know Rosemary when she stayed in Sydney in August 1940.

Chapter 8

Opened by Censor

1941–1942

When they finally disembarked from the *Rangitiki* on their return from New Zealand and Malaya in November 1940, Rosemary and Raymond had nowhere to live. For eight weeks, they stayed with her parents in London, spending most nights sleeping in the cellar as a protection against German bombing. This meant that Raymond was sleeping in the same room as his mother-in-law! Raymond then managed to find lodging for himself – but not for the two of them – in Cambridge, where he had been relocated with the LSE during the war. Rosemary spent most of the next two months in Sidmouth in Devon, helping her younger sister Elizabeth after a difficult childbirth.

Whilst she was in Sidmouth, their erstwhile first-class passenger from the *Rangitiki*, the 'Admiral', visited Rosemary on his leave. Stanley Watkinson was a New Zealander and Rosemary showed him a bit of England. It seems that he had grown a little smitten with her since they became friends on the *Rangitiki*. Shortly before his vessel HMS *Hood* left for battle on 22 May 1941, he wrote to her, 'I am still faithful to my first love. . . . You have and had something from me no one else could have. Remember that, won't you? Now let me know how often I may write to you.' He died when the *Hood* was blown up by the German battlecruiser *Bismarck* just one day later, on 24 May 1941.[1]

It was not until the beginning of March 1941 that Rosemary and Raymond found accommodation for the two of them together, in Bateman Street, Cambridge. Six months later, they rented 2 Sylvester Road, the house of Raymond's closest friend, Munia Postan, who had moved to London for the duration of his war work. While Rosemary and Raymond lived in the house, they took lodgers and socialised with LSE geographers and economists, including the Kaldors and Hayeks.[2]

By that time, Raymond had taken up part-time work for Admiralty Intelligence (Geographical Section). In July 1941, the Japanese – not yet at war with Britain and the United States – had occupied all of Indo-China (Vietnam, Cambodia and Laos), threatening an assault on the oil-rich Dutch East Indies (now Indonesia) and also threatening Malaya, an invaluable source of rubber. Raymond proffered a report on the Malay east coast. 'I was summoned to the War Office . . . I had made a report on communications and harbours – river mouths . . . as a result of our trip . . . in 1940. They told me it was the best information they had from the area – which made me angry, that military intelligence should depend on a layman's report incidentally gathered. They also asked me if the Japanese could land in the monsoon. I replied of course they can!'[3]

Raymond's remaining time was employed writing up his research on the economics of the Malay fishermen.

At the end of October 1941, Edmund and Celia's daughter Louisa (Loulou) was born in Maymyo, Burma. Earlier that year, Edmund had been promoted to captain. For most of the year, he was unable to do any anthropology as the army occupied him in Mandalay and Maymyo, where life was 'comfortable, well fed and luxurious and just bloody awful!'[4] Letters were a lifeline: Edmund devoted much detail to the advantages and disadvantages of the different routes they could choose: 'Lashio–Chungking–Hongkong–Manila–Transpacific . . . only 5/- . . . Air Mail via Durban – avoid this like the plague . . . Air to Hongkong, then by surface route Transpacific and Transatlantic, said to take only five weeks, cost 1/-.'[5]

Although Edmund was well able to develop nuanced arguments in his academic work, where political matters and everyday behaviour were concerned, he had a lifelong inclination to set forth ideas in black-and-white terms – and even to believe his own polarised formulations. This is nowhere more evident than in his letters from Burma during 1941. In a colonial backwater, amongst expatriates with values redolent of the late nineteenth century, he reacted with fury. Highly intelligent, he understood that war generates great and sometimes unexpected changes in society, and with regard to issues such as colonialism, he saw the big historical picture. But his anger with the faults of British imperialism made him talk and write as if he were blind to fundamental distinctions between radically different societies.

And 1941 brought dramatic changes in the war.

Nazi Germany, which had had a pact with the Soviet Union to enable the two countries to divide Poland between them, invaded the Soviet Union without warning on 22 June 1941. At the end of the year, the Japanese launched a surprise attack on the United States at Pearl Harbor in Hawai'i on 7 December 1941. Within hours, they also invaded Malaya without warning, landing along the very coast at Kota Bharu where Rosemary and Raymond had lived during their fieldwork a little over a year earlier – just four months after Raymond had informed a rather surprised War Office that an invasion such as this was indeed perfectly possible at the height of the monsoon in December. A week later, the Japanese invaded the southernmost peninsula of Burma from their ally Thailand.

Rosemary and Edmund were corresponding regularly until the beginning of 1942. Edmund had been becoming increasingly frustrated and cynical as his time in the army stretched on. By the time Edmund received Rosemary's letter of 3 January 1942, the Japanese invasion of Burma was well under way: the Japanese had launched a second offensive further north, much closer to where Edmund was stationed. His reply has not survived.

Edmund and Celia's life was about to be turned upside down by the Japanese assault on Burma.

ROSEMARY TO RAYMOND

28 January 1941   **Livonia House, Sidmouth, Devon**

My dearest

I was glad to hear from you. . . . Sidmouth is simply packed with the funkers[6] now – mostly inconsiderate old ladies who feed their lap dogs on meat or rabbit and whose bitterest cry against the war is therefore the price of rabbits and impossibility of getting them!

Yes, I *will* go and get a G.M. [gas mask] at once. I quite agree with you about a sudden surprise attack [German invasion] very likely this spring. The military are in much evident activity around here, doing all sorts of comical diggings and buildings and making messes of various kinds all over the place. Things may blow up pretty stiff this Spring I think. Remember I shall always do my utmost to *stay put*, as we are asked, if anything *should* happen; especially while I was at Thorncombe [her cottage in Dorset]. It would be futile to start meandering about the country or trying to get to London or Sidmouth or anywhere. I could live a long time on Mrs Browning's[7] potatoes!! . . .

I have just sketched out the opening chapter of my book and am beginning to get rather thrilled about it. But I think I need to be quite alone, to get on with it fast. I always worked better at Edinburgh on a paper if I could get away quite by myself. . . .

Well my darling, write to me again . . .

All my love my dear . . .

I keep meaning to finish and find myself on another sheet of paper. Yes, I do miss you; but what fun it will be when we meet again. I've always held that fainting, being sick, toothache etc. is worth-while because of the marvellous feeling afterwards, when it is better. It really is rather fun to be away on my own for a bit for that reason – I feel as I did when engaged to you about meeting you again. I am a beastly hardboiled independent bird aren't I? Incurably unable to settle down to uneventful pacific married life day in and out as Margaret[8] has done. I can always do with a little flitting!

But you don't mind do you? You alone know where my heart is . . . There is only one place in the world for me in the end, as you know, my darling, and that's by you.

Goodnight now, really I must say goodbye.

Your own

Rosemary.

4 February 1941   **Sidmouth, Devon**

My dear,

I have just listened to whom I suppose was Lord Haw Haw[9] on the wireless. He certainly has an awful voice – speaks through his nose. He was mostly occupied in telling us how 'the biggest military problem facing Churchill is shipping' but I think we all know that from the lips of our own leader, so it's not startling. How he does hate Churchill. I think this obvious hatred of a leader is a very bad form of propaganda. I daresay when we say things about Adolf like this it makes the Germans smile just the same. Propaganda ought to be much more subtle, and *apparently* friendly I think. If obviously from the enemy it defeats its purpose by antagonising the listener straight away . . .

All my love

Rosemary.

လ‍ဎ

It had taken some considerable time for news to reach Edmund that Rosemary and Raymond had survived the Atlantic crossing safely.

EDMUND TO ROSEMARY

16 March 1941   **Maymyo, Burma**

Dear Rosemary

. . . It was a tremendous relief to hear from you as I was convinced you were either a prisoner in a German raider [battleship] or else had been put ashore for the duration on some uninhabited island in the Pacific. As things turn out it seems that you have been nearer to death than that . . .

My anthropology has more or less died. . . . Write again soon and let me know all the gossip . . .

Love Edmund.

20 June 1941   **Maymyo, Burma**

Dear Rosemary,

[My] dear you have no idea how delightful it was to get your letter. Celia and I both gorged on it. It's true of course that you can't really explain what it is like being blitzed, but at least you give us the feel of life, and we are both so homesick for Bloomsbury that even to be told that it is just dust and ashes is comforting. Please, please write again and do your utmost to describe the feeling of wartime England. You see our existence here is so wholly artificial and anachronistic, that we are stunted; we can't grow at all, and quite obviously everyone at home is growing very fast. Goodness knows whether we are going to win or lose this war and perhaps it doesn't matter so much either way; but what is certain is that a complete social revolution is taking place and you back at home are right in the thick of it, while we out here are just stranded on a sand bank . . .

Before commenting on your news a little of ours. . . . My entire existence is a complete waste of time. I am supposed to be in charge of a company of Chins (not Kachins), whose language I do not understand, and with whom I am supposed to converse in Burmese, a language which neither they nor I understand, and which I am given no opportunity to learn . . .

About my life in the army of course I may tell you nothing. Suffice that. . . . If the Japs do decide to come in this direction, I myself think it will be a very brief affair of fifth columnists and parachutes, so perhaps I shall have my chance of winning the V.C. yet.

. . . My real supreme grouse [is] a prospect of four, five, umpteen years in this **%"@** Burma Army. Do you wonder that I get to the stage of asking very seriously 'Would it really make much difference if we did get defeated?' At home on the other hand it apparently takes you all the other way, and the more you get bombed the more patriotically last ditch, backs to the wall, and death and glory you all become. Psychologically I suppose it's what one would expect, and presumably the German reaction to being bombed is precisely the same.

The war apart and strictly as a married couple we continue to be very happy; Celia has had appalling luck with her health with a whole succession of dysenteries, flues and what nots. She loathes my fellow *pukka sahibs*[10] with a far more virulent hatred than I do and we lead a quite marvellously asocial existence. Taken all round, the physical side of life is very tolerable; (we have no rations to contend with for instance); but the lack of intellectual, or even intelligently human, companions is soul destroying. We are quite damnably lonely. Celia is expecting a baby in October, and though its arrival will be a complicated business in war time, it should do a lot to give us both a more positive interest in life as it hits us.

. . . Love to you both and to everyone else. Please write again soon. . . . E.

ROSEMARY TO EDMUND

25 October 1941   **Sylvester Road, Cambridge**

My Dear Edmund

Your letter of 29 August just arrived – opened by censor for the first time for some time, but in spite of your discussion of the Japanese situation, nothing deleted. . . . So far, Raymond is doing fire-watching only,[11] and now we are in this house, I think I shall be doing it too. I am due to register[12] on Nov 8th, (I am 29, my dear I feel quite old, it is dreadful!) but I do not think they will actually call me up as I am at the moment running a large house, servant-less, for two men[13] both engaged on war work. I want to do some war work, as a matter of fact, and could get a very interesting job in the Board of Trade, interviewing traders and shopkeepers about rationing and the limitation of supplies, finding out their complaints and discovering what their stocks are etc. but it is quite impossible until, a) I have finished my monograph on Malay Housekeeping for the L.S.E. series, and b) find some kind of domestic help. We have taken over Munia Postan's house which he built for Eileen Power, before she died [he was seconded to the Ministry of Economic warfare in London]. It's a large house, and I have never had a house before; to have started this game just [now], is no joke . . .

The oddest things are unobtainable. Matches are worth their weight in gold. A friend offered to exchange me half a pound of sugar (one week's ration) for a single box of matches the other day. I said, make it a pound, and I might consider giving you half a box. Vinegar, olive oil, oatmeal, soap, more surprisingly mustard, semolina, cereals, baking powder, biscuits, chocolate are all unofficially rationed by grocers now. This is not to say we are really more than slightly inconvenienced. All these things are obtainable in small quantities, and it is astonishing how well you become in economising in them, and even in doing without what we should have regarded as necessities in peace time. Also the occasional thrill of finding a haul of such things as chocolate, biscuits, and cigarettes, or lemons, makes up amply for the previous famine. As a matter of fact the food situation is much, much better than it was six months ago. You can see this in the increase of our jam, fats, cheese, sugar and meat rations recently. The 'short supply' goods are also much easier now that all grocers are organised, and won't sell except to 'registered' or regular customers, and then at so much a head only. It means that there is really very little, except bread, rice and coffee that you can buy in a strange shop . . .

The outlook is bleak here, but not too grim. . . . You poor darlings doomed to an ever-increasing exile! It would be marvellous to see you again. I should perhaps say, it *will* be marvellous to see you again!

It was said, at one time, that the collapse of Russia might lead to the fall of Churchill, and though I doubt if that would ever have been the case, I think it is not thought so now. . . . Some people have suggested that if and when Russia collapses there will be a strong peace move here. All my experience with char-ladies, country people, my butcher, grocer, and so on contradict this for me. I think the people of this country are firmly prepared for harder and harder times, if necessary . . .

I do not think, still, that we shall have an invasion, even in the spring, [supposing] all being over with Russia. Hitler has, after all, in spite of his resounding successes, lost the Battle of Britain, the first round of the Battle of the Atlantic and so far is stymied in the Eastern Mediterranean. . . . That is all something to remember when one feels depressed.

. . . Of gossip: . . . My brother Terence, is also Captain, and has been . . . put in charge of a subsection of Italian intelligence.[14] Elizabeth, my sister, has unaccount-ably parked her child on its grandma and joined the WAAFS [Women's Auxiliary Air Force] . . .

I must stop and do some work. Cambridge is full of reminders of you! . . . The 'Festival' – do you remember (or now that you are a father,[15] ought I not to remind you?) where we had a dinner and fell in love before the Clare ball – is expensive and only middling worth it nowadays. . . . Who would have then thought that I should end up in my thirties (nearly), a sober provincial housewife in Cambridge? What a funny world this is since the war – and even having paying guests – except that almost everybody has some sort of alien in their house now, either paying guest, or evacuee, or civil servant billetee, or something . . .

Au revoir. I make various resolutions to write to you every month at the least, but honestly I am so busy, it is difficult you know . . . here's my love to both of you.

. . . Do let me know about your infant![16]

Ever yours [Rosemary]

EDMUND TO ROSEMARY

14 October 1941   **Maymyo, Burma**

[This letter probably arrived sometime in December. The Japanese invaded Burma at about the time when Rosemary would have read this letter.]

Dear Rosemary

. . . The tremendous patriotism of your last letter rather shocked me, for at this range it certainly appears that war time England is rapidly becoming an almost exact replica of the Nazi Germany we are so busily destroying. But it is good to know that on a somewhat meagre scale you can still get enough to eat, and that in general 'morale is high'. Morale here is just wonderful, no one ever mentions the war at all! There are indeed times when I am positively glad that I am not at home; not that I should be in the least pacifistic about it, but I should disagree so violently with everyone about all the aims and methods of war; here everyone is so completely and utterly stupid that one simply doesn't worry.

But the point of my grouse is this: The one thing that makes any sense about this war is that all the nations which survive it will be more or less completely totalitarian and collectivised, and a damned good thing too . . . and what we are fighting for is to see that the top dog at the federal tea party wears a union jack and not a swastika, we are not trying to 'destroy the Nazi system'. It would be madness: here has Hitler unified all Europe for the first time in 130 years and all our propaganda experts can think of is to bleat around as if they wanted to split it up into fragments again. But it's no good talking at long range like this, if I was in England I would probably agree with you, out here the system that makes me a white *pukka sahib* in an ocean of multi-coloured slaves makes me completely sick, and I feel that German, Russian and English Imperialism are all equally worthy of fires eternal. Mind you I'm not so depraved as to want to lose the war, but I do feel from time to time that it doesn't really matter very much who does win it, and that all that does matter is that it should finish as soon as possible. Since however I still feel that the odds lie in our favour at about 51/49, I am quite an enthusiastic soldier! Frankly I simply loathe soldiering, but I'm quite good at it.

. . . And what is Raymond doing now? Has he any students, or is the Admiralty all time? And are you yourself really writing a book? . . .

Please, please write again and soon.

My love to you all

Edmund

ROSEMARY TO EDMUND

3 January 1942   **Capel Curig, Carnarvonshire, N. Wales**

My dear Edmund

. . . Perhaps now war has come so near to you, you will not need any more reassurances as to why we, even as intellectuals, are fighting. Really Edmund you have written me some maddening letters in your life time but in some ways none equals the stupidity of this last of yours [of 14 October 1941, above]. You say my 'patriotism' shocks you; that as we are all organised in the same way as the Nazis to fight them, it won't make any difference who wins; and yet you end up characteristically with the languid remark: 'And yet I am not so demoralised as to want to lose the war.'

Listen, my dear. It isn't easy to write about the issues involved or to put one's faith, doubts and convictions on paper. The issue is not simple, and you ought to know that for people like you and me our feelings cannot be simple either. Putting them on paper, especially in defence of a defeatist attitude such as you had, may over simplify them. But you know this is not a game we are playing. And over here, it is not a game we are watching either. For good or evil, morale wins the war, and morale has got to carry those of us who are struggling with the grimness of blackouts, air raids, the irritations of food shortages, the dullness of ordinary family life being broken up, the exasperations of shortages of supply and the temporary and local inefficiencies of organisation and administration; not to mention the real tragedies of things like the loss of the *Hood, Ark Royal, Prince of Wales*,[17] and so on. . . . When you are *in* it you cannot lie back and placidly say, 'True, I do not want to lose the war, but I can't say I think we shall gain much by victory'. One has simply got to will and want victory with one's soul, one's imagination and one's brain and to stifle criticism (except constructive) and scepticism, for the duration. For frankly, all we care for is at stake, and this is the only way to preserve it. Don't you see, there is a difference between patriotism and jingoism? But it isn't even patriotism we fight for. It's the preservation of all the ideals of intellectual freedom for scientists, artists and thinkers all over the world we are fighting for.

Out there, you may think we are as organised and as regimented as the Fascists. But you know it really isn't true! The restrictions which seem so spectacular to you, outside there, are no more than common sense dictates to a people besieged, and are not really either particularly irksome, unfair or hard. Even if they were, what is the use of talking about liberty of choice for instance when one's house is on fire? You have got to submit to organisation dictation and discipline to put the fire out. Then you can talk about living in glorious freedom in the house, when it is saved.

The difference between our organisation and the fascist is two-fold. First in degree, second in kind. It is only a discipline voluntarily entered into, for temporary reasons only, to win the war. And the end is as different as night from day, which is much more important than any superficial resemblance between the means. We do not shut people up in prisons for listening to foreign wireless talks, for worshipping their own religion, for criticising specific government mores, for teaching scientific sociological theory, for being friends with people like the Scheys, Fortes, Schapera, Malinowski.[18] We don't torture political prisoners, set friend to spy on friend, and child to denounce parents. Do you think the LSE could continue its present teaching and staff in the same way if we lost the war as if we won it? Do you think R. could continue his anthropological work unhampered, or that you would be free to champion the social cohesion of the Kachins?

. . . If we lose libraries by bombing, this is better than having them voluntarily destroyed by a crowd of hooligans acting under official instructions; if men are

killed in battle, better they should die there than be murdered under civil authority by police in prisons. If children are bombed, better this than that they should
learn to become traitors to their parents.

. . . Clothes rationing is a healthy limitation on extravagant spending when we
should all be saving. It involves no physical hardship. The blackout is a nuisance
only because we are long accustomed to well-lighted streets in towns. Fuel shortage is only acute enough to force unnecessary waste to cease, not to cause us
to be cold. We have always saved brown paper and string for re-use, why not
envelopes and notepaper and newspaper? Plenty of books can and are still published. People have parties, go to the theatre, ballet, cinema, concerts, listen to
the wireless, watch football and horse racing as ever. Travel is congested but we
can still go in trains at our own sweet will. No! Life in England is still comfortable,
warm, well fed, not devoid of amusement, nor unduly restricted in movement,
discussion or action. We can be ten times worse off before we begin to feel some
of the things which the 'liberated' countries of Europe are suffering, in their salvation and new unification.

Pull yourself together, and think twice before you write again as you have done,
please!

. . . I'll write to you again sooner this time I hope, but God knows when letters
reach you now. Your last, at end of Oct. took about 6 weeks by air. But don't write
such nonsense to me again, my dear please.

Your ever loving Rosemary

23 January 1942   **Sylvester Road, Cambridge**

My Dear Edmund,

I wonder where you are now, and if this letter will reach you before our dear
friends the Japanese. If I felt there was no other reason for fighting this war, I
should now be prepared to go on to the bitter end out of pure rage at what they
have done to our beloved Malays.

. . . In these inauspicious circumstances, I have just finished a Monograph on
Malay Housekeeping, No 7 in your series.[19] It is not likely ever to see the light
of day in Malaya, where its chief interest and market should have been. In fact it
seems as if I should now alter all my verbs to the past tense in the book. It is really
heart breaking . . .

I am daily expecting a job of some kind, but they have even suggested that I
should consider going into a munitions factory, of which there seem to be some
near us crying out for labour. (Is that allowed [by the censors], I wonder?) I can't
help feeling that there are already enough stupid people running this war from
the top, and that the few moderately intelligent ones would be rather wasted on
such work; I am not liable to be actually conscripted yet, being married, but this is
so to speak moral pressure. However, if more moral pressure is exercised on me,

Figure 8.1. Edmund, January 1944. He inscribed it, 'This at least explains my crooked nature'. Photographer unknown.

I should prefer to go into the Wrens, where one would at least have a chance of getting a commission if one was worth it, whereas once in a munitions factory, there you would be stuck in a reserve occupation at two or three pounds a week for the duration . . .

The actual worry of the war situation is however still the worst we have to suffer. I repeat that the food situation, to anyone with imagination, is really not more than inconvenient; it is not serious. Most people have felt the milk shortage of winter more than most things. . . . I never stand in queues, and I still hold that it is not really necessary ever to do so. For cigarettes and chocolate, biscuits, cake and before 'points rationing', tinned salmon, people who queue do so to my mind because they have nothing better to do; none of these things can be called essential. . . . If we had to queue for milk, meat, bread and fats we might think we were really hard up, as they do on the continent. If we had to give up our warm woollens for the troops, as in Germany, we might feel unhappy at clothes rationing. But it has been an enormous success, and I think everyone admits that. It is in the Board of Trade that I hope to find a war job that I feel I might be useful at. But you may still find me in the Services perhaps!

We had a sad Christmas, all to ourselves, patriotically not travelling up to London for a family reunion, as we were all asked not to do. We had rabbit, jugged with a glass of very good Burgundy in it, which we opened for the occasion, and afterwards an excellent shop bought plum pudding. For tea, we had a real iced (with ordinary sugar! It worked!) rich plum cake, full of currants and things carefully saved up for the occasion, and made with stout, since brandy and sherry and such things are now really difficult to obtain. But somehow the spirit was not there for Christmas. . . . But we must keep our peckers up, I suppose, and if we go down, at least let us go down fighting; if there is to be any shooting, I would rather get shot in the hazards of war, than [be] put quietly away under an ostensible system of civil law and order by some Fascist bully, either Red, Black or Yellow! . . .

I do hope you will keep us informed if anything drastic happens to you. I wonder if Celia is still with you? Or if you at last [are] really doing some fighting yourself. I was really terribly thrilled about your daughter and long to hear what is her name, and what it feels like to be a parent.

I have an uncomfortable feeling that by the time this war is over, I shall have come to the change of life. . . . I only hope I shan't have put [having a baby] off till too late, and regret it afterwards. If Raymond were called up it might be reconsidered. After all, you were the child of parents not so young,[20] and it does not seem to have entirely blighted your young life – or has it?!

Did you get my cable about [your] daughter? . . . One worries much more for one's friends at the corners of the earth than one does for oneself, you know. And we are really in clover here compared to what you may be before we have finished with the Japs.

. . . All our love to you, my dear, and good luck to you. I think of you a good deal more than I get time to write to you, you know.

Bless you and take care of yourself.

Ever yours [Rosemary]

Notes

1. Stanley Watkinson (1919–41) was born in Barrow-in-Furness, but his family emigrated to New Zealand in the mid-1920s. He was on a training scheme for New Zealand naval officers. The letter extract is from Rosemary's engagement diary, 13 May 1940.
2. Nicholas Kaldor (1908–86), a Hungarian-born, post-Keynesian economist, lived in Cambridge for most of his life. Friedrich Hayek (1899–1992) was an Anglo-Austrian economist and philosopher.
3. Raymond Firth, 'Chronology', unpublished.
4. Edmund to Rosemary, 31 March 1941.
5. Edmund to Rosemary, 20 June 1941.
6. Those who 'funked out' and fled the war to the safer countryside.
7. A good friend and neighbour in Thorncombe village.
8. Margaret was Rosemary's elder sister.
9. 'Lord Haw-Haw' was the nickname given to William Joyce (1906–46), an American-born fascist who broadcast Nazi propaganda to the British during the Second World War. He was later hanged for treason.
10. *Pukka sahib*: literally, 'first-class master', but used here derisively to mean 'white British top dog'.
11. Initially voluntary, from 1941 onwards all work sites were required to have designated firewatchers on duty at all times. Firewatchers went on lookout and took initial action in response to incendiary bombs.
12. At the end of 1941, the National Service Act (No. 2) introduced conscription for childless women aged twenty to thirty (later extended to ages nineteen to forty-three).
13. Dudley Stamp, their paying guest, and Raymond. Dudley Stamp (1898–1966) was vice-chairman of the government committee on Rural Land Utilisation (Scott Committee).
14. Terence Hodgkinson (1913–99), Rosemary's stepbrother. Terence later became a major in military intelligence. After the war, he joined the Victoria and Albert Museum (V&A), becoming keeper of sculpture from 1967 to 1974.
15. Rosemary knew that, all going well, Edmund would be a father by the time he received her letter.
16. Louisa (Loulou), born a week later.
17. Rosemary and Raymond had lost their friend from the *Rangitiki*, Stanley Watkinson, who died when the British battleship HMS *Hood* was blown up by the German battle-cruiser *Bismarck* on 24 May 1941. HMS *Ark Royal* was torpedoed by a German U-boat in November 1941; HMS *Prince of Wales* was sunk by Japanese aircraft off Malaya in December 1941.
18. These were all colleagues and friends of the Firths who would have been anathema to the Nazis as they were either Polish or Jewish. Beate Schey, whom Raymond had met in Austria in the early 1930s, was a personal friend of Raymond's. Meyer Fortes (1906–83) and Isaac Schapera (1905–2003) were both South African-born anthropologists who had prestigious careers in Britain as anthropological colleagues of Raymond. Schapera (known as 'Schap'), in particular, was a lifelong friend of both the Firths and Edmund and Celia. Bronisław Malinowski was Raymond's mentor and friend.
19. Edmund had provided financial help to enable a series of LSE monographs to be published.
20. Edmund's father was aged fifty-nine and his mother thirty-seven when he was born.

Chapter 9

One Suit and Two Blouses

1942–1943

The day before Rosemary wrote her 23 January 1942 letter to Edmund, the Japanese launched a full-scale assault on southern Burma from Thailand. Ten days later, the Burmese capital, Rangoon, fell to the Japanese. Edmund and Celia were only some 400 miles north, in Maymyo. During February and March 1942, the Japanese moved progressively further north, bombing cities and towns heavily. Around the end of March or early April, Celia and her five-month-old baby daughter Louisa (Loulou) evaded the Japanese advance by walking from Maymyo to Schwebo airport by night for a whole week, hiding from the Japanese by day. They escaped on one of the last planes to fly out to Calcutta in the intervals between Japanese bombing raids; it was only because she was a nursing mother that Celia managed to get a seat on the plane with her baby. From Calcutta, they made their way by train to Bombay and then by ship via Cape Town to Scotland, where they landed some four months after they had first set out from Burma. Both were nearly starving; the baby weighing only eight pounds at nine months old. Celia immediately went to stay with her mother, Barbara Buckmaster, in London. Loulou's grandmother took one look at her and said, very firmly, 'She needs feeding.' She spoon-fed the infant puréed spinach, which, apparently, she adored; whenever Loulou saw her, she would open her mouth like a fledgling. Before long, they left London to stay with Edmund's brother Walter and his wife Meg, who lived and worked on their farm in Buckinghamshire. Celia then looked for a place to live and found one in Hertfordshire, about forty minutes' drive both from

Walter and from Edmund's mother. Celia moved there with her daughter Louisa towards the end of 1942.

Edmund, as an engineer, and now linguistically competent in Jingpho, the Kachin language, was seconded in January into a 'crazy cloak-and-dagger outfit' to disrupt the Japanese advance by blowing up bridges and leaving a network of officers behind Japanese lines to work with the locals as spies.[1] 'Never having actually demolished anything I was scared stiff that my charges would be inadequate. On the first bridge – a big concrete and steel girder affair – I worked all out from 2 p.m. to 2 a.m. single handed non-stop – then went back to the other bridge where I nearly got shot up by the Chinese sentry. I could not finish the job until morning. [I] then went back to the big bridge again, checked over the charges and added some gelignite to help crack the concrete. Fortunately it went off in text book fashion.'[2] The bulk of the British army retreated westwards in disarray to India, while Edmund remained in eastern Burma. After losing his radio and being cut off by the Japanese advance in May, he then had to retreat eastwards, walking with three other men for seven weeks over the mountains into China, under appalling conditions. Part-way through this period, he noted: 'There is no doubt that by this time I was really getting very tired; it showed itself in increased irritability and increasing dislike of my fellows. I grew less and less interested in whether we went forwards or backwards.'[3] Ten days later, he 'was feeling extremely ill by this time. The weakness of the dysentery and fever and chill continued to make me slightly delirious – a mere blubbering child.'[4] When they eventually reached Kunming, he was flown to India over the mountains and Japanese-occupied Burma and hospitalised to aid his recovery.

In late August 1942, he was flown back into Japanese-occupied Burma, where he recruited Kachin irregulars to gather intelligence and disrupt Japanese communications. Supplied periodically by air, this task involved trekking on foot through the jungle in fearful conditions for hundreds of miles over a period of months. It was probably around this time, in late 1942 or early 1943, that 'Colonel Gamble . . . more or less had me court-martialled . . . reduced in rank from acting major to substantive second-lieutenant [and] transferred to the Civil Affairs service'.[5] By the end of 1943, Edmund had 'in the course of this very unorthodox personal war, travelled very widely indeed in the Kachin hills and got to know a great variety of different sorts of Kachin', which influenced his thinking about small societies 'at a very fundamental level'.[6]

ᨀᨗᨒ

From April 1942, Raymond was seconded full-time from the LSE to Admiralty Intelligence, based in Cambridge, employing his knowledge of the

Pacific to edit handbooks for use as part of allied operations against the Japanese. In October, he was sent to the United States to learn about the naval and military intelligence work of the Americans and explore opportunities for further exchange of skills and material. This was Raymond's first visit to the United States. His most vivid impressions were of the journey back: flying in a stripped Liberator bomber at 19,000 feet, sitting on the floor, wearing flying gear and oxygen masks. Sadly, his erstwhile professor, Malinowski, had died in New Haven just six months earlier. As ever, Raymond was in touch with friends and colleagues, alert for information regarding government thinking on planning for the administration of Europe when liberation came, or potential funding for anthropology after the war.[7]

A year earlier, in 1941, with manufacturing increasingly directed towards the war effort, the Board of Trade had established a small Consumer Needs research unit to monitor shortages of any and all household goods and clothing – from blankets, kettles and raincoats to corsets and razorblades – in the face of wartime constraints. Cycill Tomrley[8] was the regional Distribution Officer, first appointed to cover East Anglia. Rosemary and Raymond had got to know her quite well over the previous year; through her, they learnt about this work and its similarities with the economic fieldwork they had done in Malaya. Having finished her book, Rosemary wanted to be working. She thought the research would suit her, so she applied, was accepted, underwent training, sat the exam (instructive in its rigour)[9] and was posted back to Cambridge – as one of the few married women in the unit, it was expected that she should be with her husband, if at all possible. Her boss was Cycill Tomrley. The job – 'anthropology all over again . . . finding out what stocks retailers hold, what customers can't get, why manufacturers can't supply, and [advising] about salvage, replacement and so on for bombed traders'[10] – was indeed something Rosemary was good at. In September 1942, she was promoted to Area Distribution Officer, working all over East Anglia.

Rosemary started a diary of the work, recording both her routine research and many humorous anecdotes. On a visit to the town of March, there was 'more talk of babies in the shops this afternoon. "All these fanciful mothers" I was told by the shopkeeper, complaining in a tolerant way of their desires and prejudices in the way of infants' clothes! . . . Elastic shortage tragedy: it seems the vicar's wife's knickers really came off in a shop last week. What *will* the Board of Trade do?!'[11] Another day, in a small general shop in Haverhill, 'A large notice "Vinegar In" greeted my entrance to the shop'.[12] Sent to Southwold following what she initially believed to be a major disaster, Rosemary noted 'the main problem appeared to be the provision of [a suit for] a 44" waisted man, who had escaped [a blast] without a shred of clothing'.[13]

Early in 1943, Rosemary was involved in a piece of in-depth research on the effects of bombing, which caught the attention of senior staff in London.

In April, she was headhunted to join three other staff on the first national Mobile 'spotlight' Team within the Board of Trade; the team leader was Gordon Sackett. The team was to make detailed studies of areas that had been particularly affected either by bombing or other supply problems. The letter of invitation commented that: 'I know this kind of work is very much in your line. . . . If our town assessment and spotlight work is to be developed really well we must, in my opinion, have really good people doing it in the early stages. . . . It would mean, of course, working away from your base for pretty long periods of time, and being pretty full on the move all the time.'[14] Rosemary found the idea exciting and replied to say that she had Raymond's support: 'this is a war job, and I think he feels as I do that the war might easily separate us a good deal more than it has done so far.'[15] She also negotiated Cycill Tomrley's support and duly joined the team when it began its work in June.

As part of this Mobile Team, Rosemary travelled to South Wales, Tyneside, Lancashire, Coventry, Hull and Glasgow. She was enormously stimulated by the responsibility and the research itself, which built on the skills she had acquired during her Malay fieldwork. Rosemary was grateful to Raymond for his support: it was commonly accepted that women worked in wartime, provided they cooked and cared for their husbands (married women were exempt from conscription). But it was unusual for a married woman to leave her husband to work away from home.

Her work in South Wales was recognised by her superiors in London: their methods and results would be shared with 'eager enquirers from U.S.A'.[16] In October, she led the team during their survey of Hull; she was complimented by headquarters on her report: 'I think it presented the facts very clearly, and [gave] one of the most complete pictures we have got of any town.'[17]

Away from Raymond, she wrote to him nearly twice a week, aware of the pressures separation placed on each of them. She described the local economy and both the ugliness and the beauty she encountered: 'A world of half lights, and machinery, and an atmosphere of one of Dante's underworlds . . . that I find very interesting and attractive in its own peculiar way', as she commented to Cycill.[18] She also found time to write to Edmund, her stepbrother Terence, James Livingstone in Egypt and William Stanner in Australia. Her trained eye caught the differences in affluence and behaviour around the country. Contrasting the absence of prams in the impoverished valleys of South Wales with the number in East Anglia, she noted, 'I have begun to look with new eyes at all the mothers pushing prams in the street . . . what an indication of our standard of living even in wartime that any working woman [here] regards them as necessities! Are there prams in Russia, China, Malaya?!'[19]

ROSEMARY TO EDMUND IN BURMA

5 April 1942   **Sylvester Road, Cambridge**

My dearest Edmund,

How far away you seem now! . . . My dear, I wish I could *talk* to you. . . .

I was summoned to London for an interview by a board of seven big bugs[20] at the Board of Trade on the 26 January. The results were favourable, and I was offered a job as a junior area distribution officer. Immediately I went down with flu. . . . When I had recovered . . . I went down to Bournemouth for the rest of [the] six weeks training period – which was precisely one week. However, I passed the exam, although five were failed, and they . . . sent me back to be posted at Cambridge. . . .

I find the [Board of Trade] job fascinating. We act as scouts for the London headquarters of the Board, to find out how wartime restrictions are affecting the consumer. We travel about, interviewing traders, and discovering how much of their grouses are legitimate, how much affect the consumer, the important person, and how much is purely retailer hardship. Although it is important to get the confidence of the retailer in order to find out the facts, we are really not so much interested in his troubles as in those of the unfortunate housewife, who at the moment cannot get kettles, saucepans or frying pans, elastic, sanitary towels (!) and so on. It is field work to a T . . . notebook, general judgement of reliability of informant, sifting gossip from fact, checking up on evidence from other sources and all. In addition, I have the good fortune to be working under an extremely charming as well as efficient person. . . . We travel about a good deal, and . . . while staying at places like Norwich, have the chance to look at charming churches. Also, she takes me in her car often, and we drive through lovely country.[21] One has the feeling of being very near to the reality of helping in the war too, since one can so often *Do* something, even if it [is] only report to headquarters, but in the end our reports really do help to frame policy. I would a hundred times rather be doing this than sitting in an office writing minutes all day.

. . . I think of you a lot just now; and would love some definite news; my last from you was 25 Oct., a hell of a long time ago. All my love to you my dear, anyway. And good luck if you meet a Jap.

Yours ever [Rosemary]

ROSEMARY TO JAMES LIVINGSTONE IN CAIRO

6 April 1942   **Sylvester Road, Cambridge**

My dear James,

. . . We have got a house in Cambridge . . . and a paying guest to use up the extra room and help pay the heavy overheads. He is Dr. Dudley Stamp . . . a geographer at the LSE and a nice man. . . .

I consider myself lucky to have a job in Cambridge where R. also is. Most people over here have given up many of the social conventions . . . shopping with an old string bag and carrying your corsets home over your arm because no wrapping is allowed, are all taken for granted. So is taking your milk in a little medicine bottle out to tea-parties, if you still go to them, saving your orange peels from your children's ration and giving them to someone with sugar to make marmalade out of; sleeping . . . in the most extraordinary promiscuity, staff and employers and all sexes in one basement room, parents and married children and all. Sleeping on other people's couches because travelling at night is so difficult, and bringing your own cigarettes wherever you go are other examples.

. . . But if I start talking about the war I shall write pages. . . .

Edmund is now father of a daughter. . . . I met his sister in law [Philippa Buckmaster, Celia Leach's younger sister]. . . . She thought I was his cousin, and finding not, asked how I came to know him. I repressed the desire to say, *I* nearly married him, instead of your sister! . . .

I never had your letter which you sent to N.Z. It must have been sunk. So I do not know anything about your 'young woman'. . . .

I must attend to my sick husband; goodbye for now and good luck.

With love, [Rosemary]

ROSEMARY TO HER AUNT KATHERINE

26 September 1942   **Sylvester Road, Cambridge**

My dear Katherine.

. . . I love my job. We are concerned with the distribution of all things except food – cups, kettles, children's shoes, towels, protective clothing for agricultural workers, overalls for factory workers, and so on. There has been some particularly interesting and worthwhile work to do with Norwich after its series of quite nasty blitzes. We are, as it were, the eyes and the ears of the Board of Trade, visiting traders, wholesalers and manufacturers, and discovering how all our orders affect their output, production, distribution and so on. A large part of our work consists in acting as safety valves for all the grouses of the trader – we are supposed to be the traders' friend! The work has brought me into contact with a whole section of English people with whom I had not the faintest contact or the slightest knowledge before. The backbone of England, aren't they supposed to be?! I find most of them alarmingly anti-Semitic already, but in spite of lamentable narrownesses, and very deep seated prejudices, with a certain very admirable quality of guts and goodwill and general sturdy independence; and a more genuine realisation, very often, of the exigencies of war which restrict the supply of this and that, than the average customer, who must have a pair of little white kid boots for Johnny, or plum coloured gym tunics for Sarah at High School. . . .

Accommodation and food, especially for lunch if you are stranded in some tiny village on early closing day,[22] is often a problem; and sometimes, as I stand in the corridor of a crowded train, I grumble between my teeth to passengers who step on my toes: Is your journey really necessary? But a good deal of our travelling is done in Mrs Tomrley's car. She is my 'boss', and a wonderful woman to work under. In fact, I could not choose a better war job, if I had the chance of all that is going.

. . . All my love Rosemary.

P.S. I have just had the very charming wife of Edmund Leach to stay with me! She escaped between bursting bombs and other horrors with a small girl from Burma. E. is still out there in the army. Celia is very nice – I like her enormously, enough not to be a bit jealous – which is just as it ought to be! R.F.

ROSEMARY TO WILLIAM STANNER IN AUSTRALIA

2 December 1942   **Sylvester Road, Cambridge**

My dear William

. . . Our most exciting news is that Raymond has been in America for about five weeks. He was sent out to Washington by the Admiralty board for which he is working to find out what they are doing in his line of work over there. Authorised on Sunday, he left on Tuesday evening to travel by fast independent liner; he returned more excitingly by bomber.[23] I know he thoroughly enjoyed the experience and he was also able to contact some anthropologists over there. How sad that he should have been six months too late to see Bronio![24] . . .

Personally, we lead a remarkably comfortable if energetic life. Lack of *time* to do things, through everyone doing several people's jobs besides their own, is the chief lack we have I still believe. It would be nice to be able to go slow for a change and do things at leisure. I suppose this rush tells on all of us a bit, there is no real mental worry from blitzing now, except in isolated cases – no lack of plain food and we are not in the least cold, in spite of the save fuel campaign. Travel is the worst thing – and as this is half my job, I mention it personally with feeling. Late and overcrowded trains and precious few of them at inconvenient times! . . .

I have been promoted in my job, and now I am ashamed to say, earn very nearly as much as Raymond does at the miserable wage the Admiralty pays him. . . . In spite of all this extra earning, money flows in and *rushes* out – prices have risen quite considerably all round, and one really wonders if one ought to smoke with cigarettes at over a 1d. [old penny] a piece. Nevertheless, everyone does smoke just as much if not more than ever.

Do you know that I have only heard from you once since we left Sydney?

. . . Bless your heart, oh fickle and silent one!

Love from both of us. R.

ROSEMARY TO JAMES LIVINGSTONE

1 June 1943 **Sylvester Road, Cambridge**

My dearest James

I was more upset than ever I expected to be to hear your news of Beeth.[25] . . . James, I do send you all my sympathy, if it can reach across the vast spaces of war and time which seem to separate us. I know he was your best friend, and these days one can ill afford to lose any of one's friends. . . .

We live in a sort of breathless atmosphere of urgency, fear, anticipation or excitement. At the moment, the two latter are the uppermost emotions, thank God. But one still has the feeling that all this time of war is just an interlude in one's life, which one is waiting to be over, in order to continue the ordinary routine of living. When it is all over, one will appreciate with a shock that a goodly slab of life has gone by for good. I suppose this is one of the uppermost feelings of my mind which has made me put off being 'domestic' [having a family] till after the war. I do dimly begin to perceive that when that blessed time comes, it will damn nearly be too late for all that!

[. . . A] really good social development of the war has been the British Restaurants. In quite small country market towns, as well as in bigger places, there is now usually one of these. In some large room, very often a disused Georgian library . . . a crowd of people assembles and gets fed in an astonishingly short space of time for the price of about 1/- [one shilling]. Everything possible is organised to save time now, and in lots of little ways, like helping yourself in shops, queuing in an orderly way for buses, serving yourself at quite swish restaurant places in town, sharing taxis as if they are public conveyances, (policemen organise taxi parties now!); people are doing things which would be unheard of pre-war. . . . I think the operative factor in all our shortages is and will remain labour. It is a fact that no country is so totally organised in all aspects of its war effort as we are, I believe, not excepting our enemy. And in respect of farming, a little-known fact is that we are now the most highly mechanised agricultural country, even higher than U.S.A.

Rigid price control of all food and non-food goods which could at a stretch be called essential has prevented inflation. The astonishing thing is that people cheerfully go on smoking with cigarettes at 2/4 [two shillings and fourpence] for 20! More cheerful still is the widespread willingness and indeed enthusiasm both among government and public, for a measure of these controls to remain after the war, some permanently, some for at least a time. There are a number of people engaged in planning for after the war, a very healthy and necessary thing, even in total war, I feel sure. We shall be too tired afterwards to think of all these things unless we put a certain measure of organisation into being now. . . .

Good luck to you, James, I don't forget anything.

Yours ever, [Rosemary]

ೞಬ

It was in early June 1943 that Rosemary started work with the Mobile Team in the Welsh coal-mining valleys.

ROSEMARY TO RAYMOND

20 June 1943   **Sunday**   **Aberdare, S. Wales**

My darling

. . . I find the valleys not without their own beauty, which is almost Chinese. Against a background of great rolling mists and beautiful lines of rising hills you get these almost incredible geometrical patterns of man-made little grey boxed-in rigid lines of unimaginative habitation. Behind or below them plunged into the depths of the valley, tower the chimneys and wheels and inferno of the industrial machines. Grey, shining wet slate, rows of mean little houses, and then the astonishing beauty of hills, green pastures where sheep feed, waterfalls and wooded slopes. It is such an astonishing contrast, that it makes one gasp.

. . . It is astonishing to me to find kettles in really acute short supply, and saucepans comparatively plentiful, cups all right and plates almost non-existent, so different from our region, where there are stacks of plates, and saucepans are unseen, and there is in places a glut of kettles. . . . We begin to think, however, that these valleys are not in fact so badly supplied as was first thought! It will be interesting if this in fact proves to be so, though it won't, I suppose, increase the popularity of the Mobile team if it proves that regional reports were in fact not quite so accurate as they thought! . . .

There has been some hitch and my bicycle has not yet arrived. I remember that I omitted to bring a pump. Could you send me one, please, to Aberdare? Also the padlock, which is on the window sill in the hall I think.

. . . Look after yourself, my precious. I think of you!

. . . Ever yours, Rosemary.

24 June 1943   **Pont Neath Vaughan, near Aberdare**

Darling,

. . . My bicycle arrived at Newport this morning I ascertained by phone today, one week late! I have told them to send it on to Llanelli. It is ridiculous it chasing me all over S. Wales.

You would be so amused to see where I am now. We are staying in a mining electrician's cottage at a village at the top of the valley above Aberdare called Pont Neath Vaughan. We arrived at the rather scrubby little Boot Hotel in Aberdare where we had booked rooms only to be told they had ratted on us and no room available! . . . There is nothing else in Aberdare, which is just a mining town, so we drove up to this village . . . and threw ourselves on the mercy of the Inn keeper there. It was about 7 o'clock and pouring with rain and us with no prospect of a bed! He had no rooms but sent us up to this cottage where the couple are Jehovah's Witnesses! We have two nice rooms here with oil lamps, lavatory outside and no running water, but very clean and comfortable;[26] we bought our rations [locally] and have breakfast with Jehovah's Witnesses, and the Inn gives us our supper. It will certainly be cheap, and it is lovely to come up to this country village among the hills out of grim Aberdare. Feeding at the Inn is just like a holiday – Sackett had <u>two</u> fried eggs and I <u>one</u> for supper the first night! We spent the evening in the bar learning Welsh and arguing with an anti-Semite until 11.30. Closing hours[27] are 10.0 but no one seems to pay any heed to them at all up here. Next evening we went to another little Inn where the men were singing Welsh songs after playing darts. There is the sound of running water all night, and the quiet noise of sheep bleating on the hills. Tonight we went for a nine mile walk after an early supper – got back from a walk right up into the hills at 11.30 just as it was growing dark.[28] . . . But we do work between nine and six as well, you know!

All my love my precious. Rosemary.

RAYMOND TO ROSEMARY

24 June 1943   **Sylvester Road, Cambridge**

My darling,

. . . It was nice of you to ring up. . . . It has been delightful getting letters from you so soon and I am glad you are finding compensations in the country[side]. Audrey [Richards] rang up on business this evening and gives you her love – after a warning to remember how wily the Welsh are! I saw Cycill [in Cambridge]; before dinner we had a beer together at the riverside pub. . . . There is talk of training (French) ADO's [Distribution Officers] to take over in France when the occupation is on – a scheme analogous obviously to those the Americans have for general training of administrators for occupied areas – and she may be asked to lend a hand in the training. Both these items are probably not public property so you had better not refer to them.

I have hardly begun to miss you yet, but no doubt will once the novelty has worn off! So far it's only like the middle of the week feeling! . . .

FAME has come to me: *Who's Who* has written for my life history, with a demand for 'immediate' return and a promise to publish in the next edition in December 'if in time'. Why or how they have suddenly discovered me I don't know. But I shall presumably now exist officially.

Must close and go to bed. All my love my dearest. Take care of yourself.

Ever Raymond.

ROSEMARY TO RAYMOND

4 July 1943   **Sunday**   **Ammanford, Carmarthenshire, S. Wales**

My darling,

. . . The mining villages around Aberdare have a very definite character of their own, remote, turned in on themselves, apart, which is difficult to describe, but is felt; and I can well understand the so called 'miners' mentality', detached from the rest of the world at war, egocentric if not selfish, thinking in terms of his own problems only. . . . Poverty is visible . . . in the marked absence of prams, and the women carrying quite tiny babies enfolded in the large shawl, peasant fashion. Few women wear stockings, and the shoes in the shops are of the cheapest kind. . . . Groups of black men [coalminers] can be seen dismounting from buses about three o'clock in the afternoon, as the shift is a seven hour one, beginning at eight a.m. The chip shop is a great social centre about eight or nine o'clock in the evening, as the street is the other social centre. People stand in groups in the roadway with babies, and men squat on the pavement or steps of their houses chatting in the sun, in the evening. There are hundreds of misshapen little curs[29] about, said to be due to the Welshman's fancy of breeding dogs; and a strange race of mongrels he has managed to produce – indecent long bodied fat things on little legs, all out of proportion. The cats are nicer, but distinctly grubby too. . . .

Yesterday has been haymaking day all up this valley. I went to Pontarddulais, seven miles towards Llanelli, on my bicycle, to see whether it should be surveyed. The hedgerows were all caught up with tufts of hay and the smell of the hay filled the air. Rows of men and women were working in lines on as steep slopes as you might expect to see in the Tyrol. I have found my bicycle of as great value at weekends for pleasure as for the job. . . .

Take care of yourself, my precious. I wish you were here to enjoy all these new experiences with me, which I am *loving*!

Your Rosemary.

7 July 1943   **Llanelli, Carmarthenshire**

My darling –

I've been thinking of you such a lot lately. . . .

Some day soon now we'll have a family of our own, to take the place of so many of those of our friends who were there under the red roses drinking sherry [at their wedding on 24 June 1936] and are now scattered or gone – Bronio, Eileen, Agnes,[30] and lots more who are just far away. My dear, I hope you are not working too hard and are happy. I am enjoying this journey of discovery enormously and I shall never regret taking it; but I do realise time is flying and the homing instinct is welling up in me, for making and keeping a home, a real home, I mean with you.

You have been extraordinarily compassionate and understanding with me and my selfish desires of self-fulfilment, you know. There aren't many husbands who would be so tolerant, and patient and yet *care*. I do think it's about time you had your heart's desire, and I think I know now what that is. God bless you, my dear. I'll give you a child all right. Don't worry! . . .

My love to you my precious.

R.

23 July 1943   **Royal Hotel, South Shields, County Durham**

My darling,

I had one night in Newcastle, a big black city sprawling up and down steep slopes on either side of the Tyne. Which has a somewhat spectacular single span steel bridge rather like the bridge at Sydney Harbour, over it [. . . and] the funniest little tin trams with open ends.

At S. Shields, ten miles away, we have landed in clover. An unenterprising front reveals inside a really comfortable and rather inexpensive hotel . . .

It has been bitterly cold and sunny here in the last 2 days, and we were glad to have a fire in the lounge. I've got a fire on in my room, now, believe it or not, but it is *really* cold! . . .

The town is ugly but not grim. It has some amazing parks, and the sea front is exciting. There are four collieries here, one bang in the centre of the town, but the docks are the main source of livelihood.[31] There is every indication of recent extreme poverty. Some of the back streets are rows of really squalid dwellings, and the women, and especially the children almost in rags. But the friendliness of the slum dwellers is, as always, disarming. The women call you 'love' always, and take immense pains to direct you, help you and so on. The dialect is not so pronounced as I expected, broad of course, but not nearly so marked in its way as Welsh. . . .

I am afraid I shall have to take my Bank Holidays up here. . . .

Look after yourself my dear. I did enjoy that little homecoming![32]

All my love, Rosemary.

9 August 1943   **Royal Hotel, South Shields**

Darling,

You sounded rather lonely and neglected on the telephone, I felt a proper pig for not having written to you regularly. . . . You're not regretting letting me go away, are you?! It's so much easier for the person who goes, it always must be – it's a pity this didn't coincide with your American trip – I remember how I wanted you back just to fill the house and make it home instead of a place to eat and sleep. When one is travelling, and there are always new things and people to see, as well as a hell of a lot of work, one forgets to miss people quite so much. And I have to

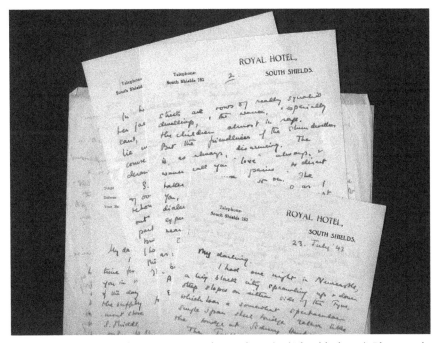

Figure 9.1. Rosemary's letter to Raymond, 23 July 1943: 'A big black city'. Photograph by Hugh Firth.

admit that in a sense – a curious sense – it is a restful and simple life this. I suppose it is rather like being in the army or on active service in the sense that you do the work, as much as you can, and then everything connected with living is done for you: food, shelter, provided and paid for, no worries about housekeeping and very little washing and general 'maintenance' to do. I have cut down the etceteras to living to a real bare 'male' standard; [I] live in one suit and two blouses week in and week out. . . .

All my love, my precious.

Yours only Rosemary.

Notes

1. Adam Kuper, 1986, 'An Interview with Edmund Leach', *Current Anthropology* 27(4): 375–82, p. 377.
2. Edmund Leach, writing of his retreat from Burma, undated diary entry, possibly 26 April 1942. Unpublished.
3. Edmund Leach, diary entry, 30 May 1942, unpublished.
4. Edmund Leach, diary entry, 9 June 1942, unpublished.

5. Adam Kuper, 'An Interview with Edmund Leach', p. 377.
6. Adam Kuper, 'An Interview with Edmund Leach', p. 377. Stanley Tambiah, 2002, *Edmund Leach: An Anthropological Life*, Cambridge: Cambridge University Press, also discusses this period: see p. 44 and p. 417. In August 1942, Edmund was flown into Fort Hertz, a landing strip created by troops parachuted in earlier.
7. Raymond Firth, 'Reflections of a Centenarian', unpublished.
8. Cycill Tomrley later became secretary of the Council of Industrial Design (now the Design Council). In 1969, she published *Let's Look at Design*, London: The Book Service.
9. The exam tested knowledge of regulations, but also demanded a response to scenarios. The interview included roleplayed situations with difficult 'shopkeepers'.
10. Rosemary to William Stanner, 6 April 1942.
11. Rosemary, diary entry, 4 March 1943.
12. Rosemary, diary entry, 6 April 1943.
13. Rosemary, diary entry, 17 May 1943.
14. Miss Bell to Rosemary, 1 April 1943, from the Board of Trade headquarters at Millbank, London.
15. Rosemary to Miss Bell, 7 April 1943.
16. Reg Hicklin, Board of Trade, Millbank, to Rosemary, 28 July 1943.
17. Reg Hicklin to Rosemary, 17 December 1943.
18. Rosemary to Cycill Tomrley from Aberdare, South Wales, 20 June 1943.
19. Rosemary, diary entry, 15 March 1942.
20. Seven important personages: the expression 'big bugs' was used during the 1940s and 1950s.
21. While she was learning the job in the first month or so, Rosemary's boss, Cycill Tomrley, drove them both. Later, Rosemary travelled by train.
22. Until the mid-1960s, most towns and villages had one day a week when all shops closed for the afternoon, typically on Wednesdays.
23. Travelling out on the *Queen Mary* alone, not in a slow convoy.
24. Bronio Malinowski, previously Professor of Anthropology at the LSE, had died in Connecticut in May 1942.
25. One of the circle of undergraduate friends who had been members of the Cosmopolitan Club at Edinburgh University.
26. Very similar amenities to those at Holway, the cottage Rosemary had purchased in Thorncombe in Dorset, in 1937.
27. Licensing hours: it was only legal to sell alcohol in a bar or public house until 10 PM.
28. From the spring of 1941, two hours daylight saving time in summer meant that it was bright until very late in the evening.
29. A mongrel dog, typically roaming without an owner.
30. Bronio (Bronisław) Malinowski (1884–1942) died in New Haven, Connecticut, on 16 May 1942. Eileen Power (1889–1940), the wife of Raymond's best friend Munia Postan, died on 8 August 1940. Agnes and her husband Hermann Adam had returned to Basel, Switzerland.
31. The four collieries to which Rosemary refers appear to have been Westoe, just half a mile from the Town Hall, Harton (closed in 1969), Boldon (just inland from South Shields; closed in 1982) and Marsden – also known as Whitburn – on the coast, just south of South Shields (closed in 1968). She may, however, have been thinking of St. Hilda's, also within half a mile of the Town Hall, which had closed in 1940. Westoe colliery was sunk in 1909 and continued working until 1993. The docks included two 'staithes' for loading coal.
32. Rosemary had been able to spend two nights at home en route from Wales to Tyneside.

Chapter 10

Clogs, Cotton, Commerce and Cream

1943–1944

In the summer and autumn of 1943 Rosemary, Raymond, Edmund and Celia were all living apart from each other: Edmund in Burma, Celia in Holwell, a village in Hertfordshire, Raymond in Cambridge, and Rosemary was constantly on the move around England, Wales and Scotland. Edmund was possibly still based near Fort Hertz, Putao, an isolated airstrip in the extreme north of Burma, supplied only periodically by air.[1] Much of the time, he was on foot in the jungle amongst the Kachin, frequently behind enemy lines, in cloak-and-dagger operations that most likely involved managing Kachin spies passing on information on Japanese operations. Edmund's war was alternately exciting and boring, but above all exhausting and frustrating. Consequently, he was only able to write very occasionally and letters took months to arrive.

Rosemary's life was busy – at times even hectic – travelling back to London for meetings, then to Cambridge for the odd night at home before she travelled back north for another in-depth survey.

Gordon Sackett, the senior Board of Trade official who had helped select the Mobile Team, also led the team and was Rosemary's immediate superior. He was clearly fond of her. Cycill Tomrley had picked this up and warned Rosemary of possible difficulties if they worked closely together. But Sackett was very professional – he never raised his fondness for Rosemary while they worked together. He did write a letter in October 1945 in which he said, 'You know you've given me so much pleasure as to make life worthwhile if it were to end tomorrow. Bless you and God keep you. Gordon.' During these war years, Rosemary had attracted the attention not only of Gordon Sackett and Stanley Watkinson, but also of William Stanner in Dorset in 1937 and Dudley Stamp (their lodger in Cambridge).

After Wales and Tyneside, the team was sent to Lancashire, then Hull (where Rosemary herself led the research), Coventry and Glasgow at the end of the year. Rosemary wrote perceptively on the contrasts between Hull and Coventry. Hull had suffered from periodic bombing throughout 1941, 1942 and 1943, including eight major raids; nearly 95 per cent of all houses in Hull were damaged. Coventry, by contrast, had been heavily bombed early in the war, in November 1940, when over five hundred people were killed, but suffered much less subsequently. Coventry was a centre of war materials production. To accommodate the influx of workers, a number of vast Industrial Hostels had been created, on the same principle as British Restaurants, each accommodating from five hundred to a thousand people, at a charge of £1 a week, with spacious buildings, a restaurant, lounges, games rooms, a post office and a shop where goods in short supply, such as chocolate and cosmetics, were available for hostel members only. Rosemary commented, however, 'All the signs show an enormous purchasing power in this part of the world. We do not like it nearly so much as Lancashire and the North. There is a certain core of hardness, graspingness and a cool reservation lacking in the northern industrial areas.'[2]

While she was in Hull, Rosemary received a visit from senior staff in London – including a 'Mrs. Goldie . . . Assistant Principal in charge of bombing and such like' – keen to discuss the numerical data and better understand the work of the Mobile Team.[3]

At the end of their time in Glasgow, Rosemary was due to return to her normal job in Cambridge. The team intended on having a little celebration: 'We took Miss Bread from the region out for a drink last week, but unluckily chose a Thursday, on which day and all Sunday, no pubs are open! Barbarous country, and they close at 9.0 anyway.'[4]

∽∾

Rosemary returned to Raymond for Christmas 1943 and took up her previous post in Cambridge again in January 1944. Her book on Malay household economics was now in print. Raymond was still preparing his work for publication, besides working full-time on Pacific Island handbooks for Naval Intelligence and finding time to keep up some of his anthropological contacts.

While he and Rosemary were spending Christmas with Celia at Holwell, Raymond became ill with bronchitis, to which he was prone, and pleurisy. Rosemary wrote to her mother-in-law in New Zealand: 'I have had my hands really full . . . the last fortnight. Your tins of dried milk have come in as an absolute godsend. . . . We are planning to have a really proper pre-war holiday.

. . . That is what he really needs most of all I think, so that he can build up a bit of resistance: we shall look for a nice war hotel with good food where he can be nice and lazy for a time.'[5] Rosemary duly arranged a four-week holiday in Mousehole, Cornwall, in March 1944. The holiday started bitterly cold and spartan, but gradually warmed. On 26 March, they listened to Churchill speak of 'deliverance from the mortal U-boat peril' and of plans for a National Health Service after the war. It was his first public speech in more than a year. They visited St Ives, 'full of the sight and smell of oranges' – most frustrating, because they had no ration books on them! On their last day, clear and hot, at Gurnard's Head, they lay on their backs in the sun and 'watched what turned out to be German planes far overhead, dropping sheets of silver paper strips – apparently anti-radio[6] detection. They were rather a beautiful sight.'[7]

ROSEMARY TO EDMUND

2 August 1943   **Alston, Northumberland**

My dear [Edmund]

I go on getting your letters with pleasure though I do not reply as often as I should. In a job rushing about all over the country . . . leisure for writing does not come so easily as it should. But I keep touch with you through Celia, of whom I get more fond each time I see her, as I think I told you. I have not yet been able to see her in her new home in Hitchin . . .

At the moment the chances are a bit more remote as I have been seconded . . . for six months of complete mobility, during which time a mobile team of four of us are liable to be sent anywhere in the Kingdom . . .

For a brief Bank Holiday weekend I've come 45 miles out of Newcastle to a charming village of Alston, right up in among the rolling hills of the edge of Cumberland, with those little stone walls marching crisscross across the naked hills, sheep populated only . . . the fresh air and long walks in the fells are like a break of pre-war holiday atmosphere.

. . . All my love as ever – [Rosemary]

ROSEMARY TO RAYMOND

19 August 1943   **Cross Keys Hotel, Burnley, Lancashire**

Darling,

I had a very good journey up here. . . . I had that excited sensation one usually has when one is on a northbound train and this pleasant companionable attitude of my fellow passengers added to it. At M'chester [Manchester], the train filled up with locals, and the real Lancashire dialect started. I was thrilled to the bone. . . . I've been called 'luv' I don't know how many times and each time I glow within as if they really meant it; as in a way I suppose they do – open friendliness is certainly a great characteristic up here, and the endearments are a socially recognised symbol of it. I just feel silly about the north country accent, it seems to me the most endearing of all the dialects, and I feel that my 'lardy-da' southern cold English is quite precious, I am almost ashamed to open my mouth and show myself forth a stranger in the land!

It is quite different here from Newcastle. We are in the centre of the cotton industry, mostly spinning and weaving. The cheerful clatter of clogs on the pavement is the all-pervading street sound. Men, women and children wear the typical clog with black stockings, which stamps the real local. The clogs are shaped . . . with a distinctive point, steel tipped, and an upper of black shiny tough leather, and a little strap for the ankle. The metal tips ring on the stone streets and as children run it makes a delicious clatter. Women have always worked in the mills here, and I understand it was to use in the damp, dirty oily factories where the waste and raw cotton is dealt with, that they adopted the clog. I do not know what they do with their children up here, for one sees neither the shawl as a carrying garment for small babies, as in Wales, nor the pram of the richer south.

[As] a result of women coming back to homes after a day in the mills, shops remain open till seven o'clock, and in peace time, until nine some nights. There are *no* queues here, which is the most noticeable difference between here and Newcastle, which was full of queues at shoe shops, stocking shops, fruit shops, cake shops and restaurants. I think the women have no time to queue here, bless them! As a result, there are tomatoes and plums on view in shop windows, cakes, brushes and handled cups. We are so near the potteries and supplies are evidently so good, we are not doing crockery at all. Up here, the pint mug with a handle is the great vessel in demand. (In the south they won't look at such a thing, except for the army!) Girls brew their own tea in these mugs[8] and drink it straight out of them in the mills – a thoroughly sensible habit, obviating the need for the teapot.

High tea is of course the local habit, and even hotels pack up their restaurants soon after seven.

My hotel bedroom looks out over a stream rushing by a mill, and I sleep to the sound of running water which is delicious. Like most of the hotels here, it is primarily a pub . . .

A girl has just left this restaurant with the broadest dialect I've heard. 'Goodbye lass, and be good while I'm away' – 'All right, luv, come back' – 'Well, I may not come back that's 'trouble' she replied. The elision of the definite article is widespread. 'You want to take 'bus down yon road till you come t' railway station' they say. It's delicious.

. . . Take care of yourself and 'mind t' kitten'!

Yours ever.

Rosemary.

ROSEMARY TO CYCILL TOMRLEY

29 August 1943   **White Bull, Blackburn, Lancashire**

My dear Cycill

. . . I get the impression of pre-war poverty up here but none of the sense of a slum atmosphere we had in Tyneside.[9] Burnley is a weaving town, mainly upper end of the trade, but there is also spinning. . . . I gather the conditions in the mills pre-war was terrible. You see young girls in the buses returning home with cotton fluff in their hair and on their clothes. Of course all the women have always worked here. Apparently, grandma looks after the baby . . .

I expect you wonder how I am getting on with A.G.S. [Gordon Sackett]. There just don't seem to be any emotional crises at all: . . . I was expecting things to be far from simple. But they aren't – thank goodness. It just seems as if we were both very fond of each other and worked together very well and no problems raised. He's got a tremendous (sometimes comic) sense of professional etiquette, I think . . .

I was amused when I was in London discussing recruits with Miss Bell.[10] She said to me at the end: 'Well, goodbye and good luck. And look after Sackett! I think he's awfully fed up having all these difficult women to manage.' He really is a dear, you know, and just needs I think a little looking after, poor soul. . . . I suppose my affections and desire to look after somebody are all really thwarted maternal instincts. I shall have to give my real maternal instincts a chance soon, I think, before it's too late. But in the meantime I am quite happy with a substitute.

. . . Bless you, and have a nice holiday.

All my love

Rosemary . . .

ROSEMARY TO RAYMOND

29 August 1943   **Burnley, Lancashire**

Darling,

. . . We have had torrents of rain every morning this week. . . . But the cheerful clatter of clogs through the wet streets relieves this gloom, and makes you real-ise why they wear them up here! The afternoons have usually cleared up, and a delicious freshness come[s] over the town. Along the streets['] end you can see the purple slopes of the Yorkshire moors, between a flutter of washing hung up between back rows of houses to dry. The houses are mostly stone built here, and I have not yet seen any such awful slums as I saw in N'castle. Nor do the children look so uncared for. The women are rough and often poorly clad, but they give that feeling of the poverty of peasants, still able to call their souls their own, more than the killing poverty of humans caught in the industrial machine . . .

Well, my precious, I am still enjoying life: but I think your little pigeon which longed to travel will be quite ready to return to the nest and settle down after this six months are up. Then I shall have to make up to you for all the time you've been alone on my behalf!

Look after yourself. I do love you, you know that. I think of you often. Couldn't do without you at home as an anchor, for all my straining at the family leash!

Ever your own. Rosemary.

RAYMOND TO ROSEMARY

31 August 1943   **Sylvester Road, Cambridge**

My darling,

. . . I have been thinking of you, despite the lack of evidence on paper . . .

This last week I have spent on the Malay book, and I feel at last that it has got somewhere. . . . I think I ought to be able to send the MS off in a few weeks to the publisher . . .

I suppose you have seen in the newspapers that Nuremburg has been 'obliterated'. Let's hope an exaggeration but there can't be much of the old town left. I feel that it's got to be done, but it's a cheerless business.

. . . How the days draw in – not much past eight, and nearly time for blackout. It will be winter when you return!!

All my love, dearest. Go on with the job and don't worry about me; I am doing quite well. Take care of yourself, darling.

Raymond.

ROSEMARY TO RAYMOND

22 October 1943   **The Guest House, Beverley Road, Hull**

Darling

. . . I feel myself bursting with energy and health surrounded by the overworked on the verge of nervous breakdowns! . . . I think the team we've now got is really good – a man, Douglas, and Miss Brunsden the conscientious one. We all get on well together too . . .

The searchlight crews have been having practices each night, and there has been a lovely little silvered aeroplane lit up in the sky by a cone of piercing light shafts, as it travels slowly across the heavens.

Apart from practices, we had one night with an alert and a little gunfire, but nothing much. I didn't get up [to go to the nearest air-raid shelter].

Hull's centre is almost non-existent, and if you ask a person in the street or even a policeman where a well-known large shop is, they say, 'Well let me think – yes, it's so and so'. The big shops have been blitzed so often and moved [so often], that no one can remember where they are . . .

My roses have been lovely; they arrived in perfect condition and have filled my room with scent . . .

Ever your own R.

Will ring up Sunday.

24 October 1943   **Hull**

Darling

. . . I am enjoying Hull. It's extraordinarily interesting to try and find out just how badly off a bombed town is, and is a bit of a new job in a way too. Of course it's rather fun to be doing it on one's own too, although I enjoy working with Sackett . . .

There is a great deal of good humour and goodwill up here – the Yorkshire spirit undaunted by the terrible fate its city has suffered. It's extraordinarily exhilarating; Hull doesn't depress one a bit, because its spirit is so very undaunted.

. . . Ever yours Rosemary.

11 November 1943   **Coventry**

My dear,

. . . The first thing which strikes you and which dominates all your later thoughts of the town is the three spires which still leap up into the sky in sheer beauty over the city. . . . There is something almost obscene in the spectacle of a fifteenth century timbered house bulged out in ruins over the road, its timbered windows gaping into its blasted, burnt out shell. . . . It seems proper that the products of modern engineering should suffer from the effects of modern aerial warfare, or even, one sadly accepts the effects on our immediate cultural past, the Georgian houses. But it seems outrageous that a building from the days of handcraft which has survived some four hundred years without decaying should eventually have to be vanquished by steel and explosive. It is out of proportion.

. . . Standing near the cathedral one can look down on either side over really considerable areas of devastation, but willow herb, dandelion, and daisies grow in the shells of houses, all of which have been carefully razed to the ground, and neatly fenced off. Unlike Hull, the wounds all seem very old, as indeed they are. But the people of Coventry, one gathers, have nursed and exhibited their one wound, while Hull has accepted wound after wound without a great deal of fuss.

I understand that Coventry is now one of the very fullest of the war industry towns, and that wages are higher here in general than almost any other place. Spending power seems enormous, and there is said to be little forethought for savings. The Secretary of the local Chamber of Commerce told us that Coventry was too self-conscious about its bombing; that it, being the first to suffer, has had too much limelight altogether in proportion to its real trouble. And that in consequence, the Coventry people were spoiled and did not have that great sense of realism, that spirit of ability to distinguish genuine and secondary hardships which we found in Hull. . . . [Also] the frank friendliness both of manner and the openness of speech of the North is lacking: one is called 'Madam' by the chambermaid not 'luv'! . . .

Accommodation is the most difficult thing in the world to get. We finally landed up in a Trust House in Nuneaton, about ten miles out. . . . We are told that in Coventry itself landladies let their lodgings to both day and night shift workers at once – thus using beds and rooms on a 24-hour shift and collecting full rents from two sets of lodgers!

. . . All my love my dear.

Yours ever R.

2 December 1943   **Queens Hotel, Gourock, Scotland**

My darling,

I am glad I rang you up in London. Fancy your having been ill again and I knew nothing about it! I can see, it's high time I came back again and looked after you properly . . .

I had rather a successful day in London . . . talked to four new recruits on the work of the Mobile Team. I think they were a bit affected with enthusiasm, which is what is wanted . . .

[Accommodation] is even more difficult to get here than in England . . . this part of the world is absolutely stiff with the RN [Royal Navy] and these men come and go so erratically that hotels are never willing to book far ahead. At any rate we have landed in the most comfortable hotel we've struck so far by a long chalk. . . . But the food! Well, when I say it's pre-war, that's putting it mildly. Cream on the top of the milk with porridge in the morning is thick, and jugs of this fresh milk appear all day. Wherever else we've been, milk has been acutely short and mostly dried at that. Then we get what appears to be fresh butter in large quantities at *every* meal, breakfast, lunch, tea and dinner. The lamb and beef melt in your mouth, and one has enormous helpings, with deliciously cooked vegetables. . . . Puddings are full of raisins and egg custards, and for tea we get more scones and butter and cake than we can consume.

The hotel is as near to the sea as our house was in Malaya. It looks over a delectable stretch of water to great mounding hills behind. The estuary is alive with all manner of shipping, which is lit up by night[11] and sparkles like a peacetime party in the blackout.

The call of these hills, the smell of the sea, the gulls wheeling over the ships, the massive grey brick Scotch buildings,[12] the generous atmosphere of friendliness, hospitality and plenty about, have infected us all with enormous zest, and we are as excited over Scotland as children on holiday.

. . . Don't be too jealous of me for having such a fling just before I come home . . .

Yours ever, Rosemary.

15 December 1943   **Belhaven Hotel, Glasgow**

My dear,

. . . I haven't rung up because calls to the South seem to take anything up to two hours to get through[13] and then are very indistinct . . .

Glasgow is the home it seems of fogs. A ghastly yellow darkness descends on the city every afternoon and thickens as the night sets in, as it does at 5 o'clock or earlier.

Our work here has not been made any easier by the attitude of the Regional Officers, who have been most unhelpful, even discourteous. . . . Either they are incompetent or malicious, for they were unable even to give us a suggested list of the main shops to visit. This has all made our work in an enormous city like Glasgow (a million population) much lengthier and more laborious than it need be. It's stupid: such a difference from the previous region . . .

We have had to lead a more abstemious life on the drink line though, due to the local habit of the pubs [only] opening 5 to 9 p.m. One really doesn't feel like a drink so early – 9.30 is about the time. . . . We have taken to the solace of cards: you'd be amused to see the four of us driving the thoughts of trade from our minds by rounds of Rummy. . . . Four people working, eating, and playing together for several months easily get on each other's nerves . . .

Let me have a word before I leave Glasgow darling. Drop me a postcard over the weekend . . .

Tell Miss Le Pelley to warn the butcher there will be my ration book for the meat in the Christmas week. I'll bring it along on Friday, but he'll need to be prepared I dare say.

Darling, it will be lovely to come home to you. I feel you need me now, and I do want to come and look after you and feather our little nest. You know that, precious, don't you?

I love you.

Your wife, Rosemary.

Notes

1. Adam Kuper, 1986. 'An Interview with Edmund Leach', *Current Anthropology* 27(4): 375–82, p. 377. Stanley Tambiah, 2002, *Edmund Leach: An Anthropological Life*, Cambridge: Cambridge University Press, p. 45. See also https://en.wikipedia.org/wiki/Fort_Hertz.
2. Rosemary to Raymond, 22 November 1943.
3. Rosemary to Raymond, 27 October 1943.
4. Rosemary to Raymond, 20 December 1943.
5. Rosemary to Marie Firth, 12 February 1944.
6. 'Chaff' was an anti-radar device: small strips of aluminium that confused enemy radar. Both Britain and Germany had developed radar location systems in great secrecy before the war. By 1944, public awareness of the existence and use of radar was growing, although the technology remained secret.
7. Rosemary, diary entries, 15 March, 26 March, 27 March 1944.
8. Brewed as in a teapot; teabags were still a rarity in England.
9. Rosemary had remarked on some extreme poverty and squalid dwellings in Tyneside: Rosemary to Raymond, 23 July 1943.
10. Miss Bell was a senior civil servant in London, responsible for the Consumer Needs Division, including the Mobile Team.
11. Presumably with minimal port and starboard red and green lights to avoid collisions in the busy estuary.
12. Grey stone and red brick.
13. Long-distance or 'trunk' calls had to be requested through the operator. Operators needed to request a line through other intermediate exchanges. With limited telephone lines, this often took a long time. Eventually, the (female) operator would call back and say she had the call and then put the caller through.

Chapter 11

Twenty Hens, Three Cats and a Fish

1944–1949

At the start of 1944, Edmund was still fighting an uncertain battle with the Japanese in Burma, but Rosemary and Raymond were able to begin to look forward to a future in peacetime Britain. After four years of war in Europe and two years fighting the Japanese in the east, the allied British, Soviet and American forces were confident of eventual victory. In the winter of 1942–43, the Soviet defence of Stalingrad had resulted in nearly a million German casualties and decisively reversed the Nazi advance. For the next two years, both the Germans and the Japanese were in almost continual retreat. Now, in different ways, Raymond's, Rosemary's and Edmund's thoughts were all turning towards home, towards rest, recovery and another phase of life.

ৎৄৎ

In the spring of 1944, Edmund had been promoted to staff major; thus, he attained the same rank he had held before he was demoted a year or so earlier. During most of 1944, he was on the move, amongst the Kachin or with the British army, pushing south very slowly as part of a punishing campaign to drive the Japanese back out of Burma. He was both physically and mentally exhausted.

By early 1945, he had risen to be deputy to the chief military officer responsible for administrating 'liberated' Burma, possibly near Mandalay, barely 100 miles from where he had lived amongst the Kachin nearly six years earlier in 1939.[1]

He was, for once, in a position to be 'in the know about what is happening', at least in his own theatre of war in northern Burma. Characteristically sceptical of what the press published about the progress of the war in Europe (and scathing about the apparent neglect of the war in the east by the British press), he was eager to understand what Rosemary was now engaged in after her Mobile Team work and possibly slightly jealous of Rosemary's apparent role 'at the core of reconstruction planning'.[2]

Above all, Edmund was very anxious to get leave to visit Celia and his daughter, whom 'I long to see'.[3] '"Repat" and "Leave" fills everyone's thoughts. There is a tremendous amount of real tragedy in the background, the number of unfaithful wives and shattered romances that have to be dealt with is appalling. I reckon that three years is about the limit of tolerable marital separation. . . . I have fits of the utmost gloom but that is just the outcome of general sexual frustration'. . . . 'In the circumstances, birthdays and all sorts of anniversaries get rather painful.'[4] But the struggle to oust the Japanese from Burma was not finished. In March, he wrote that 'we are very much in the middle of the battle hence letter-writing is difficult. . . . I don't think anyone at home realises the quite incredible nature of this campaign' (all supplies had to be airlifted into the jungle).[5]

Edmund was unable to get back to England until May 1945.[6] When he returned, he was still weak from recurring bouts of malaria and dysentery and was not at all happy to encounter a daughter, aged three and a half, who resented his presence.

Rosemary and Raymond were together again in Cambridge for six short months in the first half of 1944: Raymond with the Admiralty, Rosemary working all over East Anglia once more. Then, as part of planning for postwar development, Raymond was invited to become secretary of the first Colonial Social Science Research Council (CSSRC), a post he filled for eighteen months on a full-time basis through most of 1944 and 1945. But this meant Raymond living in London while Rosemary stayed in Cambridge. In July 1944, Raymond moved into a temporary flat in Hanover Square near Oxford Circus in central London, where he was greeted by one of the Nazis' new flying bombs, which landed just a couple of hundred yards away. Luckily, he was unharmed.

ॐ

Rosemary now applied to move to London. At the start of 1945, she was able to join Raymond in London (in another temporary flat, in St George's Drive, Pimlico), and in May 1945 she was given responsibility for the London Region of the Consumer Needs Division of the Board of Trade.

Yet no sooner had Rosemary and Raymond rented a permanent flat together in June 1945, in Maida Vale, London, which was to be their home for the next seven years, than Raymond left to spend nearly three months away in West Africa, because he felt that as secretary of the CSSRC, he needed some experience of African problems. Although the war against Japan continued until 15 August, Germany had been defeated in May 1945 and peace in Europe was allowing more normal government at home, as well as allowing government thinking about development in the colonies to begin again.

Rosemary later recalled of this period: 'wandering about Regent's Park. . . . I used to come here during [these] war years, with various not very serious "admirers" – such as I used illegitimately to collect in my early married life when I was not sobered down by motherhood!'[7] One such 'not very serious' admirer was Reo Fortune.[8] 'Raymond was in Africa and Reo used to visit me regularly when he had time . . . one fine Spring day we lay in the sun in Kew Gardens and became mildly amorous. I remember saying: "I'll be fond of you till the autumn leaves fall Reo, and Raymond comes home!" All that seemed quite appropriate to the times of war and live-for-the-moment which we were engulfed in.'[9]

EDMUND TO ROSEMARY

14 July 1944   Burma

Dear Rosemary

. . . Out here we are trying to steel ourselves to the prospect of another two or three years . . . the resultant state of indefinite divorce is gradually sapping my innate [resilience] completely. How Celia stands it I don't know, I just don't. . . . I find it extremely hard to imagine either the house or my daughter though I have photos of both. Indeed I am such a stranger to my family that it is hard to plan ahead. . . . I fear [I] will have to think again and find some more lucrative employment than Anthropology which . . . might be a pity . . .

My personal war has been fairly quiet – I have not been in a battle area since December though for months now I have been standing by for a somewhat hair-raising enterprise. . . . Please write when you can . . .

All my love Edmund.

17 October 1944   Burma

Dear Rosemary

I have to thank you for parcels of papers; you can have no idea what pleasure they give. I wish I could send something adequate in return but . . . it now needs so many permits even to send off a pound of sweets that really I can't do it at all unless I am actually in Calcutta. I was intrigued by the 'illustrated' account of Consumer research; you are certainly engaged in a much more positive sort of war-work than I am . . .

Love to you both, Edmund.

9 February 1945   **Burma**

Dear Rosemary

. . . We are in the midst of a very extraordinary military campaign and my life is very interesting but very bleak and uncomfortable, no 'amenities' whatever. However the food is good. But I know what Mandalay is like in April and the prospect of being anywhere in the vicinity is not pleasant.

It is a long time since I had the chance of doing anything even vaguely anthropological but I ought to be an expert on economics by the time [I do]. . . . The race between inflation and the army as to who reaches Rangoon first will be intriguing to watch.

We are steadily bombing Burma to pieces and none of the towns survive except as heaps of rubble. Fortunately most of the population have cleared out into country villages and the jungle . . .

Sorry no time for more.

All the best, Edmund.

ᏨᎵᏬ

Edmund came back to England in May 1945, but thankfully he was not required to return to Burma after the destruction of Hiroshima and Nagasaki and the Japanese surrender in August 1945.

Rosemary resigned her Board of Trade post in March 1946 to be able to start a family – something she and Raymond had been wanting to do for some time.

In the main, women in the late 1940s either remained unmarried in order to pursue a career or gave up their career to bring up children. Rosemary chose the latter option. Only in the 1960s, with the next generation, would women hold down professional jobs whilst bringing up their families.

Rosemary became pregnant almost immediately after she left her job.

Rosemary and Raymond's son Hugh was born in December 1946, at the start of the coldest winter in a century. Household pipes in buildings, almost none of which had central heating, were frequently frozen that winter; it was an extremely anxious time to be caring for a small baby. Moreover, Rosemary caught German measles in the spring of 1947. Nevertheless, she was determined to continue breastfeeding, and by the summer she was thoroughly enjoying being a mother.

ces

Raymond became preoccupied with his work at this time. He had been formally appointed as the Professor of Anthropology at the LSE in late 1944,
after Malinowski's death in 1942 – although, as he was still seconded to the
Admiralty and the CSSRC, he did no teaching before 1946. At the very end
of 1945, he ceased to be secretary to the CSSRC (a senior civil service post).
But he was now invited to become a member of the council itself. Much
of his energy went into the politics of the CSSRC. His involvement in the
CSSRC proved challenging as rivalries between anthropologists in London,
Oxford and Cambridge caused problems and setbacks that troubled him.[10]
However, Raymond's efforts with the CSSRC were extremely successful:
research money from the council and government funding for higher education helped anthropology to embark on a long but steady process of growth
in terms of both numbers and influence. Besides these challenges, Raymond
was also working hard to build the profile and the establishment of the LSE
anthropology department, of which he was the head. Anthropology itself was
also changing: in 1947, Raymond would start an anthropological study not
of a faraway society, but of Bermondsey in London.

In late May 1945, very soon after Edmund's return to England, Raymond
received 'a letter unexpectedly from [him] . . . and we picked up threads
again'.[11]

In the years immediately after the end of the war, as in 1938, Edmund
experienced a period of self-doubt. He was still registered for his doctorate,
with Raymond as his supervisor, but he had lost all his field notes and papers
in the desperate retreat from the Japanese in 1942. Edmund himself said, 'I
was not at all sure that I wanted to have anything more to do with anthropology, but between us we agreed I should read all the literature and reassess
it in the light of my on the ground experiences. I completed the thesis in the
spring of 1947.'[12] In September 1947, Edmund went to Sarawak in Borneo
using funding Raymond had secured from the Colonial Research Council.
On his return, he joined the staff of the LSE.

At this time, the contradictions and uncertainties in Edmund's view of
himself began to coalesce in a way that eventually led him to propound some
radically new ways of thinking about power and political structures in remote
and little-known societies. In one sense, Edmund remained an engineer all his
life. He admitted that 'I am, I must confess, frequently bored by the facts. . . .
I cannot arouse in myself any real interest in the cultural peculiarities of . . .
the Tikopia. . . . I read the works of Professor Firth . . . so as to learn something about the principles behind the facts.'[13] He wanted to understand the
big levers underlying social behaviour and particularly social change; detailed
description alone did not interest him. He wanted to lecture on anthropo-

logical theory, and he was uneasy in an LSE department that was dominated intellectually by Raymond's ideas about the importance of economic organisation and 'practical anthropology'.

This was possibly the one period in their lives when there was real tension between Raymond and Edmund. At that point, he did not 'fit in' at the LSE. Edmund wrote to Raymond:

> My present total feeling is that I would like to get out of academic anthropology altogether for some considerable time. . . . My intellectual doubts make me, as you must have noticed, aggressive and iconoclast in argument. . . . [Also] The fact that I cannot distinguish the personal and academic elements in our relationship is both embarrassing and highly confusing. These arguments were the ones that I presented to you in the first place on the occasion of our evening talk at your flat and you apparently found them unconvincing. But when I approached the issue from another angle this last Thursday you took me seriously; instead of saying that I was dissatisfied with my own intellectual position, I said that I was dissatisfied with yours; surely this is the same thing. Intellectually I am out of step and confused; I feel I can only appreciate the real issues by getting away from them. . . . This . . . has lately, it seems to me, been further aggravated by my own iconoclasm, a state of affairs which I thoroughly deplore. . . . Hence again my feeling that in order to see the wood for the trees in proper proportion I must get right outside it. . . . All of which is highly unsatisfactory especially as I know very well that in six months' time I may, and probably will, feel quite differently about the whole issue.[14]

But Raymond wanted to try and keep him there. He recognised and greatly respected Edmund's 'intelligence, his mathematical background, his acute critical scrutiny and his creative theoretical approach [which] made him an instant asset to the anthropological seminar'.[15]

Edmund, however, was ill at ease with the empirical, descriptive, 'static' approach of both Malinowski and Raymond. The ideas he found himself mulling over did not accord with the detailed 'ethnographic' approach he had agreed to adopt for his doctorate. He had become 'overwhelmed' by these issues and by his own intellectual doubts, which he discussed at length with Raymond during late 1948 and in 1949.[16] He resolved to resign, and took a year out, working full-time on the ideas that were to become the hugely influential *Political Systems of Highland Burma*. To Raymond's delight, he then returned, promoted to a new post of reader.

Rosemary, Raymond, Edmund and Celia were now regularly seeing each other socially and, despite occasional professional tensions, Raymond and Edmund became close friends.

In these post-war years, Raymond was immersed in his career, whilst Rosemary was occupied almost full-time looking after her small son and often one or more of her sisters' children. In the summer of 1947, Raymond was again away, this time for three months in Malaya on a Colonial Research Council mission. Rosemary wrote to Raymond that it was 'time to start another baby when you get back'.[17] Sadly for her, that never happened.

Although Rosemary and Raymond were still close in many respects, it seems to have been at this time that the seeds of later difficulties between the two of them were germinating. Raymond's preoccupation with the rivalries and tensions in his work life was probably the major contributor. It seems likely that Raymond became somewhat depressed at times as a result of the setbacks he experienced in his work. Rosemary's mood appears to have become more fragile in response to her experience of a husband who was no longer 'there' for her. She may well also have had anxieties about where her own life might be leading. As a housewife with a young baby, she was becoming increasingly separated from Raymond, Edmund and the stimulating life she had so much enjoyed when she was working.

She did, however, develop some very important relationships with a number of women in their circle of friends: some, like Betty Belshaw, were the wives of anthropologists. Betty's husband, Cyril, was a New Zealander like Raymond. He was a student of Raymond's at the LSE in 1947; Cyril and Betty then moved to Australia in 1950 for a period before settling in Vancouver. Betty and Rosemary saw each other frequently and became good friends; when Betty had a daughter just a little younger than Rosemary's son, their friendship strengthened.

The years of austerity and reconstruction in late 1940s Britain had much in common with the last years of the war. Bread was rationed, for the very first time, from 1946 to 1948 and meat was rationed until 1954, while money for universities was also extremely tight.

Plentiful fruit and vegetables were thus a wonderful and welcome relief from scarcity for Rosemary whenever she stayed somewhere with a bountiful garden.

During the United Kingdom's long dry summer of 1947, while Raymond was away in Malaya, Rosemary spent time first in Bristol with Elizabeth and her son Christopher, and then at her elder sister Margaret's extensive home at Merton in Wimbledon,[18] where she looked after Margaret's young daughter Debby while the rest of the family went for a holiday. This was a period with many new experiences and much pleasure – but also loneliness. Rosemary wrote to Raymond almost every other day; besides missing him, a big part of her was yearning for the intellectual life she was no longer living.

Two years later, Rosemary's elder sister Margaret, who had recently broken a rib, was due to give birth to her fifth child. Rosemary looked after Debby again for some eight weeks during this period. They spent much of the time in Dorset at the little cottage Rosemary had bought in 1937. It still had oil lamps for lighting, a coal stove for cooking and cold water pumped by hand into the kitchen. 'All the tradesmen call, including the fishmonger and the ironmonger,[19] and in spite of drawing oil and water and struggling with an outside lavatory there seems far less rush of things to do than in London.'[20]

ROSEMARY TO RAYMOND IN MALAYA

30 July 1947   **Redland Court Road, Bristol**

Darling,

. . . I haven't missed you so, since you left, as this evening . . .

It seems such an odd life for me, being away from you and looking after children all day, that although I dearly love Hugh sometimes I feel so strange, I have to remind myself this is the same Rosemary who lived at 32 Gt. Ormond St., and in Cambridge and went everywhere with you! When I'm actually doing some service for Hugh I feel quite natural and happy. But it's the by ends of having a baby that are odd: for instance a cousin of Daddy's comes in and 'talks baby' for an hour. . . . Sometimes all this becomes a nightmare of strangeness, and I long for you to wake me up and remind me who I am, and that I do belong to you – as I do, darling don't I?

. . . I know you must be terribly busy and have lots of notes and things to write, so I shan't fret about letters if I feel you are receiving my own.

We both send our love.

(I am better by the way).

Rosemary.

22 August 1947   **Merton Cottage, Wimbledon, London**[21]

My darling

I feel rather like an actor in a repertory company, the scene has shifted so completely. . . . I left Bristol on Wednesday. . . . Here, there are six children and five adults in the family – beginning at Hugh 6 months, Deborah [Debby] 13 months, cook's daughter 2 yrs., Susan 3, Andrew 5, Oliver 8, and Cyril, Margaret, Grete a Swiss girl, and the cook. A woman comes in 3 times weekly. Then there are about 20 hens, 3 cats, (one suckling kittens!) and an enormous garden reminiscent of Andrew Marvel. Plums, apples, pears, mulberries, tomatoes, grapes, sweet corn, marrows, potatoes, lettuces, carrots, etc. etc. rampant so that it is difficult to make much impression on them. The lawns are strewn with fallen fruit no one has time to pluck, bottle, stew, jam, or even *give* away any more! You know it has been a spectacular summer – weeks of fine cloudless warmth reminiscent of the continental summer. Life here is rather like that in a Victorian country house. Never have I seen so many children, so much fruit, milk, eggs, such long passages and numerous bedrooms – so many prams in odd corners. It is amusing: I have to take control here tomorrow when the older children go away and I am left with Hugh, Deborah and the Swiss girl, chickens, cats, and fruit trees. God help me!

Your son is much admired by all. He can a l m o s t c r a w l.

Ever your own Rosemary.

25 August 1947   **Merton Cottage, Wimbledon**

My darling,

. . . Sometimes you seem a very, very long way away and Hugh and I quite alone in the world – as if I had always and always been living in other people's houses, getting up at six, feeding the baby, washing nappies, bathing him, shopping and cooking and so on. I suppose this completely domestic life is so new to me anyway that it makes me feel even more strange, living it with you away, than just having you away while I was getting on with my accustomed work, as in 1945 when you were in Africa, and I was with the B.o.T. [Board of Trade]

At other times, particularly in the evening, when these spectacular warm nights fall at the end of a blazing summer day . . . and a cricket drums quietly in the grass: when the lights gleam from open windows across a lawn and one can wander without thinking of temperature into the garden: at these times I often feel back in 1939 and that I am in Malaya with you. You have missed one of the most splendid years of the last few decades I suppose. Day after day we have clear blue skies, sunshine, warmth. . . . I've never seen such plenty in such beautiful weather as here.

. . . Now the entire family have departed for their holidays I am left in charge of an eight bedroomed house with 3 bathrooms . . . and a fish of Oliver's which causes me more anxiety than the feeding of all the other animals and people put together, and a caterpillar also of his! . . .

Here there are so many children (six when all at home) no one has time to worry overmuch about a single cry, quarrel or smack. How much better for the child than all the emotion and attention poor Christopher evokes![22]

I am learning a lot about children and babies and I hope about husbands too. I hope I may never give so much attention to Hugh as to spoil him as C. is spoilt, nor yet get so absorbed in my children as to be almost impenetrable to you, as Margaret is to Cyril, who lives, moves and has his being on the edge of her domestic world.

. . . Ever your own special

Rosemary.

ҨКѺ

Meanwhile, Raymond's international academic reputation was growing. In 1947, he was asked to become one of four advisors, along with the nuclear physicist Mark Oliphant and Howard Florey – who had isolated penicillin together with Alexander Fleming – on a major project: to establish and build a National University for Australia, in Canberra, the new capital. In 1948, Raymond, Rosemary and Hugh (aged fifteen months) spent four weeks in Canberra as part of this work.[23] This was the first of two such visits they would make to Canberra; the second would be much longer and more significant.

Towards the end of this 1948 visit, Raymond was invited to become the first director of the School of Pacific Studies at the new Australian National University (ANU) in Canberra. He discussed it with Rosemary: 'Rosemary and I did not take [it] too seriously . . . and after some reflection I declined it.'[24] They then travelled on to see Raymond's parents in New Zealand. When Raymond returned to his LSE job in London in April, Rosemary and Hugh stayed on for three months with her parents-in-law, returning by ship via Melbourne.

Figure 11.1. Raymond, Rosemary and Hugh on arrival in Canberra, March 1948. Photographer unknown.

ROSEMARY TO RAYMOND IN LONDON

28 June 1948   **R.M.S.** *Strathaird*, **Melbourne, Australia**

My darling

It was sad parting from your parents in New Zealand and your Father was particularly moved. He held Hugh in his arms till the last minute, and I felt quite cruel, taking him out of those loving arms, perhaps forever. Your father has shown to me an unexpected degree of affection for Hugh. He says he never had time to play with his own children, but there is no doubt he thoroughly understands the handling of small children. He is gentle, firm, affectionate, playful, and not over anxious. I had half a mind, while you were away, to go off on my own and get a glimpse of the South Island. But I soon saw that the chief burthen [burden] of responsibility for looking after Hugh would be bound to fall on Mother, to whom it was really rather a matter of tension. Hugh is adventurous and bold and independent, and loves the fresh air and free play in the garden, all of which things somewhat alarm your mother!

But your mother strikes me, in relation to her family, as a loving hen who has reared a family of ducks, and looks on with alarm and despair as they all troop into the waters of intellectuality and independence. I believe the real reason your mother so longed for a daughter was that she expected the daughter to be non-intellectual like herself. I think fundamentally she could not accept me as a substitute, because to her chagrin, she finds I also fall into the male category of intellectual independence. But she is, of course, not the less generous in her affection in spite perhaps of wishing I were otherwise. But I think rightly or wrongly, I represent to your mother, reason and England, two things of which she is afraid because they have taken her children. I write this because I got to know your parents really well this time and can look on them all round. We had some lovely times together, especially with Hugh, and I was pleased to notice that later on as Mother got used to Hugh's ways and found out that he did not kill himself every day, they established very good relations.

Hugh . . . sends you dear love.

R.

ജ

After their return from this first visit to Australia in the autumn of 1948, Rosemary appears to have suffered a period when she was low in mood, something she experienced intermittently for the rest of her life. In her diary, she quoted T.S. Eliot: 'It seems I shall get rid of nothing / Of none of the shadows I wanted to escape.'[25] What is less clear is what these shadows were. (In the late 1940s, her diary consisted only of quotations from poetry.) Certainly, her relationship with Raymond was under some strain. With reference to Raymond, she transcribed, 'I that was near your heart was removed therefrom'.[26] Was Raymond preoccupied with work, perhaps under strain himself, or had he started an affair around this time, as she speculated much later? Socially, she saw Edmund regularly during this period; it seems possible she was plagued by doubts about her marriage to Raymond and wished that she could have spent more time with Edmund. What would her life have been like if she had waited for him to return from China?

In many ways, Rosemary was probably ambivalent about her current situation. On the one hand, she very much wanted children – she wanted more – and she enjoyed looking after young children and observing their development and their interactions. On the other hand, she was clearly lonely at times and yearned for adult company, financial independence and especially intellectual stimulation. And, like many women, she doubtless felt burdened by the many mundane, routine and time-consuming tasks involved in raising children.

ROSEMARY TO MARGARET

16 March 1949   **Holway Cottage, Thorncombe, Dorset**

Dear Margaret

. . . Deb and Hugh both distinguished themselves in the railway journey here altho' their reactions were very different. . . . She cried at all the engines and at the train starting, all of which things were causing Hugh to shout with delight. . . . Once arrived they seemed to settle down very well. Hugh and Deb are really funny together. H. most concerned when Deb cries from nervousness, tells me and points at her with face of distress himself. Deb is also comic in her superior morality towards H. Altho' she gives very little attention to injunctions about sitting up properly or not banging her plate about, or spilling her milk, all these pieces of advice are regaled to Hugh. She even once said to him 'Not talk while mummy talking, Hugh'! She calls him 'Poppett' and tries to teach him to speak. 'Say more pudding please' – and she leans anxiously towards him . . .

Ever yours R x H x D x

Notes

1. Stanley Tambiah, 2002, *Edmund Leach: An Anthropological Life*, Cambridge: Cambridge University Press, p. 45.
2. Edmund to Rosemary, 28 November 1944 and 8 October 1944.
3. Edmund to Rosemary, 1 May 1944.
4. Edmund to Rosemary, 28 November 1944 and 17 November 1944.
5. Edmund to Rosemary, 11 March 1945.

6. He was back in England on 27 May 1945 (Raymond Firth, 'Chronology', unpublished), but was not formally demobilised until January 1946 (Adam Kuper, 1986, 'An Interview with Edmund Leach', *Current Anthropology* 27(4): 375–82).

7. Rosemary to Hugh, 19 May 1971.

8. Reo Fortune (1903–79), New Zealand anthropologist. His relationship with Margaret Mead and Gregory Bateson was fictionalised in 2014 by Lily King in *Euphoria* (London: Picador). Rosemary's admirers appear to have also included William Stanner (in 1937) and the geographer Dudley Stamp (in 1942).

9. Rosemary to Ralph Bulmer, 26 April 1980.

10. David Mills discusses these difficulties in excellent detail in David Mills, 2008, *Difficult Folk: A Political History of Social Anthropology*, Oxford: Berghahn, chapter 5.

11. Raymond Firth, 'Chronology', unpublished.

12. Adam Kuper, 'An Interview with Edmund Leach', p. 377.

13. Edmund Leach, 1954, *Political Systems of Highland Burma*, London: Athlone Press, p. 227.

14. Edmund to Raymond, 11 December 1948 (LSE Library, Firth/8/1/67).

15. Raymond Firth, 'Reflections', unpublished.

16. Raymond Firth, 'Reflections', unpublished.

17. Rosemary to Raymond, 10 July 1947.

18. A large house and grounds owned by the John Innes Centre, housing the director (Cyril Darlington, Margaret's husband) and other John Innes staff.

19. A fishmonger, a butcher, a greengrocer and an ironmonger all toured the villages, each by van, selling from house to house. The village had two bakeries, two grocers, two pubs and a post office.

20. Rosemary to her sister Margaret, 16 March 1949.

21. The house owned by the John Innes Centre.

22. Christopher, born in January 1940, had had a disrupted childhood as a consequence of the war, only living with both his parents for the first time when he was aged seven (Christopher Clay, *My Parents and I,* unpublished).

23. See S.G. Foster and Margaret Varghese, 1996, *The Making of the Australian National University*, Sydney: Allen & Unwin, pp. 26–55 and 126. The other advisor was Keith Hancock, a historian.

24. Raymond Firth, 'Reflections'. Yet correspondence from Edmund to Raymond on 11 December 1948 (LSE Library, Firth/8/1/67) suggests that Raymond was still debating a move to Canberra at that time.

25. T.S. Eliot, 1939, *The Family Reunion: A Play*, London: Faber and Faber. From Rosemary, diary entry, undated, September 1948.

26. T.S. Eliot, 'Gerontion', a poem. From Rosemary, diary entry, undated, September 1948.

Chapter 12

The Cost of Change
1951–1952

The start of the 1950s offered both Raymond and Edmund new job opportunities with the potential to change not just their careers but their whole
lives. Edmund took such an opportunity by moving to Cambridge in 1953.
Raymond and Rosemary faced a more radical opportunity – to emigrate to
Australia. Their decision was to have a huge impact on Rosemary over the
next decade.

In 1951, Raymond was invited to go out to the Australian National University (ANU) in Canberra for the second time – on this occasion, for a whole
year, as acting director of the School of Pacific Studies, to build its staff and
research capability.

Raymond also secured ANU support and funding for a six-month return
expedition to the island of Tikopia, to examine how the society had changed
in the twenty-five years since his first visit in 1928. An examination of the
process of social change affecting a non-western society over such a timescale
had not previously been attempted amongst anthropologists.

Anthropology was moving on from static descriptions of isolated 'primitive' cultures. Raymond was most interested in the processes of social change
within a society, whilst Edmund wanted to get away from traditional anthropological studies of a single supposedly discrete society and understand the
messy interactions *between* adjacent people and cultures. Edmund published
these ideas in his *Political Systems of Highland Burma*.

Around this time, Edmund undertook further fieldwork in 1954 in the
dry central area of Ceylon (now Sri Lanka), and Celia joined him there for a

time. She described the country as the most beautiful place she had ever been to. In addition to painting, she had already written two novels, *Village Story* and *Family Ties*, both published by the Hogarth Press.

Rosemary, Raymond and their four-year-old son journeyed out to Australia by air in July 1951. Travel by aeroplane was still an expensive novelty. Very few people in Britain could afford to fly, and even amongst those who could, most flew rarely, if at all. Destinations beyond Europe, including the United States, were still only within the reach of a small number of very fortunate people. Rosemary, Raymond and their son made the journey in stages, stopping off in New York, Chicago, San Francisco, Hawai'i, Fiji and New Zealand, where they stayed with Raymond's parents. The first few weeks in Canberra were difficult as they were in a flat so cold that a friend lent them extra blankets; but they subsequently rented a beautiful modern house for their stay and were able to enjoy the climate and the lifestyle. Rosemary enjoyed the contact with other academics, such as Margaret Mead, the high-profile American anthropologist. Whenever she was away from the family home in London, Rosemary wrote regularly to her father, sharing delights, triumphs and tribulations, but particularly seeking advice or solace when she was feeling lonely or uncertain. In November, Rosemary confided to her father that 'Sometimes I feel I could not bear to return to England with its noise, dirt and austerity; sometimes I feel desperately alone in the glaring sunshine of a country [so] fundamentally brittle'.[1]

As it happened, one of Rosemary's closest friendships was cemented during their five months in Canberra. Cyril Belshaw was a Research Fellow in Anthropology there, and Betty and Rosemary, already friends since they met in London in 1947, helped each other with their two small children in Canberra, as well as supporting each other in their precarious positions as intelligent women married to successful professional men. They met at least once a week for a meal and nearly daily to take their children to nursery school. During this time, Rosemary also re-engaged with university life in a way that may have led her to think about rebuilding a career.

Raymond's expedition to Tikopia would involve at least five months away from Rosemary. It would take him a month to reach Tikopia by plane and boat. He would spend three months there and return when the government boat next called – an event which happened about every three months, but very unpredictably. Rosemary would be unable to communicate with Raymond from the moment he left for Tikopia: the island is over 120 miles from the Santa Cruz Islands to the west and the government boat was the only visitor to the island. Although Raymond and his colleague Jim Spillius did have a 'telephone-radio' weighing 120 pounds, it was only designed for emergency use and was not reliable. While he was away, Rosemary and Hugh would live with Raymond's parents in Auckland, New

Figure 12.1. Raymond, Auckland, 1951. Photograph by Clifton Firth.

Zealand, before which they would all spend Christmas with his extended family in Auckland.

Shortly before they left to visit Raymond's parents, and before he left for Tikopia, Raymond was offered the directorship as a permanent post for the second time. This presented the couple with the real possibility that they might emigrate to Australia.

While still in Canberra, Rosemary and Raymond had long talks and were working toward reaching a joint decision on whether to emigrate. Rosemary discussed the implications of such a move for Raymond's research and teaching in depth with him, as well as the impact of emigration on their personal lives.

Despite this, by the time they travelled to Auckland for Christmas with Raymond's family, Rosemary and Raymond had not yet reached a conclusion about whether or not they should emigrate. Raymond left Rosemary in Auckland in mid-January 1952. They had agreed that he should make the final decision on his stopover in Canberra and let the vice-chancellor know before he left for Tikopia in mid-February. Rosemary and Raymond corresponded with each other during those few weeks, setting out their thoughts. Rosemary also talked at length to the Professor of Anthropology at Auckland, Ralph Piddington.[2]

Yet, curiously, in her balancing of the merits of Australia versus England, Rosemary neglected to highlight one major issue, which mattered fundamentally to *her*: the close contact she had in England with her family, most especially her father Gilbert.

ROSEMARY TO HER FATHER, GILBERT

30 July 1951   **En Route to Canberra, via New York and Chicago**

Dearest Daddy

. . . We are now in the air on our way to Chicago . . .

Alas, what shall I remember out of all this crowd and bustle of experience to tell you of? First, perhaps, the almost enrapturing experience of riding high in the night sky, stretched out on one's bed canopied like a tent in the plane, and watching the full moon beside, or as it almost seemed below one.[3] This peculiar machine which man has produced is in very truth one realised then, at night voyaging over sea with the moon and stars, a space ship. There, if one woke in the night were the familiar sheets, pillows, blankets and close drawn curtains; but just above, one stretched one's head and saw the whirling universe, the surprised moon, appearing a little squashed. . . . Somewhere below one, if you looked, lay the ocean of a little world in this universe. But so sure, so steady, so strong the engine thrusts and so broad and safe the wings stretched out on either side, one felt in the hands of the arrogant creators, not the tiny inhabitants, of that little world below.

Appropriate enough that this magic should precede landing in America. . . . we stepped out into a land where the buildings, machines, cars, clothes, property, everything betokened apparently limitless wealth, work and resources . . .

New York City we met and left in a raging thunderstorm. Driven in from the airport to a city of towering black buildings swirled around with ugly black clouds and darted with streaks of lightning, the rumbling thunder sharing the din of overhead railways and screeching traffic, I felt Dante himself could not have driven me into a more ominous city of destruction and fear . . .

The wealth . . .

But also what poverty! We were driven though Harlem and side and back streets where I saw housing conditions as bad as in London, and streets far, far, dirtier than any London slum; folk too, untidy, ill clad, dirty. . . . One begins to understand why there is a drug addiction problem in America, juvenile crime, lynching . . .

It is as well that America should be the home of democracy. For if by any chance she should lean towards fascism, the ways and methods of that type of society would not look so very strange to her people as they would no doubt like to have others think.

Love and best wishes to all in London.

Ever your Rosemary x

23 August 1951   **PO. Box 4, Canberra, Australia**

Dearest Daddy

. . . The journey [from New Zealand] to Sydney was rather fun – by flying boat. It's exciting getting up out of the water like a great heavy bird and then landing *splash* at the other end . . .

. . . We have just seen a delightful modern house which is to let . . . and we have hopes of that. It has huge glass windows looking out onto a big gum tree and beyond a delightful mountain view, and is beautifully equipped, washing machines and all . . .

The air is of a heaven like clarity and the hills round us and the gum and wattle trees breathtakingly beautiful. We shall like it when we have got used to it all I suppose and especially if we get this lovely new house.

Hugh sends his love, so do we all.

Rosemary x

30 September 1951   **Empire Circuit, Canberra**

My dearest Father

. . . We have been entertaining and entertained a good bit. Margaret Mead has been here. . . . She is a remarkable woman – not handsome or smart in the very least, with a rather nice round simple friendly face, but of course an enormous fund of egotism of an intellectual nature. I think she has gone to seed scientifically myself in the last 5–7 years: she is so famous and there is so much pressure to do quick publicly interesting surveys and give 'interesting and topical' lectures, that I think she has lost her fine intellectual standards and has got very slipshod in her pronouncements. I heard her lecture and it was full of near brilliant but highly misleading generalised statements without documentation or detailed evidence in support.

. . . She was disarmingly nice to me, expecting apparently to find a bony angular faced English aristocrat (I can't think why!) and finding instead she said 'an English rose'. Still they do have thorns as I reminded her.

. . . All my love my dear.

Ever your affectionate Rosemary.

4 December 1951   **Empire Circuit, Canberra**

Dearest Daddy

. . . I know I shall often, often dream of these . . . months here – in some ways perfect: a lovely house, pure climate, friends for Hugh and a garden,[4] a small community of friends, a great deal of entertaining, days out in the bush and mountain country with a car, wonderful food, and wine. . . . But for different reasons I think neither R. nor I wish to become Australian, and leave Europe. . . . However as I said two years ago, regretting a wrong decision if I must, I would rather regret it *in* England, longing to be here, than here, longing to be back again! . . .

We all send our love for Christmas.

Rosemary.

ᏣᏝᎾ

On 19 January 1952, Raymond left the family in Auckland, for Canberra, on the first stage of his journey to Tikopia.

ROSEMARY TO RAYMOND

22 January 1952   **Otara, Otahuhu, Auckland, New Zealand**

Dearest Raymond,

. . . After you'd gone I felt positively homesick for Australia. . . . But it is odd how even after a second chance we can't bring ourselves to renounce Europe. I tried to rethink it out this way – we know only too well the different advantages of going and of staying in England. Are we afraid to pay the cost of a change? And so what are the costs of either decision? I decided they were as follows:

Costs of Staying in England	*Costs of Canberra*
1. Raymond's probable bad health.	1. Little music.
2. Poor general living conditions.	2. No traditional [i.e. classical] art.[5]
3. Lower spendable income.	3. Out of scientific touch with European
4. Possibility of few students or no	thought.
research funds.	4. Away from main friends.
5. Danger of actual future atomic war.	5. Uncertain political future of Australia
6. General malice of other	and therefore of University.
anthropologists.	6. Fred's temperament.[6]

Looked at in that light the factors in the first column all seem more solid, real and of greater weight than those in the second column.

The things of which I am most apprehensive on my return are general housing conditions, bad weather, diet and poor food, rather than a lack of cars or washing machines, and also a return of your bad health. This is probably the greatest single factor which we have really not much discussed . . .

But health apart I suppose we just are not attracted by tangible advantages or sensible living but feel emotionally European. How perverse we are!

. . . We all send our love.

Ever your Rosemary.

RAYMOND TO ROSEMARY

25 January 1952   **Canberra**

My darling,

. . . I am very evenly poised about the decision. The thought of being cut off from Europe makes my heart sink, and it would be a wrench to think of not going back to my room at the School [LSE], and all the work associated with it. But I think I would be prepared for this, if the situation here were clearer, and if I were *quite* sure that you really would be prepared to make a life here. What about Hugh, his schooling and his interests?

Write me again in the next day or so, to add to your analysis . . . or if only to say that you leave the decision open to me.

. . . My love to Mother, Father and HUGH.

Ever Raymond.

ROSEMARY TO RAYMOND

30 January 1952   **Otahuhu, Auckland**

Darling,

. . . I think I begin to see a new crystallisation.

I do feel that one should follow one's heart. The fact that after all this adding and subtracting and weighing up of advantage, we still feel we don't really whole-heartedly want to go [to Canberra] even on second chance, must be significant. It means really that one thing, that is Europe, has a far greater weight than the mere sum of items as concerts, theatres, friends, which simply overbalances all the rest.

. . . I am prepared to leave it to you – Raymond. But I think I should follow my heart – and your heart says 'Europe' . . .

Love R.

RAYMOND TO ROSEMARY

2 February 1952   **Canberra**

My darling,

. . . It is hard to realise that we shall be off in a fortnight. By then I must take the great decision. I am expecting a letter from you on Monday. If I don't get one soon I shall cable or phone. I feel as if a slow fate is pushing me to stay here – and wonder almost in horror if it is right. The answer is probably that either course is right. All my love, and to Hugh. I miss you both.

R.

 osto

On Tuesday, 5 February, Rosemary received a telephone call in her parents-in-laws' house in Auckland, from Raymond in Canberra. Raymond told her that he was going to accept the directorship of the Research School of Pacific Studies. Rosemary, unprepared for the reality of such an irrevocable decision over the long-distance phone, was filled with dread and found herself barely able to speak.

She was acutely aware that she would not be able to see, or probably even talk to, Raymond again for some six months. In eleven days, he would leave Australia, bound for Tikopia with nearly a dozen crates of supplies for months of isolated fieldwork.

After a sleepless night, on 6 February 1952, Rosemary sent the following by cable.

ROSEMARY TO RAYMOND

6 February 1952   **11.05**   **Otahuhu, Auckland**
TELEGRAM

I AM AFRAID FOR ALL THREE OF US PLEASE LET US RETURN I AM PREPARED FOR EVERYTHING AT HOME UNLESS THIS BREAKS YOUR HEART. ROSEMARY

ROSEMARY TO RAYMOND

6 February 1952   **Wednesday**   **Otahuhu, Auckland**

My own Raymond,

What will you think of me – will I ever be able to look at you I wonder or will you think I have really put out my hand to hold you back from something you badly wanted, just when you had made up your mind? But all the time I was trying to be so fair in presenting the case to you, I never really thought you would say yes, and so I think in my bewilderment I was dishonest with myself and put off making my *own* decision. I thought I needn't make one and would not need to be responsible. . . . When I heard you say on the telephone you were going to accept I felt such a panic in my heart as I've never felt before. My dearest, I felt sick, I went away and wept and I honestly tell you I did not sleep all last night turning the matter over in my mind.

. . . Raymond, our two instincts must be better than all the balancing – I felt last night as if the wrong person was to marry me – something dreadful about to happen . . .

And it made me see myself. I have wanted my cake and [to] eat it, and have been selfish with you I think. Things have been difficult between us but I have learnt a lot on this trip and specially from your father. I think things will be better in future. I'll help you to do the work and get the time and rest you need in England and I shall accept all the 'austerity'. I am sure of that now; before when you asked me I wasn't sure. R., I trust you'll agree to this; don't let's allow Fate to push us into something we both really dread.

All my love. R.

RAYMOND TO ROSEMARY

7 February 1952   **Thursday**   **Canberra**

My darling,

. . . Your cable yesterday wrung my heart – it was so simple and direct and seemed to speak the very soul of you. I judge it represents your innermost feelings, despite your letters. If this is so I would not want to stay here. I shall take the decision myself, and I shall not take it in your interest simply. But we are too much alike in interests for the basic attitudes of one not to be a guide to those of another. What I have wanted to do is to be sure as possible of your feelings as well as of my own – to try and distinguish between panic at decision to change, and deep-rooted unlikelihood of being able to adapt effectively in the long run. I share all these feelings . . .

All my love darling. R.

RAYMOND TO ROSEMARY

12 February 1952   **Tuesday**   **Canberra**

My darling,

Just a note . . . I am beginning to sort things out and pack away . . .

The telephone call this morning was a good clarifier for me – I tell the V-C [Vice-Chancellor] tomorrow (He isn't in today). I feel sorry for the people here, who have been hoping I would come, but one can't take decisions just for those reasons. We shall congratulate ourselves in a year or so!

All my love

Ever Raymond.

☙❧

On 13 February, Raymond met the vice-chancellor and gave him his reply: 'I have given most careful consideration to this invitation and with the greatest regret I feel that I must decline it. . . . The basic reason is that my roots in Europe go too deep. Indeed it is only by trying to pull them up that one sometimes realises how strong they are.'

On 14 February, Rosemary wrote one more letter to Raymond, intending to reach him before he left. Her letter arrived too late: Raymond had already set off for Tikopia.

ROSEMARY TO RAYMOND

14 February 1952   **Otahuhu, Auckland**

Please to deliver on board plane –

Passenger to Honiara via New Guinea

My dearest Raymond

I suppose the occasion will never likely occur again, but I hope I may never have to go through such another week as that between your first telephone call and your last. . . . In spite of all our earlier discussions and of my carefully phrased last letters, I never had had from you any real deep conviction that you would seriously accept, and the shock I got over the telephone stunned me. It all seemed so inadequate communicating through phone and cable and all your letters came so late that what you said was already of no value. I feel I have lived a year since last Tuesday week and now there is another five months at least for me to chew over . . . those frantic last minute almost blinded decisions!

How impossible it is to see rightly into what really goes on in another person's mind, even in conversation. Words are as often as much a cloak or a test for experience or thought as an indication of thought. And we believe so fondly we have freedom of choice when in reality a hundred tiny things gradually manoeuvre us into positions from which choice becomes inevitable. A terrific emotion of despair seized me at the sound of your voice saying you were about to take the plunge, and all my intellectual arguments for accepting your decision forsook me as an overturned bottle is spilled of liquid. At the moment I almost hate the recollections of Canberra whose attractions were the cause of all this anguish . . .

All well here and send our love.

R.

ROSEMARY TO HER FATHER

24 February 1952 **Otahuhu, Auckland**

Dearest Father,

. . . No such vital decision should ever be left even nominally unsettled till the two people concerned are separated, and certainly not left prior to a separation without possibility of contact destined to last four or five months.

[. . . I had said] that I would leave the decision absolutely to him. So I hoped to be able to do: so I should have done. I had always said if Raymond really felt something was sufficiently important for his work I would not wish to stand in his way. But I don't think I ever really imagined in my heart of hearts that he *would* choose to stay. We had never really seriously talked together on these lines. So when on that memorable 5 Feb. he rang up and told me he was about to take the plunge and accept, I was drained of all emotion but fear and shock. I could hardly speak over the long-distance phone; Raymond said to me 'Are you crying?' I wasn't but I almost wished I could cry. So he said: 'You still have two days, if you can't stand it cable me "Lets return" and we will.' So he rang off.

I shall never forget the next 24 hours. I was nearly sick. In spite of all my resolutions to stand by what Raymond's professional and health interests really demanded, I found I couldn't regard the prospect of living in Australia, even with three yearly leave, without anything but terror. I foresaw that Hugh would return to England and I would lose him as the Firth parents lost Raymond. And yet I felt responsible for this decision: for had I not written the carefully balanced letter finally which turned the scales, and had I not promised R. to let him take the decision and to abide by it? I felt, after that, I couldn't go back on my word . . .

And there was no chance of discussion. . . . The cable wires were all too confused for real talk on the phone. I have never passed such another night. . . . I felt torn between loyalty to Raymond, to my promised word to let him decide, and loyalty to myself which felt I could not live and die in Australia, and separate Hugh from England and European culture and standards and all that I felt I loved.

I never understood till then what exile could mean . . .

In the end in despair, my own egotism won – or so I must now think. I cabled early next morning – the morning of the King's death,[7] of which I had no leisure to think, 'Please let us return to England'. . . . Now he has left Sydney and is out of reach of all communication, explanation or apology till the end, perhaps, of July.

And I have a heavy load of conscience to bear. If R. suffers continually from illness I shall always now have secretly to blame myself . . .

Oh, daddy – I was quite happy when R. left. . . . I would not really have over much minded the five months with no communication. I am not afraid of real dangers –

of outside hazards, of loneliness even. It is of my conscience I am afraid; of my imagination as night after night I again balance up the pros and cons of Australia or England; of the effects of my going back on my word; of my having made Raymond do something for me which he may secretly regret all his life . . .

The only cheerful thing is Hugh. . . . Grandfather has become so all embracing a companion, and is so gentle firm and good with him . . .

Tomorrow, your birthday. Raymond is due, or so I believe, to arrive in Tikopia. . . . It will be a memorable trip scientifically. A revisit by the same man after exactly 25 years to an island knowing all that time only sporadic contact with the outside world . . .

Your deeply loving Rosemary.

RAYMOND TO ROSEMARY

13 March 1952   From Tikopia: cabled by Captain after ship reached port

ARRIVED SAFELY TIKOPIA AND HAVE A HOUSE. SOME MODERNISATION BUT MANY OLD FRIENDS. ISLAND HARD HIT BY HURRICANE. LOVE RAYMOND.

Figure 12.2. Raymond with Pa Fenuatara, Tikopia chief, informant and friend, 1952. Photographer uknown. LSE Library Firth Photographs/4/20/5.

ROSEMARY TO HER FATHER

10 April 1952   Otahuhu, Auckland

Dearest Daddy,

. . . From feeling like a fish out of water in this old fashioned lower middle class provincial society which I endured as a duty for Hugh's sake, I have discovered for myself a little circle of friends. . . . My old friend . . . Betty Belshaw took me to lunch. . . . There were four women there besides myself and immediately I entered the house I realised I was back on my own ground again. No lace curtains and drawn blinds against the lovely New Zealand sun, no china or glass orna- ments, no vast and uncomfortable leather chairs . . . modern paintings on the wall, a used 'cello in a corner, an open piano, plain modern curtains, and *books* all-round the room. Just to enter such a house made me draw a long breath of contentment. . . . The conversation was free and ranged wide, we talked of every- thing and I thoroughly enjoyed myself . . .

All my love. R.

1 July 1952   Otahuhu, Auckland

Dearest Daddy,

. . . I do not think I could ever have got through this six months alone without Hugh's company in an alien class structure with people who, apart from those I meet myself on my precious days in town, think, see, and feel, in a totally differ- ent manner to mine. . . . In the houses of most of [Raymond's] Mother's friends where we visit there is hardly a single book; ideas are never discussed.

As a consequence all social intercourse is as rigidly sexually divided as it might be in a Moslem country. After polite greetings, the women get in one corner and discuss births, deaths and at much greater length disease and all preliminaries to death of their mutual acquaintance. And the men their motor cars, gardens, bowling clubs or more infrequently the state of New Zealand government . . .

And yet . . . I have been loaded with kindnesses from these people, with whom I have not one thing in common, presents given to me for Hugh, and for myself, quite unsolicited, make me feel ashamed that I criticise so much in my mind!

. . . All my love to you and to Kathryn . . .

Ever. R.

෴

At the beginning of June, a boat called at Tikopia with rice to relieve the famine that followed the hurricane.[8] Raymond sent a note via the boat: 'I think of you both very often. . . . The whole Canberra decision, as I see it . . . was made unnecessarily prolonged and complicated by our (my) failure to focus the issues finally before I left New Zealand. . . . What made me in the "almost to the brink" attitude was one of your letters pleading for the benefits of clean modern living in tones which I felt were final. But the brink is different from the plunge, and having drawn back, I feel regrets at the memory of a dream rather than acute feelings of disappointment.'[9] Raymond said that he expected to be back in New Zealand during July. Rosemary hoped to hear from him as soon as he reached Canberra.

But July came and went with no more news; in early August, she had only silence. Rosemary's anxiety steadily rose.

Notes

1. Rosemary to her father, Gilbert, 18 November 1951.
2. Ralph Piddington (1906–74), New Zealand anthropologist, who was censured in Australia for criticising racial discrimination against native Australians in the 1940s.
3. In 1950, flying was still a luxury. Seats converted into full beds, with all the frills.
4. Their London flat at 56B Warrington Crescent had no garden or yard of any kind.
5. Rosemary meant the lack of art galleries with Renaissance and classical art collections. She did like and was interested in aboriginal art.
6. Although personally friendly, there was some professional jealousy on the part of Fred Nadel (1903–56), an Austrian-born anthropologist who had studied under Malinowski in the 1930s. Nadel was head of anthropology at the ANU, whereas Raymond, as acting director of the School of Pacific Studies, was Fred Nadel's academic superior.
7. George VI died on 6 February 1952.
8. This was a rare occasion when the Tikopia needed assistance from outside. Tikopia society is remarkably sustainable. See Jared Diamond, 2005, *Collapse: How Societies Choose to Fail or Survive*, London: Penguin, pp. 286–94.
9. Raymond to Rosemary, 14 May 1952.

Chapter 13

Goblins

1952–1953

On 17 August, Rosemary received another major shock. Raymond arrived back in Auckland. But he had been dangerously ill with pneumonia on Tikopia. The boat in which he was due to return was a month late; when it did arrive, he was invalided off the island by the Tikopia on a makeshift stretcher. He later confessed to Rosemary that he feared he would not leave Tikopia alive.

He had been hospitalised and given massive doses of penicillin when the boat reached the Solomon Islands and he was hospitalised again when he reached Sydney. He did not contact Rosemary from Australia, as he had 'not wished to alarm her'.

Raymond had had a history of bronchitis over the previous decade in England. This latest illness likely redoubled Rosemary's feelings of guilt at her role in persuading Raymond to decline the job in Australia, with its clear, dry air. Despite Raymond's reassurances that they had indeed made the correct decision, a number of factors now combined to unleash in Rosemary a tide of anxiety and low mood. Triggered by the loss of security about Raymond's health, and regret at her decision to tilt the balance away from a new life in Australia, Rosemary succumbed to a fearful depression: she felt at times 'like one who has come back from the dead'.[1] After their return to England, Rosemary's anxieties about major decisions became amplified, especially when they sought and purchased a new home in Highgate, a short walk from her father, her sister Margaret and her stepbrother Terence – a three-storey house with a garden, which, in the event, proved eminently suitable. Many of her regrets, she thought, were the result of her habit of looking back on the past, longing for something that maybe no place could give her again: the feeling of security, perhaps, that she had had before her mother died?[2] Raymond would probably have found Rosemary's continued preoccupation with the Canberra decision difficult. He himself was gradually becoming more distant over this period, working longer hours and growing more preoccupied with LSE politics and writing up his Tikopia material. Rosemary tried not to show much of her real feelings. She alluded to 'difficulties' between them – she later deduced that it had probably been during this period that he started having affairs. Crucially, although she was, socially and intellectually, very much at the centre of the expanding anthropological network in Britain, Rosemary had, since 1946, lacked the status and self-esteem that comes with employment. In the absence of an effective, close, supportive relationship with Raymond or Edmund, the vital but socially unacknowledged role of mother left her without a publicly recognised role to sustain her self-belief over nearly a decade after 1946. Publicly successful marriages hide a multitude of sins.[3]

In October 1952, three days after they arrived back from their year abroad, Raymond's close friend and colleague Isaac Schapera invited them for a meal with Edmund Leach. It appears from Rosemary's diary that Edmund paid her little attention on this occasion. He had recently spent a year working on his controversial ideas about the instability of social 'structures', about which he no doubt wanted to talk with Raymond and Isaac. Rosemary was feeling very low and liable to perceive rejection where none was intended. The old flame was rekindled briefly, she noted. Nevertheless, Rosemary's sense that Edmund only wanted to spend a little time with her must have deepened her gloom. Her depression no doubt distorted her perception. Goblins were getting in the way of the relationships between herself and both Raymond and Edmund.

ROSEMARY TO HER FATHER

18 August 1952   **Otahuhu, Auckland**

Dearest Daddy,

Raymond came back yesterday by seaplane from Sydney. He walked off the gangway in a very uncertain fashion. . . . He had to be carried off the island in an improvised litter made very ingeniously by his companion Dr Spillius, who organised a relay of Tikopia to carry him. At Vila, where he had to wait four days for a plane . . . he was put into hospital, and at Sydney Ian Hogbin met him and carried him straight off to hospital . . .

In Sydney he was examined by two very eminent and evidently competent specialists; they said he had now a permanent 'dry pleural rub' in one lung, and . . . seriously told R. that he must lead a very easy life, keep the lung warm (flannel waistcoat!) and avoid getting overtired . . .

. . . I had been half dreading a return to England and to this bad health later on, but to be told straight out that he has this permanent scar or wound, which only an easy life can prevent getting serious, six months after the chance of accepting the job which, whatever its other disadvantages, would without doubt have given him the chance of a life as easy as he wished to make it, in a dry exhilarating climate, is almost too much. It just confirms all my half-suppressed suspicions and inflames my feelings of guilt. I feel now I thought only of myself and shall suffer for it for the rest of my life. I will write again later – its lovely to have R. back but it's all mixed up for me with biting remorse.

Ever – Rosemary.

15 September 1952   **Orient Liner SS *Orcades*, Melbourne**[4]

Dearest Daddy,

. . . I had it all out with R. the second morning in Canberra, and I must feel released of guilt as far as he goes: he made it quite plain that, had he felt at all strongly about it, he would have not given over so easily for me. [. . . Sometimes] I feel returning is worthwhile; at other times I feel like re-entering a prison in London.

. . . Love as always. Rosemary.

ROSEMARY'S DIARY

13 October 1952   **Warrington Crescent, Maida Vale, London**

Arrived Tilbury – drove by [taxi] to Warrington Crescent. Journey thro' London on a raw wet grey day depressing, and both R. and I were I think indescribably shocked to re-discover the dirt and decrepitude of the flat. Coming from the light – grace and ease of the [journey by ship] . . . quite apart from Australia, New Zealand, our home seemed an incredible retraction of standards.

Throughout the day, as I endeavoured to unpack, to fit in to the old life mentally, I became almost overburdened with gloom. Dirt, indescribably ugly brickwork, and signs of untended decay struck me everywhere.

In the evening I quite broke down: cried bitterly to R. and told him I thought we had made a ghastly mistake to come back. He also bewildered, [but] still took his stand on [the belief] that when we got acclimatized again, we should find it worth it.

16 October 1952   **Maida Vale, London**

[We] Dined at Isaac Schapera's flat – to meet E.R.L. [Edmund]. The Freedmans also there.[5] I was looking forward to it, but Edmund might [as well] not have been there. He just goes away somewhere whenever I am around. Am I unreasonable? I only want to talk to him, as we did in 1945.

The old flame rekindled momentarily at dinner, but faded . . .

20 November 1952   **Maida Vale, London**

My lowest ebb today. Worried about [finding] a house, Hugh being difficult, grey skies and cold, I felt like gassing myself all day. Elizabeth Downs was to come to dinner and I didn't want to see her. . . . When I came into the sitting room at last having put H. to bed and greeted her, I suddenly realised here was my old friend again, alive, that faint emanation of my mother about her which had first inspired me to a kind of adoring admiration when I was eighteen. And after kissing her I just sat down and without being able to say anything, burst into tears. Elizabeth was quick to recover, on her knees beside me as I just repeated 'I am so unhappy I am so unhappy', [she] asked me to tell [her] why. I said 'I can't, I can't it's too long – Raymond knows it all too well' – then Raymond tactfully went upstairs. . . . To Elizabeth, I said 'Who should talk of unhappiness to you?' 'Why not' she said 'who knows more about it then than I?'[6]

I told her I was overburdened with remorse about Canberra and making R. reverse his decision. 'You couldn't have done that!' she exclaimed, shocked. 'How could you! If he had really wanted to go, he would never have let you do that surely.' 'Well no, I suppose he didn't mind all that [much] but a wife should be wiser. . . . He left the final word to me.' 'Well then that was unfair'.

Afterwards thinking it all over I realised it wasn't quite like that.

I think Elizabeth suddenly made me see that what I have been nursing in my mind as guilt for R. is really plain selfish remorse and regret for myself. R . . . doesn't feel involved in my reversal. He has accepted the return, with its costs. It is I, I, I, all the time who hark back to it. He tells me, occasionally, 'Why cannot you let Canberra out of your mind and stop looking back? . . .'

27 November 1952   **Maida Vale, London**

Returned from a morning's house hunting with bad ear ache in a ferocious cold wind . . .

At first it was a positive relief to have some physical pain. I could no longer worry about houses and the major decisions of life. With slow recovery I realised glumly . . . whatever happens, I worry, and worry over. Whatever I most want, that I am afraid to go through with.

After all, looking back, why had I such a compulsion, even in 1930, to reject Edmund whom I was beginning to love? I was afraid of the possibly entailed complications? But why?

Even then after I had married R. I remember on that brilliant morning in June [1936] in Great Ormond Street when I wore a red rose to go down to Oxford to meet R., thinking I had made a mistake! Foolish I!

The same in 1941. I was afraid to take up the greater responsibilities involved in Munia's house in Cambridge and made Raymond's life miserable arguing over it.

Yet that period turned out one of the happiest, probably the very happiest of all my life.

Also in 1946, when Hugh came, I was afraid of that – wanted to go back! . . .

Raymond has seen a rather lovely house in Bromley. It has character, size. It is cheapish. But it is full of big rooms facing north, and east, and seems so far away, by half hourly electric train from Waterloo. Again I want to go and live there; but I am afraid. Afraid of going so far away, of making such a break with my past, but also afraid of undertaking new financial responsibilities . . .

Fear, fear; I can feel it surging through me as a physical sensation – as a chemical in my blood – I can feel panic reaching to the extremities of my limbs as clearly as heat and cold . . .

Raymond, to whom I have divulged some of this, ends by answering 'Pull yourself together, look around you and compare your troubles with those of others. Neither in personal relations, health, or finance are we in any great difficulty.'

I can only feel as I accept his dictum, as I felt [as a child with delirium] about the nurse telling me there were no goblins on her bed. I believe there may not be, but still, *I* see them, and what *I* see frightens me – even if it be not there.

8 May 1953   **Southwood Avenue, Highgate, London**

Christmas came and went and with it an intermission to house hunting. Hiding in childhood's delight in Christmas we all forgot for a bit to be unhappy. Then we tried again and in a kind of desperation made a half-hearted bid for a great old Victorian terrace house [off] Southwood Lane, Highgate.[7] Near to my family, I thought . . . and lo and behold, today we came into possession.

I longed for it when on the verge of possession; enjoyed a brief respite from unhappiness and worry during the months of preparation, but was suddenly plunged back into a reality of despair on entering that empty house today.

. . . All that I covet turns to dust and ashes on accession. I feel again I would willingly die rather than go thro' with this, were it not for Raymond and Hugh. The more I feel I wrong them by making ghastly wrong decisions, the more I love them. . . . Perhaps then shall I one day find myself again: my lost self, who knew what was right and wrong, had courage, faith, conviction, and a will to act.

Notes

1. Rosemary, diary entry, 14 October 1952.
2. Rosemary, diary entry, 3 November 1952.
3. However, both Rosemary and Raymond had good friends. They were not lonely in the way Ann Oakley suggests Richard and Kay Titmuss were (Ann Oakley, 2014, *Father and Daughter: Patriarchy, Gender and Social Science*, Bristol: Policy Press, p. 65).

4. Rosemary, Raymond and Hugh returned together, sailing from Wellington to Sydney, then, after visiting Canberra, via Melbourne to London.

5. Judith Freedman, née Djamour (1921–2009) and Maurice Freedman (1920–75) both trained at the LSE under Raymond, and became not only colleagues, but also very good friends of the Firths. Maurice's work on Chinese families was particularly significant. Judith worked in Singapore and London before editing the *Jewish Journal of Sociology* from 1975 until her death.

6. Elizabeth Downs (Rosemary's second cousin) had suffered the breakup of her marriage, after which she emigrated to the United States with her young son, who was killed, age nine, by a truck shortly after they had settled there.

7. Number 33 Southwood Avenue, just off Southwood Lane. Her father and sister Margaret lived within five minutes' walk. Rosemary was born and lived the first eight years of her life at number 37 Southwood Avenue.

Chapter 14

Dancing Days and Orchid Nights

1953–1961

Things were about to change. The next time Rosemary met Edmund, their relationship was subtly different. Moreover, the 1950s also brought a new relationship with a woman, which proved a great source of happiness for Rosemary and played a crucial role in initiating a gradual transformation of her life.

So despite the despair Rosemary experienced on entering their empty and as yet unfurnished new house in 1953, the start of this new relationship a few years later lifted her out of her depression.

ফটফ

Raymond was, as ever, travelling away from home frequently. He was abroad on average twice a year, usually for a couple of weeks at a time, but in 1952, 1953 and 1955, he was away for three months or more at some point in the year. In June 1953, Raymond was away in New York for three weeks. Rosemary dined again at Isaac's and again Edmund was there. But this was an utterly different evening from Isaac's party in October the previous year. Knowing that Raymond was abroad, Edmund felt free to display his affection for Rosemary, however unobtrusively. They did not, it seems, spend the night together on this occasion – as they had in 1938. Yet their old love could discreetly show itself again.

ROSEMARY'S DIARY

23 June 1953, Isaac's evening party   **Southwood Avenue, London**

Somebody [Edmund] who once gave me a lovely twenty-first birthday present in spite of a great capacity to spoil all that is first given, gave what I most needed today as a kind of coming of middle age birthday present!

Past forty on my seventeenth wedding anniversary and still wracked with doubt about the validity of nearly every major decision I make, came someone who saw the same shadows I see, searched for the same light, still climbs after the same peaks. Not really just going away whenever I am around, but there all the time quietly in reality and still believing in me as a person who can be asked about the values of our way of living, the real truths.

I slept soundly tonight, better than for months . . .

❧

Edmund had set his sights on Cambridge when Meyer Fortes[1] was appointed professor there in 1950. He accepted a post as lecturer (a step down from his previous post as reader) at Cambridge in 1953 and the family moved there late that year. However, without a college fellowship, Edmund was somewhat isolated. He had hoped that Meyer would facilitate a fellowship, and when neither that nor a readership materialised, he felt cheated. When, therefore, Edmund was offered the post of Professor of Anthropology at ANU in Canberra in 1956, he very much wanted to accept. But Celia did not want to emigrate and their teenage daughter Loulou was certainly hostile to the idea of moving away from England to the other side of the world to Canberra, a place she had never previously heard of. Edmund rather bitterly felt he had to decline the offer, which he did.

Raymond and Rosemary saw Edmund and Celia periodically as a foursome throughout this period and Hugh and Alexander (Edmund and Celia's son) stayed with each other occasionally in the early 1960s.

It is striking that, although neither Rosemary nor Celia had a final say over most of their husbands' decisions about job changes, or how much time they spent abroad, both women had the power to block a decision that would have resulted in the emigration of the whole family to another country.[2] Arguably, one of the reasons why the relationship between Edmund and Celia worked was because while he wanted a partner who would not challenge him intellectually, he needed someone who would, as his mother had done earlier, firmly steer him at certain points regarding important life choices and decisions.

Although he was not involved in her art and her writing, Edmund was in awe of Celia's creative abilities, especially her painting. Yet she remained completely aloof from what Edmund was doing intellectually: she read hardly anything he wrote, with the exception of the Reith Lectures in 1967.

In the 1950s, Edmund was not popular with academics in Cambridge because of his outspokenness and his political views – he was a Marxist at this point – and because he was an atheist and a vocal humanist. But, by 1961, Edmund was on his way to achieving an academic status comparable with Raymond's: although not yet a professor, he had been elected a fellow of Kings College at Cambridge in 1960.

Both Raymond and Edmund were invited to work for a year at the prestigious Center for Advanced Study in the Behavioral Sciences at Stanford University, California: Raymond in 1958–59 and Edmund in 1960–61. There, Edmund was greatly influenced by Roman Jakobson's approach to language and linguistic categories.[3] Both wives accompanied their husbands to California. Celia presumably thought she should allow Edmund to go on this trip both because the position at Stanford was not permanent and because she had prevented him from taking up the professorship in Canberra. As it happened, she greatly enjoyed California and wrote to Rosemary about her experiences and what she thought of the place.

CELIA TO ROSEMARY

16 March 1961   **Melville Avenue, Palo Alto, California**

My dear Rosemary

I have been waiting for the shock of America to wear off before writing to you – but obviously it never will so I write still under the spell. Of all the places I have ever been to, this is the most exciting in the sense that it upsets everything one has been led to believe about the world. The abundance is enough to bewilder one completely – all the vegetables – asparagus, beans, peas, peppers, aubergines, spinach; everything you can think of all at once. . . . After the severity of shopping in England you will know what I mean . . . and goodness how we sleep. I have never slept so much in my life . . .

But there is another side, and if it had not been for the Center, which . . . is a unique experience, I don't think either of us could stand America. . . . The ugliness for instance is shocking . . . ribbon building on the edge of a by-pass . . . and no end to it because it leads to nothing, there's no centre-point, no town – just sprawl.

I like Americans very much (always have done), yet of course we only meet academics and I must say I sometimes long to get outside the little group if only to come up against those vulgar, pushing, sure-of-themselves Americans one reads about in novels.

. . . We want to know how *you* are. Please write us a long letter if you can. . . . Because despite having such a wonderful time I do feel lonely at the back of me

if you know what I mean. In this country everything and everyone goes forward. I'm used to feeling the past as least as strong as the future and I don't want to lose touch. . . . This goes with much love from us both to you both –
With lots of love from Celia.

ରୁ

Edmund's reputation stemmed particularly from his 1954 book *Political Systems of Highland Burma*, for which he had asked Raymond to write a foreword. Edmund had written a book that was challenging and critical of Raymond (provocatively, he said he was 'frequently bored by the facts . . . of Tikopia').[4] Raymond responded politely, but in kind. He posted a critical review of the book under the guise of a foreword. Raymond knew Edmund well – here was the subtle sparring of two intellectual heavyweights who might flinch a little in response to the barbs thrown at them, but who, like close-knit siblings, liked and respected each other.

Not all mutual criticism was so friendly. Meyer Fortes, as Edmund's professor at Cambridge, did not approve of Edmund's ideas, and the two became increasingly tetchy towards each other. Edmund's belief that 'we first devise for ourselves a set of verbal categories . . . and we then fit the facts to the verbal categories'[5] anticipated the slow turn in anthropology – and indeed in the humanities more generally – to a greater questioning of the objectivity of social scientific accounts of 'reality' and the critical role of language in that process.

ରୁ

If Raymond and Edmund were happy jousting intellectually, Rosemary was less happy in this respect. Edmund appears never to have considered Rosemary to be his intellectual equal; even in their correspondence in the early 1930s, he seems to have regarded himself as intellectually superior to her. In the 1950s, they socialised when Edmund was in London and looked after each other's sons occasionally, but Edmund's correspondence with Rosemary had become infrequent and more distant during this period, as attested by his (only) letters from this period, which concerned a theatre outing and joint holidays for Alexander and Hugh. In the 1950s and the early 1960s, it was Celia who wrote to Rosemary from Cambridge more often than Edmund.

This attitude of Edmund's was consistent with his behaviour towards very many other women, whether or not they were academically qualified. It might be thought that Edmund's role in facilitating the admission of women to King's College in the 1960s was an indication of a commitment to the importance of women in academic life. However, in personal relationships, as in his relationship with his daughter Loulou and his attitude towards her education, this was not evident, and it is doubtful whether he ever saw any but a tiny handful of his female academic colleagues as intellectual equals. Much later, Edmund was also sometimes disparaging about Rosemary's lack of academic training in anthropology. In the 1950s, he was absorbed in his university work and making his way in college politics. Throughout both this and the following decade, Edmund undoubtedly saw Rosemary as being merely preoccupied with wifely and motherly activities.

Rosemary was later to reflect that 'E.'s greatest betrayal was not his jilting of me in regard to engagement for marriage, but his casting off one who had become so intimate intellectually, emotionally and culturally; so to speak. His overweening ambition and vanity made him find excuses to throw me off.'[6]

 birds

In the mid-1950s, Rosemary hesitantly began to try and regain her lost self. Their son was nearly nine. Soon, she thought, she could start to carve out a role for herself beyond that of housewife and mother. But pursuing an academic career in anthropology would have been inconceivable for her at that time; by the mid-1950s, academic posts required a doctorate, which would have required Rosemary to spend a year or so abroad – and she felt quite unable to do so given her commitments to her son and her husband. From Rosemary's account, Raymond appears to have paid little attention to her attempts to construct a future for herself. The post-war assumptions about the place of women as housewives and providers of support to their husbands were at their most powerful at this time. Before she met Raymond, Rosemary had planned to go into social work; in January 1956, she therefore started voluntary social work with the London County Council (LCC) Education Department Care Committee, providing support for children in need.

As part of this work, in early March 1956, Rosemary met Helen Stocks, the youngest daughter of Mary Stocks,[7] a frequent and provocative contributor to *Any Questions?* Helen was young, alert, vivacious and radiated life and warmth, but she was personally still unsure of herself; Rosemary was more outwardly confident and relaxed, and interested in others.

They quickly fell in love with each other, and Rosemary invited her to spend a week together at Rosemary's cottage in Dorset in early April.

This lesbian relationship and its repercussions were of great significance for Rosemary. Yet even her own diaries over the next few years refer to the affair only briefly, indirectly, elliptically, or metaphorically. (In the 1950s, same-sex relationships were widely viewed as disturbed, perverted, even abhorrent, and homosexual acts were illegal for men in the United Kingdom.) Her engage-

Figure 14.1. Rosemary and Helen Stocks, London, late 1950s. Photograph by Raymond Firth.

ment diary records 'My dancing days' for the week she and Helen spent together in Dorset. They started seeing each other at least once a week, often in London but sometimes at Rosemary's home in Highgate. Helen's extended family shared a house at West Bay, Bridport, and that summer the two families started spending time together while in Dorset for the school holidays. The contrast with the previous few years of uncertainty and unsettled mood was dramatic.

For a year, Rosemary was dizzyingly happy.

ROSEMARY'S DIARY

19 March 1956   **London**

Lunched Helen and learnt to dance again!

On this day in 1935 I had a memorable lunch with Pio.[8] This year I had as memorable a lunch in its way with someone else . . .

Tomorrow shall be my dancing day.[9]

7 May 1956   **London**

. . . The pear at the bottom of the garden is superb today. Up-rearing its pointed white smothered head from a spreading base of early green delicately to a blue sun drenched sky.

Even so came she [Helen] all clothed in freshness of white and green, with translucent green earrings and her throat circled with jade; and through all, those blue, blue eyes, so level, so piercing, so loving, that looked at me.

5 January 1957 London

. . . 1956 was thoroughly good.

And I know it not only because it has made me happy but because I know that I am giving out, as well as taking in, now, that I am more interested in another person's happiness than in my own immediate joy . . .

. . . The strange and strong love which has supported me in the last ten months [. . . is] uniquely precious . . .

The end of June 1957 London

. . . Clean contrary to common sense, nature, and every personal precedent, in my middle forties I have been made happy, secure, fulfilled, and fulfilling in a way that amazes me when I look back to the miserable stumblings of the last eight years.

Surely middle age has a natural need for a little different form of love than youth? – has a need for more tenderness and understanding, and less hard passion? The realisation of a developing need for something a little different cannot be wrong and selfish?

❧❧

It had become necessary for Rosemary and Raymond to talk to each other about their fears and worries, and their marriage. It eventually became clear that Raymond had been as unhappy as Rosemary had been – even before Helen's arrival, which made him very jealous – and that exploring and negotiating the issues was not sufficient to solve their difficulties.[10] 'For one afternoon, hot sunny quiet, an afternoon I shall never forget, Raymond seemed to want really, truly to find out what I felt and why, and tenderly probed. . . . And the revelations were not only on one side,' her diary recorded in early July 1957. At some point in this process, it seems that Rosemary did tell Raymond of her sexual feelings for Helen. Raymond responded initially with revulsion and some vitriol. 'But it wasn't finished!' she noted eight weeks later. 'It is appalling this thing that has been created by our own words on 31 August: something horrible, ugly, and that hurts with thinking about and that never was there before . . . and it has come from nowhere, nothing is changed but the view of it and something that has been said.'[11]

Yet, over the next couple of years, Raymond was evidently able to come to terms with what had transpired, especially once Rosemary made a commitment to bring an end to the physical side of her relationship with Helen.[12] Moreover, Raymond became good friends with both Helen and her wider family; indeed, in the early 1960s, Helen worked for Raymond as one of his research staff on a study of kinship in London.

In the years that followed, the friendship between the Stocks and the Firth families grew steadily stronger, as the heady love affair between Helen and Rosemary gradually lost its potency and was transformed, during 1961, into a close friendship that lasted for the rest of Rosemary's life. By then, Rosemary could write that 'I have seen an inhibited personality break out gradually into rapturous happiness . . . break a vicious circle of failure and take a job, to learn to drive and to acquire a whole new set of her own friends'.[13]

Crucially, the relationship with Helen helped Rosemary to emerge from a period for much of which she had been depressed, and from a decade when she had primarily been a mother, wife and social entertainer in the eyes of both Raymond and the wider world.

When Raymond was invited to spend 1959 at the Center for Advanced Study in the Behavioral Sciences in California, Rosemary and Hugh joined him for four months. On the journey out to California via Fiji, Betty Belshaw – whom Rosemary had not seen since 1952 – motored eighty miles through the night with two young children just to meet them for an hour or so. Rosemary wrote to her stepmother Kathryn that 'She is a dear friend whom I hadn't seen for seven years and this hour in the heat-drenched tropical Fijian night was one of the happiest and fantastical I have ever passed'.[14]

In March 1959, Raymond was awarded the Viking Fund Medal in New York by a prestigious foundation set up to develop anthropology by the Swedish millionaire Axel Wenner-Gren.[15] Rosemary accompanied him and enjoyed being showered with orchids at the festivities.

ROSEMARY TO HER FATHER FROM CALIFORNIA

23 January 1959   **Bryant St., Palo Alto, California**

Dearest Papa,

. . . The ease of life here is quite extraordinary . . . a sort of 'remove-from-reality' of everything . . .

Of course all their food is removed from reality too, and I sometimes wonder if Americans would eat chickens which came to their kitchen in feathers to be drawn as in the old days instead of ready to roast in cellophane bag. There is no bread knife or board or carvers in this well-equipped house. The reason we sadly discover is that all bread is sliced, all meat dismembered ready for serving, chickens usually jointed, meat in portions, cheese sliced in bags. Occasionally I long to see some *real food raw* – a haunch of pork, a whole cheese, a proper piece of stale crusty bread with weight in it . . .

All our love to the whole family. Rosemary.

17 March 1959 Palo Alto, California

Dearest Daddy,

I [am . . .] full of our junketings in N.Y. . . . Taken to the most elegant N.Y. *Hotel Plaza* . . . I was given white orchids and at a sumptuous dinner the medallists were eulogised (rather as at an honorary graduation) and given the medals and the not insubstantial cheques! Some very charming things were said about Raymond – not just an ivory tower scientist and so on – I found quite moving.

I must tell you that at the cocktail party . . . I was so impudent as to ask if I could have plain sherry. There were long delays and I began to think I had made a mistake but determined to persevere, thinking that after all the medallist's wife loaded with orchids ought to be able to have what she asked for! Finally one little elderly waiter promised to bring Raymond (and me) a sherry, which he had to make a special journey for and brought back alone in glory on a silver plate! So I thought – looking at the loaded trays going round and round – this will serve me right for asking for sherry, I shall have to be content with ONE. And so I intended. But I had misjudged my waiter. Having moved heaven for this dotty (foreign) female who liked *sherry* at cocktail parties, he went through with it logically. And all through the evening he followed me about with replacements – one little slim sherry glass amongst all the gins. 'Aren't you the lady who . . . etc? And later I saw him refusing 'my' sherry to some other dame . . . I was enchanted . . .'

Love to all. R.

ণ৯৩

When Rosemary and Hugh returned to England in April, Raymond stayed in California for another five months, until mid-September. However, on Raymond's return from this long separation, the tensions in their marriage were again evident. Rosemary began to suspect that Raymond was having an affair at this time, although it took at least another year before she was certain. Raymond had indeed started an affair with a younger anthropologist, probably while he was on his own at Stanford. (It is uncertain how many other relationships Raymond was involved in during the 1950s and 1960s. There were undoubtedly a number, but they could have ranged from little more than flirtations to full-blown affairs.) These were also the years when Raymond's drinking, probably starting in the mid-1950s, became a major cause of friction in the marriage. (Raymond stopped drinking alcohol altogether shortly before he went to Tikopia in 1966, and never again touched alcohol.)

ROSEMARY'S DIARY AFTER THEIR RETURN

25 September 1959   **London**

. . . Four years ago I was miserably unhappy myself and I felt I was imprisoned in unhappiness justly awarded me as punishment. I tried continual palliatives on my judge to evade the punishment but all seemed useless.

Then someone [Helen Stocks] came from outside miraculously and showed me that my imprisonment was quite unnecessary, fortuitous and unreasonable, as well as probably self-imposed.

For over a year I was wildly happy outside in the open air and free. I hardly cared for anything else than this newfound freedom.

In the autumn of 1957 I was made to realise that he [Raymond] was still inside this wretched prison where I had used to be and more miserable than ever I'd thought possible. I concluded during 1958 that my duty was to go back inside voluntarily to comfort him.

Now I seem clearly to see that this is useless self-immolation; that as Greta [Redfield] said 'If he really loves you as I know he does, he must let you have your own head. . . .' My solution is not to go back into prison with him but to lure and entice him outside . . . so that we may all four[16] ('four people's happiness is in your hands' he told me in 1957) be free and happy . . .

Notes

1. Meyer Fortes (1906–83), one of the proponents of kinship organisation as the defining feature of a society, was William Wyse Professor of Anthropology at Cambridge from 1950.
2. Loulou recalls this clearly. See also Geoffrey Gray and Doug Munro, 2012, 'Leach Would Be First-Rate – if You Could Get Him', *History Compass* 10(802): 811.
3. Roman Jakobson (1896–1982), a Russian-American linguist whose ideas about universal linguistic structures influenced both Noam Chomsky and Claude Lévi-Strauss.
4. Edmund Leach, 1954, *Political Systems of Highland Burma*, London: Athlone Press, p. 227.
5. Leach, *Political Systems of Highland Burma*, p. xii.
6. Rosemary, diary entry, 29 January 1986.
7. Mary Stocks (1891–1975), writer and broadcaster, taught economic history and campaigned for women's suffrage. She was created a life peer, as Baroness Stocks, in 1966.
8. Pio Koller, to whom Rosemary lost her virginity in March 1935, shortly before she met Raymond.
9. English carol (traditional), first documented in William B. Sandys's *Christmas Carols Ancient and Modern* of 1833.
10. To what extent Raymond's unhappiness was a consequence of work pressures and to what extent it was a consequence of difficulties in his relationship with Rosemary is unknown.
11. Rosemary, diary entries, 2 July 1957, 31 August 1957 and 16 September 1957.

12. In Rosemary's diaries, although she rarely wrote directly about their love, there are sufficiently clear statements at intervals from 1956 onward for the shape of the relationship between her and Helen Stocks to be clear.

13. Rosemary, diary entry, 12 January 1961.

14. Rosemary to Kathryn Upcott, 16 January 1959.

15. Axel Wenner-Gren (1881–1961), a Swedish entrepreneur who became one of the richest men in the world in the 1930s as a result of his development of the domestic vacuum cleaner. He unsuccessfully attempted to prevent war between Britain and Germany, and has been suspected of having had Nazi sympathies.

16. The four people Raymond referred to here were presumably Rosemary, Raymond, Hugh and Helen Stocks.

Chapter 15

Bursting with Ideas

1959–1964

The 1960s saw dramatic changes in the professional circumstances of Rosemary, Raymond and Edmund. Raymond would retire from his position as head of one of the most prestigious anthropology departments in the United Kingdom by the end of the decade. For Edmund, these years brought academic prestige and public fame, fuelled by the publication of *Rethinking Anthropology* in 1961, a year 'which was for me a kind of watershed'.[1] He became Provost of King's College, Cambridge in 1966 and delivered the Reith Lectures in 1967. For Rosemary, the changes were also significant. Yet behind the achievements of each of them were insecurities that they needed to manage.

Rosemary, now with some experience of social work and refreshed by four months in California, was restive and itching to develop her skills. As a first step, she was accepted for a course in Social Administration at the LSE starting in October 1959. Raymond was supportive and wrote from California to congratulate her. The concluding six months consisted of a variety of social work placements, including in the North Wales Mental Hospital at Denbigh, which entailed Rosemary living away from home for much of the autumn of 1960.

It was the start of an important period of professional training and development for her.

At the outset of the 1960s, Rosemary was just completing this LSE course, but within a marriage that often seemed on the point of breaking apart, which would have left her with a teenage child to care for without anyone to support them. By the end of the decade, her son had left home and she had navigated the most difficult of the marital challenges, successfully completed and published a follow-up piece of fieldwork,[2] constructed a career and joined the ranks of professional anthropology.

ℭℑℒ

In 1961, with the LSE course behind her, Rosemary had hoped that a university job might come up – but with no academic posts forthcoming, she took a job at Battersea College, teaching an anthropological approach to health education. The job was under Margaret Hardiman,[3] who had been taught anthropology and sociology at the LSE, worked in army education during the war and then, like Rosemary, raised a family before returning to employment in a teaching role. Margaret became an enormously important mentor, and both Margaret and her husband John became good friends to Rosemary and Raymond.

In the marriage, Rosemary felt like she was walking a tightrope. Early in 1961, she succeeded in persuading a reluctant Raymond that they should both see a psychotherapist, Dr Margaret Reinhold.[4] They saw her separately, Raymond on only four occasions. Rosemary attended eighteen appointments over the following twelve months. A year later, Raymond also briefly consulted Dr Anthony Storr.[5]

Early in these consultations, Dr Reinhold commented on Rosemary's sense of guilt and her 'fear' of her own feelings – and wondered whether they might be related to Rosemary's experience of her parents when she was a child. Yet Dr Reinhold seemed to address this only fleetingly, perhaps because Rosemary wanted to concentrate on the difficulties she was encountering on a daily basis with Raymond.

Was any of Rosemary's guilt related to Edmund or her relationship with Helen? To that question, the answer is surely negative. Not only is there no hint anywhere in her diaries of any guilt about any of her sexual encounters, but Rosemary herself wrote not long afterwards: 'M. R. [Margaret Reinhold] said that a sense of guilt was what she first sensed in me! That was guilt for what I had *not* done or achieved in my relations with my husband. . . . I don't think I've ever felt guilty for loving anyone, be it Helen or whom so ever: only for *not* loving.'[6] It does, moreover, seem likely that early in her life Rosemary had acquired a sense of guilt on account of not being sufficiently loving when her mother died so soon after Rosemary had written her a letter of complaint. The impossibility of rectifying such an omission must have left a deep impression on Rosemary. Was it any wonder that such feelings were probably reactivated when she reflected that she had been responsible for Raymond ultimately refusing the Canberra job? Or that guilt might return as a result of Raymond's continued suffering – whatever the reasons for it – nearly ten years later?

Rosemary did have a lifelong fear of being left alone without an anchor. Would further exploration of the anxieties and fears triggered by the losses of her beloved Uncle Maurice when she was twelve years old and her mother just three years later have helped Rosemary to become less vulnerable to such feelings? In the event, what Dr Reinhold offered was nevertheless of great help to Rosemary, who, after a couple of months, felt she was gaining important insights into her own situation and behaviour.

In his few appointments with Dr Reinhold, Raymond acknowledged some weaknesses on his side and gained some insight into how 'remote' he was perceived to be by Rosemary. However, he was nervous of Dr Reinhold and cautious about what he told her. He admitted to Dr Reinhold that he drank too much. His relationship with Rosemary improved enormously when he stopped drinking altogether for a fortnight in the summer. The improvement was temporary, however: he continued drinking for a few more years; but in the longer term, this was an important shift.

Dr Reinhold identified a deeper difficulty for Raymond: a fear of being challenged or confronted, an insecurity and sensitivity to any implied criticism, which she ascribed to his mother's attribution of blame to Raymond for his little sister's death from measles. Whatever the truth of this presumption, it was certainly the case that at home Raymond would frequently become very defensive, patronising and even angry when challenged on any issue on which he felt he should be 'expert'.[7] In his academic work Raymond was much less defensive, although some observers might have detected a patronising style at times toward younger or less experienced academics. Interestingly, this insecurity possibly manifested itself differently in his academic work, which was typically hedged with qualifications that diminished the impact of his major insights. (When he began to set out his new ideas – the concepts of 'social organisation' – they were 'received rather frostily [. . . and] I was most conscious of "walking apart" from the dominant Oxford path.')[8]

Edmund, too, was sensitive to criticism, a sensitivity that almost certainly also had its origins rooted in his relationship with his mother, which was, however, very different to the relationship between Raymond and his mother. Whereas Raymond had had a supportive, calm, quiet relationship with his father (Wesley Firth had said to Rosemary that he regretted never having had time to play with his children), Raymond's relationship with his mother was unquestionably emotionally distant (surprisingly, Raymond did not fly out to New Zealand for his mother's funeral in 1962).

From an early age, Edmund's mother had instilled in him the idea that he was – and should be – special and a high achiever. (Edmund's father, almost sixty years older than Edmund, was a detached figure.) Edmund felt that he had to live up to his reputation as a brilliant student, but found it difficult to do so. At university, a second class in maths persuaded him to switch to engineering, but 'having failed in two successive exams', he again only achieved a second class at the end of his second year; he became seriously worried, and wrote to his parents about their false impressions of his ability.[9]

Once the uncertainties of his time in Iraq and the war in Burma were behind him, Edmund's sharp intellectual ability together with his critical mind did, in fact, prove to be a brilliant combination. Yet the insecurity remained. This was one of the major factors deep at work behind Edmund's 'betrayal' of Rosemary, his 'casting off' of Rosemary intellectually. Although he loved her and enjoyed their intellectual fencing when they were young, Edmund probably felt somewhat threatened by Rosemary even then: he was fascinated by her, but also wary of being challenged, as well as scared of any emotional commitment. Later, Edmund coped with his insecurities by rigidly demarcating those with whom he engaged in academic discourse (university staff and students) from those with whom he merely engaged socially and personally. Until the mid-1960s, Rosemary was not part of the academic world. It was easy for Edmund to distance her intellectually at this point in his life. He made quite sure that those who were close to him emotionally had absolutely nothing to do with his work as an anthropologist (and his family knew well that he would not tolerate any rivals).

Edmund was bursting with ideas during this period. Cambridge around 1960 was an environment in which any outsider to the British 'intellectual aristocracy' or the titled aristocracy had to work extremely hard to make an impression. These were years, therefore, when Edmund needed to be combative to make his mark. In this, Edmund was eminently successful. In 1961 – a pivotal year – he published *Rethinking Anthropology*, a book of essays that took on the anthropological establishment head-on. He compared social anthropologists to medieval astronomers attempting to fit empirical facts into idealised models derived from prejudiced thinking. In a characteristically contentious style, he set out to 'imply my own merit by condemning the work of my closest friends' – accusing them of 'butterfly collecting' as opposed to rigorous theoretical thinking. Strikingly, however, Edmund barely criticised Raymond and even endorsed the 'exceptional detail of Firth's ethnographic material'.[10] The book, its title and its epithet – 'butterfly collecting' – had the desired effect. Edmund Leach was auditioning as a public intellectual and he was simultaneously burnishing his credentials as a Cambridge don (he had become a fellow of King's College in 1960).

CRLR

For all that Raymond and Rosemary would argue and row about the personal aspects of their lives throughout the 1950s and 1960s, they often engaged in animated conversation about Raymond's work and the careers and work of other British anthropologists. The extent to which Raymond shared his anthropological ideas with Rosemary varied from month to month, according to the degree of tension between the two of them. Yet when the levels of friction were lower, Rosemary was very much a partner in Raymond's thinking about his own work and plans, which, in the early 1960s, centred on the subtle politics of maintaining the profile of the LSE, the profile of anthropology within government, and his own academic reputation in Britain and abroad.[11]

When Rosemary returned to anthropology in the 1960s, she and Raymond spent an increasing amount of time analysing and dissecting developments in sociology and anthropology in Britain. Evenings during the week would take one or two forms, with varying frequency. When tensions were lower, animated after-supper discussions would revolve around the ideas and publications of other academics or the politics of university appointments and the rivalries between Oxford, Cambridge, LSE and Manchester. When tensions were higher, comments made by one or other spouse would be pounced upon as patronising or ill-informed, ridiculous or nonsensical, and discussion would degenerate into either a row or frozen silence. At other times, Raymond and Rosemary would simply read, each in a world of their own, while listening quietly to Baroque or early music (they did not have a television until the 1980s).

Even during their most difficult periods, however, the spasmodic discussion of anthropological theory and politics was in complete contrast to the rigid separation of work and family life that Edmund found it necessary to maintain. And their mutual exploration of ideas was fruitful. Rosemary and Raymond became excited by the notion of returning to the fishing village at Bacho'k on the north-east coast of Malaya for fieldwork, twenty-five years after their first fieldwork there. As a joint venture, it also brought them closer together again for a while. Rosemary and Raymond each secured some research funding, and they returned to Kelantan for six weeks over the summer of 1963; their son Hugh (then sixteen) stayed some of the time at home and some with friends. Over the next few months, back in England, Rosemary wrote additional chapters for a second edition of her book on Malay housekeeping. One consequence of the fieldwork was an intestinal problem that necessitated Rosemary's admission to the London Hospital for Tropical Diseases for investigation. Adopting the same stance of the participant observer that she had adopted for her fieldwork, Rosemary kept a daily diary during her time in the hospital, which she later published as an anthropological perspective on the experience of medical illness and treatment.[12]

Figure 15.1. Raymond, Rosemary and Hugh at their home in London, late 1950s. Photographer unknown.

The Social Administration course at LSE, which she completed on the back of her social work in the mid-1950s, had restored Rosemary's confidence in her ability to contribute usefully and meaningfully to both academic debate and practical education.

The expedition to Kelantan at this time was a crucial turning point for Rosemary as it represented both a return to anthropological fieldwork and a step forward in rebuilding her self-esteem and her place as a professional anthropologist.

ROSEMARY TO HER FATHER, GILBERT

1 November 1960   **Duncroft Approved School for Girls, Surrey**[13]

Dear Papa

. . . I have no real status here and I have no ascribed duties. I have therefore been forced to adopt very much the attitude of the anthropologist starting fieldwork, and have tried to maintain a neutral friendly position of observation . . .

There are 30 girls here, all supposedly of fairly high average intelligence, all seriously 'disturbed', all with really appalling family backgrounds of one kind or another, all but two promiscuous, and of the two virgins one killed a baby she was babysitting with, in a fit of temper!

. . . The night before I arrived two girls had to be separated from a vicious fight; which turned out to be involved with an older girl who had been in two prisons, a mental hospital and several homes and approved schools, who was bullying the younger into signing a petition complaining against a member of staff . . .

The next day a girl swallowed a pin and the following morning absconded – pin and all – in the pouring rain with nothing but a dress and cardigan. She was however brought back later in the day . . .

Most of the staff . . . have, I find, worked together before at different institutions. In one way or another they form a fairly tight knit group . . . and their fairly happy trusting relationship with each other creates a warm 'family' atmosphere against which the girls have a chance to grow up a bit and get over some of their more outrageous emotional and social difficulties. But of course their tight group makes it more difficult for an outsider. . . . However I feel I have been up to a point accepted by the girls as there was a certain amount of frolicking last night being Halloween and I was 'honoured' with some physical ragging like the best of the staff, all in most good natured fashion . . .

Love to K.[14] and I hope she's much better. Rosemary.

ROSEMARY TO RAYMOND

28 November 1960   Hospital for Nervous Diseases, Denbigh, North Wales

Darling,

. . . My dear I am entranced by the work here ... the work is a nice combination of insight into the social as well as personal problems that lead to these mental breakdowns. . . . Man's inhumanity to man is shown in a dozen different heart rending ways every time one reads a new case history or goes to a conference as I've just done again this evening. Raymond, it really makes me feel that any hurt which you and I may have inflicted on each other is infinitesimal compared with what some people have gone through. Whether it is a kind of catharsis to see other people's problems so starkly or not, I don't know: but in some curious way I don't feel really depressed by these other outside problems, just very moved and anxious to know more and to help if possible. . . . It does seem possible that I may be good at this kind of job: if so, you won't think it morbid or escapist of me will you? . . . You once said to me in the summer when you returned from Austria that our interests seem to have diverged irremediably: yet to me I know I could never have got where I have got without you at the back of me to begin with. I am sure we should see it as a minor excursion or side tracking of ideas – due to the practical limitations of my being a woman . . . rather than as final parting of the ways. I wonder if you understand at all what I am getting at? You feel I have gone a long way from you and left you: but it's not so at all really – I have only gone off on a long circular tour which began with you and is bound to end with you in the end, too.

Bless you. Look after Hugh! I'm glad he's being good at school!!
Love Rosemary.

ভ১৯

ROSEMARY'S DIARY

24 May 1961   **First Consultation**   **Southwood Avenue, London**

. . . Went to see Dr R. [Dr Reinhold] outwardly collected. Much surprised to find her very young . . . rather more professional than I anticipated. I did not like her but felt she was competent.

31 May 1961   **Second Consultation**   **London**

Second Consultation: . . . 'What strikes me about you – what sticks out a mile – is your sense of guilt.' Later on she asked me to consider early 'disciplinary' relations with my mother, father – or other early sibling relationships. This my homework for the next week! . . . I was asked to talk about 1956 [when Rosemary fell in love with Helen]. It was a pleasure. . . . 'Social monstrosity of a relationship' was warmly contradicted. . . . I left actually *liking her* . . .

Came home that evening and we three [Rosemary, Hugh and Helen] had supper. It was so nice – Hugh's face does so light up when she comes: and in the ensuing week our lunches were perfect: an almost benign calm has fallen on our relationship . . .

A remarkable discussion [with Raymond] on my future job situation. It began with rage and bitterness on his part but I was astounded to be able to lead it to a rational and calm end. . . . He '*must*' be the good husband – forgiving, understanding even if occasionally driven to rudeness or cruelty by the outrageous wife behaviour!

7 June 1961   **Third Consultation**   **London**

. . . Dr R. found [Raymond] 'charming': but found him very nervous of her and the therapeutic situation: quite determined to preserve the marriage she said and not NOW unhappy about [. . . Rosemary's relationship with Helen]: confessed he had been very jealous before.

Spent some time today in analysing my early relations with Raymond, my fear of something undefined in him which I perceived in Salzburg [in 1935]: my guesses about his early childhood relations with his mother over death of Gretta, his parents' relations with each other, his earlier illnesses. . . . Something has been touched in R. by his first talk with Dr R. for he was filled with tender feelings – mostly almost of compassion for me – on his return from her. 'So I am so remote!' and we even achieved a curiously successful lovemaking as result of this. But he had asked no questions: only agreed with me no one should be told we were seeing a psychiatrist . . .

20 June 1961 **Fifth Consultation** **London**

. . . She is still asking me to look at my childhood to find out why I am afraid of my own feelings.

ᘔᔕᘛ

By the summer of 1961, Rosemary had made the decision to end her affair with Helen – or at least transform it into a platonic friendship – and she had also identified Raymond's mistress as being a visiting anthropologist, who, as it happened, left England that summer. Raymond was probably about to make a similar decision: at one point, he told Rosemary, 'I have told you before and I have told my mistress this: that you come first in my life. If you want me to give her up I suppose you have a right to ask it, but I won't be lectured at about fidelity.'[15] (This latter remark was a reference to Rosemary's relationship to Helen, which Rosemary had disclosed to Raymond in 1957. Raymond, however, almost certainly knew nothing of Rosemary's continuing love for Edmund.)

Rosemary hopefully remarked to herself at this point: 'some small voice within me says that there must be, deep buried beneath this cynical hard husband of mine, the smallest remains of someone who long ago loved me.'[16]

ROSEMARY'S DIARY

August 1961 **Supper at the cottage** **Holway, Dorset**

A curious month. R. [Raymond] withdrawn, inaccessible, cold. . . . I remember now Dr R. saying that R. was kind, tolerant and wise only to people who didn't offer him any challenge – his students . . . me as a young mouldable girl . . .

A curious episode at supper:

. . . We are discussing reality in the detective novels of Dorothy Sayers.

R. suddenly bursts out: 'You, none of you – with respect to you all – are as close to real life as I am.'

An astonished silence at table.

Hugh fortunately laughs good naturedly and says, 'Daddy that is surely impossible. No one person alive can be more or less close to life.'

'Yes, they can. You have none of you been up against things as I have been.'

He bowed his head, deeply angry, hurt, alone. I suddenly realised he couldn't take any more . . . silenced H. [Hugh] with a look, turned the conversation and felt astounded at my power and control. But I have won only to lose. I now realise I am living with a dead man.

1 June 1962   **Holway, Dorset**

. . . Angry at R.'s anger let loose by wine, I said most angry and hurtful things to him. Restless and sleepless at morning [in the early hours] he was up. Awaking after a peaceful and emotionally satisfying sleep I called him to my side apologising for having been 'rather beastly' last night. He came and embraced me as closely as ever, for long, and said: 'you have to do so little to scrub it all out: for you can hurt, you know.' . . .

ca:o

In early July 1963, Rosemary and Raymond returned to Kelantan to observe the changes that had occurred in the nearly twenty-five years since they lived there in 1939–40.

ROSEMARY TO HER FATHER

30 July 1963   **Bacho'k, Kelantan, Malaysia**

Dearest Papa

I must write now and let you all know that we have settled . . . in a genuine Malay fisherman's house which belongs to some relatives of our very good old friends Ioh and Awang,[17] who lived next door to us and from whom in 1940 we obtained a great deal of information . . .

Things could not possibly have turned out better, far better than we dreamed or hoped – many, many of our old friends are here, remember us with warmth; the language is coming back slowly but surely and we think we can do a useful job here of comparison with the past . . .

The house we had before was specially built for us and was mixed English–Malay style. This one is quite Malay: we sleep on mattresses (cost 45/- each!) on mats on the floor over which we have rigged mosquito nets lent us by University of Kuala Lumpur. . . . We have a woman who directs shopping, washing and cleaning and who with the aid of a young girl is cooking Malay food for us.

There are signs of change now, shops have more stock, children going to school, many young adults trying to learn to read, and the boats have engines as well as sails but much is as before. Tell Hugh we have two comical little speckled cats, attached to our house.

All our love.

Rosemary.

21 August 1963   **Bacho'k, Kelantan**

Dearest Papa

. . . The changes are rather like those of early nineteenth century [Britain], with great improvements in health, increasing population, better transport and

Figure 15.2. Rosemary with Ioh Lung, informant and friend, Kelantan 1963. Photograph by Raymond Firth. LSE Library Firth Photographs/19/6.

housing, widespread education: so far it seems as if some of the worst errors of [nineteenth-century] England are being avoided. But tho' far healthier than before, these fishermen are perhaps not very much better off than they were – they live a very hard life, going out early about 3–4 a.m. and returning about 3–4 p.m. Sometimes they have got nothing, line fishing, sometime just a few fish to eat, sometimes up to about 10/- or 15/- or even 60/- worth: but the average income seems to be around £100 a year or less – rather like the rural workers in England 60 years ago.

. . . Interest in education is very great, and about 30 women, boys and girls take evening classes in a neighbouring house, trying to learn to read. . . . It is dusk: I am about to bathe (outside, jar and bucket poured over me) and go to a neighbour's house to eat rice.

Love to all. Rosemary.

ROSEMARY TO HUGH

8 September 1963   Kuala Lumpur, Malaysia

Dear Hugh,

. . . We had a most extraordinary end to our village stay: we were led to depart in traditional style . . . by giving a public performance of Malay boxing, fencing and wrestling of a ritualised kind – more allied to a mixture of ballet and jujitsu than anything European – and accompanied to music. We had it outside our house on the last afternoon, the orchestra *under* the house. A crowd of 300 or more watched. Afterwards Minna [the housekeeper] with the help of sundry neighbours, fed about 40 persons: the players, the orchestra and a few relatives and hangers on of same – on a mixture of lentil-like beans and glutinous rice stewed with coconut cream and durian – most delicious a delicacy. All these people sat on the floor of our house, the chairs and tables pushed well out of the way, we watching.

The last evening [a] stream of sentimental visitors came pouring in to say good-bye . . .

. . . Besides this genuine display of affection was a comic scuffle for possession of our very valuable property left behind: such as 2 mattresses, sheets and pillows, towels, kettle, thermos water cooler, oil stove, oil lamp and what not. A certain amount of bitterness involved as our housekeeper, very well paid with 2 month's rent and wages for 40 days stay, half hoped to get all the *barang-barang* too for herself!

It is delicious luxury to sleep on a *bed*, to *sit down* in the lavatory *indoors*, to get water hot or cold out of a tap, to bathe nude and in private, and in fact not to have people always walking into your room to sit and chat. But we miss the food, the lovely beach, the sounds of goats and ducks under our house, little cat cuddling up on my feet at night, and the sound of gongs and chanting at the *Wayang Kulit* shows at night.

. . . Five days here, two in India, back on 18th. Love to Terence.[18]

Mother.

ROSEMARY TO GRETA REDFIELD[19] IN CHICAGO

3 April 1964   **Holway, Dorset**

Dear Greta,

. . . My teaching job [at Battersea College] became full time . . . in September, just after we returned from Malaya, and I sometimes feel quite frantic that I shall never be able to write even the smallest thing about the trip: and I was bursting with ideas when I was there. . . . I have begun to get madly jealous when I hear R. tapping away on his typewriter and I in the kitchen ironing, or shopping, or ringing up for the coal!

Malaya was marvellous: it did my intellectual amour-propre a wonderful job and I feel quite a different person after that . . .

R. and I have settled down to a good deal more comfortable and less tempestuous life since Malaya, which was very good for us. I feel I have become rather a different woman.

. . . All my love to you as ever. Rosemary.

Notes

1. Edmund Leach, 1984, 'Glimpses of the Unmentionable in the History of British Social Anthropology', *Annual Review of Anthropology* 13: 1–23, p. 19.
2. Rosemary's 1943 book was revised, extended and republished: Rosemary Firth, 1966, *Housekeeping among Malay Peasants*, London: Athlone Press.
3. Margaret Hardiman (1918–2011), subsequently at the LSE responsible for the teaching of social planning for administrators in developing countries.
4. Dr Margaret Reinhold, psychiatrist and psychoanalytic psychotherapist, practised privately at 12 Connaught Place, London W2.
5. Charles Anthony Storr (1920–2001), psychiatrist and psychoanalytic psychotherapist, wrote prolifically and talked on radio and television about his work. His first marriage ended in divorce in 1970; he remarried the same year.
6. Rosemary, diary entry, 18 July 1966.
7. This latter insight is based on extensive observation by two of us (Hugh and Melinda Firth). The earlier discussion is based on Rosemary's record of appointments with Dr Reinhold between May 1961 and November 1964.
8. Raymond Firth, 'Reflections', unpublished. These ideas were published as Raymond Firth, 1951, *Elements of Social Organisation*, London: Watts; and Raymond Firth, 1964, *Essays on Social Organisation and Values*, London: Athlone Press.
9. The evidence of Edmund's second-class achievements is in his own hand: Edmund to Rosemary, undated, summer 1931. His remark about failure in these exams is from his letter to his father: see Stanley Tambiah, 2002, *Edmund Leach: An Anthropological Life*, Cambridge: Cambridge University Press, pp. 19–29.
10. Edmund Leach, 1961, *Rethinking Anthropology*, London: Athlone Press, pp. 21 and 2.
11. See David Mills, 2008, *Difficult Folk: A Political History of Social Anthropology*, Oxford: Berghahn.
12. Rosemary Firth, 1977, 'Routines in a Tropical Diseases Hospital', in Alan Davies and Gordon Horobin (eds), *Medical Encounters: The Experience of Illness and Treatment*, London: Croom Helm, pp. 143–158.
13. Subsequently, between 1974 and 1979, Duncroft Approved School was visited frequently by Jimmy Saville, who abused at least fifty girls there.
14. Kathryn, Rosemary's stepmother.
15. Rosemary, diary entry, 12 July 1961.
16. Rosemary to Dr Reinhold, a letter written but never sent, 31 July 1961.
17. Ioh and her husband Awang Lung were extremely reliable informants in 1940 and 1963 and Rosemary dedicated the second edition of her book to them. He was a fisherman of moderate means, she a housewife. She appears in Figure 15.2 on p. 195.
18. Rosemary's stepbrother.
19. Greta Redfield was a great friend of Rosemary's; she worked with her husband Robert Redfield in Mexico in the late 1920s and early 1930s.

Chapter 16

Scorched Earth

1965–1966

The very success of Raymond and Rosemary's joint expedition to Malaya in 1963 may well have sown the seeds for the one of the biggest crises in their relationship, although there were certainly other factors at work. Raymond was beginning to consider his approaching retirement, due in 1968 at the age of sixty-seven. Returning to Tikopia in 1952 and diligently document-ing the changes since his first visit twenty-five years earlier had been a huge achievement. The return to Kelantan in Malaya was a much less significant study scientifically, but it had been a success. Raymond not unnaturally began to contemplate the possibility of one more expedition to Tikopia before he retired. It seems that he raised this as a possibility with Rosemary once or twice in 1963–64.

When they were working together or discussing specifically anthropolog-ical matters, Raymond and Rosemary's relationship was generally positive and constructive. Their rows usually developed as a result of comments about politics, the behaviour of people in the news and public life, or their own or others' personal behaviour. Until this point, the major decisions in their lives had been taken jointly.

Yet it was partly because of this history that their marriage nearly fell apart.

Although Rosemary's initial reaction to Raymond's proposal for another Tikopia expedition was not favourable, he went ahead and applied for leave and funding – presumably anticipating that he would bring Rosemary around to the idea. Unfortunately it was not from Raymond, but accidentally from someone else at the LSE, that Rosemary learnt that his leave – for at least six months – had been approved. She feared for his health, even his life, after the last expedition in 1952. But above all, it was the lack of consultation that hurt Rosemary the most bitterly. Moreover, it appears that Raymond had suggested she use her own money to come with him as far as New Zealand. Her anger made Raymond defensive, which further inflamed the situation. The insult Rosemary experienced was also linked with concerns about Raymond's affairs – and, unusually, his anthropological activities.

For there was indeed one anthropological matter on which Rosemary and Raymond seriously disagreed. Malinowski's widow Valetta was publishing her husband's private, and very personal, diaries – which unflatteringly portrayed Malinowski as obsessive, hypochondriacal and egocentric – against the wishes of his daughters. Raymond wrote the introduction to *A Diary in the Strict Sense of the Term*. He had, he later said, written the introduction 'somewhat unwillingly, at the request of Valetta . . . who was determined to publish'.[1] Its publication elicited a storm of criticism. As Raymond himself said twenty years later, 'In one sense the publication of the diaries was an act of betrayal – not so much because it exposed Malinowski's weaknesses, as that it assumed that his weaknesses could be part of a commercial property to be exploited.'[2]

Rosemary was deeply shaken by the fact that Raymond could lend his name to the publication of these diaries. Her primary concern was that Raymond was colluding in a process that would reflect badly on his erstwhile friend and mentor. However, there was another, deeper reason for her antagonism. It seems that Valetta and Raymond had been interested in each other before Raymond ever met Rosemary (possibly even before Valetta met Malinowski) in the 1930s, and Raymond had admitted to Rosemary that Valetta and he had had a brief sexual encounter in 1959 while Raymond was in California. Rosemary felt that Raymond's motives were all wrong.

Criticism also came from Raymond's friends and colleagues, who 'felt strongly about the impropriety of publication and the damage it might do to Malinowski's reputation'. Edmund thought publication was 'to the discredit of all concerned'; but he also recognised 'the significance of it as a cathartic record by the lonely and disoriented fieldworker'.[3]

When *A Diary* was republished twenty years on, the critical response was very different: there was increased acceptance of the publication of personal material about people of public interest.[4] In 1965, however, just as Rosemary would have seen it as deeply dishonourable to reveal the difficulties she faced in her marriage to anyone other than her closest confidantes, so she deemed it dishonourable of Raymond to portray his mentor in a poor light – all the more so, if, as she suspected, he was doing so as a 'favour' for Valetta. In Rosemary's view, Raymond was being deeply hurtful on all fronts: through his neglect of her needs, his attention to others, and his disregard for his erstwhile teacher's reputation.

Understandably, Raymond was not inclined to relinquish the chance to go to Tikopia: a final piece of fieldwork would be of scientific importance for understanding the changes that had occurred since 1928. And with more effective medicines, he would be better prepared in case of illness than he had been in 1952. Underneath that reasoning, though, there was probably a desire to secure his reputation as he approached retirement.

While Raymond was abroad for three weeks for a conference in Honolulu in February and early March 1965, Rosemary went to Cambridge to talk to Edmund and Celia about Raymond's Tikopia plans. They would certainly have wished to help; however, Edmund was probably more preoccupied with the politics of Cambridge academia: less than a year later, he would be in the throes of drumming up support for his candidacy as provost of King's College.[5]

Rosemary was already anxious about what their relationship would be like when Raymond returned from Honolulu in mid-March. Raymond was no doubt equally anxious. Once he was back in London, talk likely returned to Raymond's projected expedition to Tikopia, further heightening the tension. Some trigger made Raymond explode one evening; Rosemary's anxiety and desperation were magnified. The marriage itself was now at stake.

Figure 16.1. Celia and Edmund at home in Storey's Way, Cambridge. Photograph by Alexander Leach.

By early May, it was clear that Raymond would still not change his mind. Rosemary wrote to Edmund, probably in the faint hope that he might broker some resolution. Edmund's reply was detached, somewhat cynical, brief and unhelpful; it possibly reflected the rigid demarcation between work – his priority – and family life that he maintained. Finally, Rosemary acknowledged she could not dissuade Raymond from going away – but part of her felt that with no prospect of resolving major marital issues together, the marriage was dead. For the next year or so, she kept returning to the question of whether or not she should leave Raymond altogether.

Their son Hugh was aged eighteen and at home when the argument about Tikopia burst upon the family scene in January 1965. Hugh talked with each of them about the issue and their reasoning before he left in February for a spell of five months abroad in Norway between school and his first year at Cambridge University. Raymond wrote to Hugh in April, saying 'Things here go along fairly well. Rosemary has I think now accepted, though under protest and rather sadly, the Tikopia expedition idea – she is going to give me *Anna Karenina* to read when I am there!'[6] A letter from Rosemary to Hugh in May paints a rather different picture. She was resigning herself to Raymond's decision, but this could hardly be labelled 'acceptance'.

A week later, on 1 June, presumably after another argument, Rosemary walked out of the house, leaving Raymond.

She spent the rest of the week with her stepbrother Terence and the weekend with an old friend in Crowborough. (She wrote to Hugh from there, saying nothing whatever about what had happened with Raymond.) After some telephone negotiation between Raymond and Rosemary, Raymond joined her in Crowborough and they returned together to 33 Southwood Avenue.

Rosemary had been away from home for seven nights. Raymond was clearly shaken.

In late August, for the first time ever since she married Raymond, Rosemary went away on holiday by herself, a two-week cruise to the Greek islands. The trip was a powerful statement for both herself and Raymond about her growing independence and assertiveness.

By the autumn of 1965, Raymond had responded to Rosemary's concerns. He significantly adapted his plans so he would be absent not for six months but rather for three, spending only four weeks on Tikopia itself.[7] Rosemary acknowledged this compromise when she wrote to Hugh, who was then starting university, just after visiting him at Cambridge in late October.[8]

Raymond's willingness to compromise might just have produced an improvement in their relationship were it not for his retirement plans. Not only had he decided to go away for three months in 1966; he also announced that he was going to take up a post as a visiting professor at the University of Hawai'i for a whole year as soon as he retired in 1968.

Rosemary was therefore faced with a choice as to what she should do in 1968: resign from her job to join him and so damage her career, or tolerate her husband's absence for a complete year? Once again, it seemed to Rosemary that Raymond's decision to go to Hawai'i for twelve months was not open for negotiation with her. She felt that any foundation for a constructive working marital partnership had been completely undermined.

Furthermore, Rosemary's professional position was reinforcing her sense of independence. Rosemary had been seeking promotion since 1964, when Battersea College had failed to appoint her to the post vacated by her colleague and friend Margaret Hardiman. That lack of recognition, and the growing confidence she felt as a result of the imminent publication of her revised and extended book on Malay housekeeping, encouraged Rosemary to apply for other jobs. In March 1966, she was offered a post as a lecturer at the London University Institute of Education. The same month, the new edition of her book appeared on the shelves. Rosemary now applied and was elected as a member of the Association of Social Anthropologists (ASA).

In her professional life, Rosemary was succeeding. But she felt desperate about her marriage.

When Raymond left for Tikopia at the end of June 1966, Rosemary chose to go away on her own again – this time to the United States, where she reflected deeply on their relationship.

Unable to negotiate with each other adequately, and facing a year and perhaps more of Raymond being abroad most of the time, Rosemary felt that the marital bond was broken, even though their marriage might continue socially. Essentially, she thought that a marital separation would leave her too alone, particularly because they shared so many good friends. Moreover, she was aware that somewhere in Raymond, hidden, 'is a relic of someone I loved long ago'.[9]

Something inside her kept her going and she occasionally felt that perhaps all was not broken. Maybe she remembered how, when she was fifteen, her mother had 'poured out the story of her earlier unhappiness in the marriage with my father, and prepared me thus – just before she died – not to be surprised that "unhappy marriages" could . . . lead in the end to . . . mutual respect and affection'.[10] Perhaps her mother Blanche had been right when she told Rosemary how, with some stamina and the will to work things through, the difficulties in a marriage could successfully be addressed.

ROSEMARY'S DIARY

26 January 1965   **Southwood Avenue, Highgate, London**

I learnt casually from the LSE that R. had leave of absence to go to Tikopia! When I asked about this, half believing, this morning, he said I knew!

Later, said perhaps he hadn't told me finally as it was only arranged 3 weeks ago. Apparently it would be vacation plus one term – that is six months! . . .

Later, when I said it was bad enough him going when he knew I didn't want him to, but not to have asked me was what hurt most – he said 'I don't think I have myself yet realised all the implications' – or something to that effect. . . .

I don't think I have felt the full difficulty of R. till now. A man who upbraids his wife for minding about a mistress and also says she must pay to follow him if she doesn't want to be deserted, baffles me. I feel I am being used, cheated. . . .

17 February 1965   **London**

Little Mrs Tibs [the family cat] died today, with heart failure following kidney trouble. She who had often jumped up from her sleep to come and lick my face when I was unhappy and cried alone, struggled with death. Cried out piteously, lay with all dignity lost, her face on the earth, crawled limply under the dark shadow of the chest, whimpered and twitched and rattled her spirit out of her colding [sic] body, from morning till half past two.

When it was all over – before we could help her to a peaceful death – she lay curled in beauty as if one living in peace again. The snow fell outside: I gathered snow drops after she died. I folded her beautifully marked body and carried her to the vet to be cremated.

Hugh and I wept. We had not thought death so ugly. It was the day before he left for 6 months on his own in Norway.

So she spanned his childhood in this house, taught him all the facts of life and death and then departed, as he grew up.

She was a loving and much loved cat.

෴

Raymond was away again from late February until mid-March, first at a conference in Hawai'i, then visiting his father in Auckland.

ROSEMARY'S DIARY

16 March 1965   **London**

After three weeks on my own . . . with the help of medicine, the law, my friends and my kin I had looked at myself and at him.

I am happier alone, sleep better than I have done for months, feel comfortable, free from bitterness, singularly detached, if rather sad about it all. He is Hugh's father, which matters most. I cannot tangle with the law for what we have done to each other is mental cruelty as much as physical unfaithlessness [sic] and that is a subjective hurt, not to be weighed at the bar.

He cannot see that there is much wrong in what he has done. His need to go to Tikopia, as his need to settle the balance of accounts with [his mistress] have impelled him . . . to wrong me – and yet aver no wrong has been done. If I play his game I only involve myself more in his distorted values. I think it would be better if we could live in some way an arrangedly [sic] separate life. He is a good companion, not a bearable close partner.

Habit, sentiment, social need, our mutual past and Hugh all weigh heavily in favour of not performing the operation of cutting the bonds.

Common sense, deep institutional needs for self-preservation, professional ambition and a sense of unused power and ability in myself urge me to break free; as the healthy person unable to live with crippling, corrupting disturbance should be able to break free. . . .

I am calm tonight, shall sleep well.

21 March 1965 **London**

. . . I also see another thing with devastating clarity: I want to leave him, but I don't want to leave my home, my own house, my place in Highgate and among our mutual friends.

This is all directly related to the issue, whether R. is bound to consult me (not of course necessarily to do what I wish) on the question of [the] Tikopia revisit; [and] whether I am bound to leave my own job and accompany him to Honolulu after his retirement. . . .

We cannot even begin to talk about either of these things unless we can get clear what each of us means by the words we use – by the obligations of husband and wife to each other: what spheres of life do they cover and what spheres do they not cover?

What ought we to decide together; what have we each the right to call our own private domain?

. . . I came in heavy hearted and thoughtful from an evening walk, and made to go to bed. 'I don't want', I told him, 'to talk about my feelings just yet.' He stood physically between me and the door and said he would *make* me talk – and then began about my needing to see a doctor!!! . . . Alone, or at a distance, I am relatively safe. If he encounters me, physically or emotionally, I feel terrified. And his action in that small kitchen last night, where he put me with my back to the wall, made me terrified. . . .

31 March 1965 **London**

Have been reading the *Diary* of Bronio [Malinowski] which was the cause of the upset last week . . .

I am deeply shaken by the fact that R. could lend his protective name to the publication of this extremely fascinating, interesting, important document . . . that one should do it for a friend!

. . . What is it then that so disturbs me?

The extraordinary revelation of B.M.'s character, only sensed before; its similarity to R.F.'s – the nature of the bonds that tied them together – as well as those that could have tied both to V. [Valetta Malinowska]. . . .

Oh, how lonely are wives of 'the great'. . . .

EDMUND TO ROSEMARY

9 May 1965 (received 11 or 12 May) **Storey's Way, Cambridge**

Dear Rosemary,

. . . Both of us are very sad to think that your domestic affairs are still under such strain. Is there anything we can do to help? My own feeling is that there is something quite unreasonable about your expectation that the relations between husbands and wives should be subject to reason! But that comment is hardly helpful. But the technique of blackmail and ultimatum doesn't help either. Of course you are in the right from your point of view and Raymond is in the right from his point of view but wouldn't it be better to abandon all issues of right and wrong and just allow each to go his [sic] own way?

We really would like to help but how?

Much love, Edmund

ROSEMARY'S DIARY

10 May 1965 **London**

Something has come to an end finally this week. Raymond has broken me. I made a great gamble, and lost all. Gamblers don't leave play at the moment of greatest loss – except to cover their humiliation with death.

On Saturday I crossed the street to get some medicine for him, [he] who has been in bed since [. . . last weekend when] he finally told me he intended to proceed with his plans for Tikopia.

A car screeched to a halt, and I was horrified to find myself wondering why on earth it had stopped. The next moment I found myself crying uncontrollably in the street. I fell down, hurt my ankle and cut my knee, and two strange men helped me up to find me weeping without shame. . . .

So I have accepted defeat, and stopped asking.

I said R. should go to Tikopia.

. . . I feel deeply ashamed that I should have asked, pleaded, for so much – and been refused. When I have recovered from my shame, perhaps I shall know what the cost is. . . . But the heart of me has died for him.

22 May 1965 London

And yet it has not died yet. For although almost all trust, faith and confidence has been laid waste between us, I can still see that he is as he is, because there is no help for it. A man deeply and irrevocably alone, quite *unable* to enter into the point of view of a hurt loved person, but not *unwilling* to do so.

Perhaps for the first time he is trying honestly to look into himself and search his own soul. I, who have been doing it for so many years, and probably by nature do not find it so destructive, cannot blame him, if he finds it so hurtful that he hits out . . . in his endeavour to avoid self-destruction.

It is just possible that we might, in time, be able to approach each other again over the scorched earth which at the moment lies between us. Perhaps the analogy of fire is a useful one. Perhaps out of nothing, something new could grow.

He needs someone desperately. So do I. Could it be that we still do need each other?

ROSEMARY TO HUGH, IN NORWAY

22 May 1965 Southwood Avenue, Highgate, London

Dearest Hugh

. . . It has not been a very happy week. We have been discussing Tikopia again. You know I feel quite strongly, first that I don't want to be left alone for so long; second that it is seriously risky for R. to go so far away even with a companion, at his age and with his medical history. Last time he confessed he thought he never would get off alive. I vowed he would go again over my dead body. But it seems it is over my wounded heart that he will go nevertheless. After long talks it seems clear to me that R. regards this last scientific venture as of at least equal – if not greater – importance than my fears or objections. I have been very unhappy about this: but it now seems clear to me that R. cannot really at all understand my feelings and perhaps a man's work is something so important to him, as children are to a woman, that it is what Barbara[11] calls an 'impossible choice' to make between the two. If this is so, I have had to give up my overt objections, since it looks as if R.'s whole self-respect hangs on this venture. I don't know how I shall feel when he is gone, but some things one just has to learn to endure, when it is clear they cannot be avoided. R. cannot understand the importance to me of his not going: I cannot understand the importance to him of going! In the end, I think I value more highly my whole relationship with you and him, the home and so on, that I must give way. In times when two people who love and respect each other fundamentally disagree, one learns what the real priorities are. I'm not generally for saying a woman has to yield because she is the weaker sex. But over this I have been forced to yield. . . .

Bless you and my love always

Mother

☙❧

Rosemary walked out of the house and left Raymond on the morning of 1 June. She stayed with her stepbrother Terence, who also lived in Highgate.

ROSEMARY'S DIARY

2 June 1965   **6.00 a.m.**   **London**

Woke up in a comfortable bed in the quiet of Terence's house, after a full night's sleep on three pills (Mogadon).[12] . . .

I went to work, jerkily, with the memory of a very thin white faced R. almost reduced to nothing. . . . I gave, I think, an excellent lecture.

But T. [Terence] got me to talk; I only wanted to weep *then*. For a small moment I wanted to go straight back, be cuddled in his arms, forgive and be forgiven. . . . This morning I feel, I said, I'd go back, but by Jove I believe the wound would quite soon heal if I didn't. It is the social handicap I would not like – at the moment. I chiefly enjoy the peace.

4 June 1965   **London**

In Terence's room in peace (and luxury!) on the first really summer morning. Let me get a few important facts clear: the tremendous effort needed to take a leap into the outside; the curious orderly working of the mind which remembers to put in toothbrush and comb, but then forgets a belt: the awareness that a runaway wife is really something of a social pariah, in spite of the genuine overt sympathy.

The curious sensation of having no longer any rights vis à vis the deserted partner – the number of conversational occasions when one wishes to say 'my husband' and stumbles.

Desertion is deserting a marital state, not a place. I experienced this.

Next, after the effort, the jump, the pain, the anguished anxiety at the ringing of the telephone bell. But two days later, that has changed, separation has brought healing. . . .

But I must remember, I did want that bell to ring at first. . . .

☙❧

Seven days later, Rosemary returned home, some reconciliation having been achieved with Raymond.

ROSEMARY'S DIARY

3 August 1965   **Holway, Dorset**

Margaret Hardiman came over for a drink and a talk this evening – to my great delight.

But observing her and R. talking I saw the same intolerable arrogance as I have noticed in his intellectual relationships with all other women of his own or near his own age – Margaret Mead, Greta [Redfield], Audrey [Richards], Lucy [Mair], Judith [Freedman].[13] [His relationship with] myself seems reflected in [his relationship with Margaret Hardiman], although she is too clever to let him patronise her; but that is what he is attempting all the time to do.

Patronage – intolerable relationship!

He has been for so many years, of use to so many students, he sees this now as a great halo of unselfish devotion to the young, and is quite blinded to its implications for aggrandisement of his own self-image. He who gives, puts the receiver under obligation and that is what he is seeking all the time – a crowd of grateful persons obligated to him and of course, the greater his own social stature the more of these acolytes there are. I despise it all.

CELIA TO ROSEMARY

6 June 1966   **Hôtel de la Rose d'Or, Roussillon, France**

Dearest Rosemary

. . . I've been thinking about you today and wondering if we shall be home before Raymond goes [to Tikopia]. . . . I've been hoping for your sake that you will be away yourself when Raymond goes off. I know how horrid it is to be the one that is left. I remember you told me you were going to the U.S. – but sometime later, wasn't it? Anyway, if we are home you must come to stay with us during the departure if you feel like it. Meanwhile we bake ourselves in the sun and eat and drink too much. . . . Nightingales sing all day long. They are the only birds left since the French eat everything large enough to make *pâté* of. The speciality of the place is thrush *pâté*. Edmund refused it with horror . . .

How all this must seem to you working hard as you are – I can't think. . . . Don't take life too hard – and I'll ring you up when we get home.

Much love Celia.

ROSEMARY'S DIARY

20 June 1966   **London**

A whole year has gone by, and in six days Raymond leaves for Tikopia.

. . . I have booked – reluctantly – a passage to America to spend a month with Greta [Redfield]. Earlier this year I was offered a new job at the University of London, Institute of Education, and this has given me considerable new stability and interest along with a more solid status and reasonable companions. Also the new edition of my Malay Housekeeping book is out, and looks good!

But I've not yet fully accepted R.'s going. Till this Christmas things were better and we got fonder of each other. But R. is an odd cold fish.

He forces one into intolerable social situations – to meet [his mistress] again for instance, face to face!!! and then jeers at my distress in them. . . .

As the time of his leaving gets nearer, he gets more absorbed than ever in tidying up his own affairs – books edited, articles finished. He has a secretary now every week, altho' we can't afford a carpet . . .! He never suggested I should come out to N.Z. with him, but he is going twice to stay with his family.

Tonight, his lovemaking seemed so self-enclosed . . . I feel 'a thing' which has no other physical purpose than to ease his sexual tensions. . . . No tenderness, no imaginative insights into my own torn and ambivalent feelings about his going are visible at all – only *after* physical coitus can he show me the remotest tenderness or consideration. Yet I am to forget his imminent departure in a self-surrender of love?

. . . When we are at a social distance, he can be a charming friend; companion: and unselfish where his interests are not threatened; he can give a great deal – but only let me *ask* for something, and the shell snaps shut at once – be it tenderness, help, forbearance, or support, much less of course money, his company, his household help (unless offered). Only 'advice' he *likes* me to ask for!

. . . A gnawing guilty doubt shadows me – that I want now, that abstract thing, a husband with the commitment of home, status and income: and this one not at all? Which to me is little less than the mercenary needs of a prostitute.

Yet hidden below this odd, embittered, blind, brilliant, obsessive man, is a relic of someone I loved long ago. And surrounding him too is another creature Hugh knows and loves – a different person than I can see of course.

To keep the images of these two almost incompatible ideals together I cling to Raymond; a man who in spite of two years of protesting, tears and appeals, insists on leaving on a dangerous journey from which he may not return; and is surprised to find that the last months before this unilateral act is put into operation, his wife is torn with ambivalent feelings.

I am to accept meekly and lovingly what I don't like, if not, I am not 'a good wife'.

The most surprising thing of all is that I can still shed tears for him: or for some past that is slipping [away]?

౿ఙ౨

While Raymond was away on Tikopia, Rosemary went abroad to the United States, staying with her longstanding and close friend Greta Redfield in Vermont. She took the opportunity to go to Cornell and Harvard to visit their Medical School and Health Education programmes. Two days before she sailed for New York, she dined with an old friend of Raymond's from his schooldays in New Zealand. They ended up spending the night together. Later, when staying with Greta, she reflected at length on this: Greta and Rosemary talked much about relationships, lovers, husbands, fathers, children, women living alone, as well as themselves, their strengths and their weaknesses.

Back from her travels, Rosemary had to prepare for her new job and Raymond's return from Tikopia.

Coincidentally, the day Raymond arrived back in London in September was the day Rosemary's new job started. The post, which entailed responsibility for developing coursework, was challenging and involved a lot of thought; adjusting to life with Raymond back in Highgate just at this point was not easy. His fieldwork had been successful. He had stopped drinking. Yet he seemed to Rosemary to be seriously unhappy – probably partly because of the state of their marriage, but presumably also because he was facing retirement, with its accompanying loss of public status and the necessity of finding new goals and purposes. Although he had sufficient challenge for the time being (he had been appointed to the Social Science Research Council for three years), he had nothing planned beyond his year in Hawai'i.

Facing the 'intolerable dilemma'[14] of whether to give up her brand-new job to follow her husband or become separated once more, it is not surprising that Rosemary again experienced a period of acute depression at the end of 1966. She felt she was facing the loss of a marriage and the prospect of living with a man who would be abroad much of the time – possibly renewing his affairs – or, when at home, would be withdrawn, irritable and resentful of her independence. Rosemary was driven to review her life to date and reread many of her diaries and letters – including her letters from Edmund, with whom, despite his 'betrayal', she realised she was still, as ever, in love.

ROSEMARY'S DIARY

4 September 1966   **London**

. . . Twenty years ago my seeking for love and life gave me . . . six or so months of love and pleasure with Raymond.[15] [Hugh's] birth gave me untold pleasure as he has all his life, which by forcing me to think of *his* welfare rather than my own, released in me my true self.

. . . Now that I enter on the third major period of a woman's life, past the climacteric, I begin to feel what a woman really is, and what I have been.

Many men have loved me: before I was a mother, I took this all in my stride. I was also a goodish wife, at any rate R. thought so. He never criticised me or sneered at me or challenged my independence of mind, soul and body until after Hugh was born. Then it all began. I wonder now, curious with an analytical not moralising curiosity, whether his faithlessness began only after Hugh's birth? . . . Now that I have brought Hugh to healthy reasonably balanced manhood, and can ignore possible maternity [pregnancy], I am free to be beloved and to love other men again.

And so I have done. And the curse of the matter is, that while I loved and was loved by men before, R. was happy with me. In the period I kept myself a chaste wife to him, he was not happy with me. This is on the face of it a very curious thing. . . .

If other women's love had made him happier, fulfilled, more experienced and generous as I now think other men's love made me, would I be censorious of his promiscuity as I do not feel of my own experiences? I think in honesty not. . . .

1 December 1966   **London**

. . . It has occurred to me more seriously today than ever before that perhaps I should destroy all my letters, my diaries, even myself. . . .

But this suicidal feeling won't last. . . . I have come almost to the point of not any longer having any strong feelings, and in a way I have had to look over my letters and diaries to persuade myself that a being existed in the past who did have strong feelings, and that if I destroy all this evidence, I destroy part of myself. . . .

Why do I not feel sure of my existence unless it is written down? Other people identify themselves in other ways: Raymond and Edmund by their intellectual work, which stands for them as the outside, world recognised aspect of their existence. Perhaps because I am a woman, my sense of identity is only found in a relationship of love to someone else.

In my relationship to Hugh, [only, do I . . .] feel quite sure of my reality and my continued necessity. I have to get beyond this. . . . For Hugh has to grow apart from me. Women give life to men; they should not get life by keeping men in their emotional embrace – a suffocating embrace.

I ask myself today, am I destined to suffocate and destroy each man I love? I have perhaps allowed Edmund to live and grow by letting him free of my love; I hope to do so for Hugh. Women, friends, students, colleagues and relatives, I think have helped to grow and be happier by my love. But my husband seems unable to grow and live in happiness near to me . . .

I do not know if he would be better if I let him go, or whether I should be better also.

. . . Raymond . . . is near breaking point, I recognise that. I do not seem able either to help him or to help myself, either to support him, or support myself, or break away from the 'us' that 30 years of married life has made of the two separate identities of years ago.

I have tried, I keep trying. So does he.

Judge us with charity, those who love us both?

ର୍ପ୍ତର

Rereading many of her diaries and letters, and reflecting on her life, Rosemary took a clear decision to keep them, not destroy them. She placed an envelope addressed 'For Hugh Firth – or whoever else finds these letters?' on top of a box of letters from Edmund.[16] The note inside the envelope read:

December 1966

When I was [almost] 16, I met Edmund Leach; when I was 18, I went to Cambridge May Week Balls with him; when I was 20, I tried to break a relationship which it seemed to me was one-sided and involved me in great pain and suffering with little promise for the future from him. I started at that time to tear up all his letters, but I faltered then, and have never succeeded since. Some have been destroyed, these remain.

We met again after I was married, and E. became attached [again] to me in rebound against a love affair of his that had gone wrong. . . .

In 1940 he married, and throughout the war when he was in India [Burma], Raymond and I saw his wife. When he returned, the four of us became firm friends.

I have always loved Edmund, as I now realise, looking back on these letters at a period of almost desperate depression, loss of confidence in myself and doubts about my own work.

I have come almost equally to love Celia, and both of them have been a real source of strength and help to me at various stages of acute unhappiness in my married life.

If you read these letters ever, may they show you rather how very complicated and uncertain is the human heart. . . .

Perhaps for this reason, they should be kept.

Notes

1. Bronisław Malinowski, 1989, *A Diary in the Strict Sense of the Term*, 2nd edn with new Introduction, London: Athlone Press, pp. xxi.
2. Malinowski, *A Diary in the Strict Sense of the Term*, pp. xxi–xxii.
3. These comments are quoted by Raymond in his introduction to the second edition of *A Diary in the Strict Sense of the Term*, p. xxiii. It may be thought that there is a parallel

between the publication of Malinowski's diary and the publication of this book. The Prologue addresses these issues of privacy, value and perceived 'discredit'.

4. Anthropology was also becoming 'reflexive': there was a real interest in the fieldworker as both agent and recipient of the interaction between the stranger and the 'strange' society.

5. The provost is head of the college, responsible for both academic and financial affairs.

6. Raymond to Hugh, 10 April 1965.

7. Raymond was accompanied on Tikopia in 1966 by Torben Monberg (1929–2007), a Danish anthropologist and Chief Curator of the Department of Ethnography at the National Museum of Denmark.

8. Hugh studied at King's College, Cambridge, from 1965 to 1968.

9.. Rosemary, diary entry, 20 June 1966.

10. Rosemary to Betty Belshaw's daughter, 4 August 1982 (LSE Library, Firth/8/4/1).

11. Barbara Nadel (later Barbara Prynn; 1940–). Her anthropologist father Fred Nadel had died in 1956 and her mother died in 1959. She used to stay with the Firths periodically and became a close family friend. She has had a successful career in adoption and fostering as a social worker and teacher.

12. Nitrazepam, a mild anxiolytic and hypnotic.

13. Greta Redfield, Audrey Richards, Lucy Mair and Judith Freedman were all good friends as well as colleagues. However, the Firths only rarely met the American anthropologist Margaret Mead.

14. Rosemary, diary entry, 7 November 1966.

15. Rosemary was clearly thinking of a period at the end of the war, shortly before Hugh was born.

16. Rosemary subsequently placed her professional records, including fieldwork notes, along with Raymond's, into an archive at the LSE Library. Shortly before her death, she let her son and daughter-in-law know that there were also personal notebooks and letters of interest and possible significance, of which they should be aware.

Chapter 17

The Wheel Keeps Turning

1967–1969

Rosemary had now succeeded in establishing herself as a professional anthropologist, with a brand-new university job, a book published and membership of the Association of Social Anthropologists (ASA). In 1967 and 1968, she had several papers published; she delivered one of these at an ASA conference on the role of women in anthropological fieldwork. Although they were not working on any joint projects, Rosemary and Raymond were now able to debate and explore ideas together much more freely when they were both at home.

Rosemary was adjusting rapidly to her new circumstances. She was now far more independent as a professional. However, since Raymond's expedition to Tikopia in the summer of 1966, she had been forced to realise that she could not stop Raymond from spending long periods abroad as soon as he retired. She was used to him going away on his own for a few weeks or occasionally a couple of months, but, over the following few years, he planned to spend most of each year away, first at one university, then another, coming home only for Christmas and the long academic summer break.

This was quite new and it would take some getting used to.

⚬⟋⟍⚬

For a few years, Rosemary had been anticipating that her father would not live much longer. But when he died in June 1967, shortly after her stepmother Kathryn, the loss of this man on whom she had relied for emotional support for so long was extremely hard. The following year, Raymond retired and, in August, left to spend virtually a whole year at the University of Hawai'i. Although Raymond had often been away at conferences, this was the longest he had ever been away during their marriage – he was gone for longer even than when he had been on Tikopia in 1952. Also in the autumn of 1968, Hugh moved to Edinburgh for four years to undertake postgraduate research, living away permanently for the first time.

Rosemary felt that she had lost three men in her life almost at once: her father through death and both Raymond and her son Hugh through physical distance. She was living alone in a way she never had before.

Yet this lengthy separation from Raymond had two important consequences. It forced her to become more emotionally independent, but it also enabled her to become more intellectually independent. The long decade from 1966 until her retirement in 1978 was a period of highly productive professional work: communicating an anthropological approach to teachers and those involved in training teachers, cross-fertilising between anthropology and medical sociology, and interesting academic anthropologists in how their ideas might be transmitted to a wider public.

She was particularly committed to helping both educators and anthropologists understand how people's social roles influence what they 'see' and think – and to showing the analogies between rituals of initiation, which seem so striking in societies other than our own, and the rituals of professional training in education, anthropology and academia.

As part of the change in her own roles and relationships, she started corresponding regularly with Hugh, now an adult, seeking his feedback – for example, on the draft article subsequently published as 'From Wife to Anthropologist'.[1] She also wrote to him around this time to say how 'relations with Raymond are so much better since I have been earning, and have some say in what I do, spend, and so on'; Rosemary had keenly felt her lack of financial independence during the period when she was not in paid employment. She also described the 'odd, unreal' sensation occasioned by adjusting to Raymond's retirement at a point when 'something else is happening to me in the professional world, the reverse of age and retirement'.[2]

Raymond might have been on the brink of retirement, but he was still publishing and he was at that point in his career when he was beginning to be showered with honorary degrees from foreign universities, such as Oslo, Canberra and Chicago.

Edmund was elected provost of King's College, Cambridge, in 1966, and the following year he and Celia moved into the Provost's Lodge at the college. By this time, their two children, Loulou and Alexander, had left home and were living in London. Celia unwillingly accepted the role of provost's wife and hostess of many convivial parties, entertaining notables such as Yehudi Menuhin and Prince Peter of Greece.

The following year brought honour, fame and notoriety of a more public kind to Edmund: he was invited to deliver the 1967 Reith Lectures. These were intended to promote public understanding and encourage debate about important issues. Edmund characteristically set out to challenge accepted truths about British values and assumptions – to encourage debate. His theme was 'A Runaway World?', based on the assumption that there existed a widespread fear of change, challenge and the younger generation's taste for rock music and 'pot and purple hearts, long hair and LSD, mini-skirts and love-ins, student strikes and political demonstrations'.[3] He was nervous about the weekly broadcasts and asked Celia for advice on their presentation – probably the only time he ever asked for such advice.

His first broadcast opened by asking: 'Men have become like gods. Isn't it about time that we understood our divinity?' His second lecture tackled philosophy through a discussion of the nature of reality and free will. The most incendiary, on 'Ourselves and Others', caused uproar as Edmund stated that, 'Far from being the basis of the good society, the family, with its narrow privacy and tawdry secrets, is the source of all our discontents.' In the printed version, he professed himself 'astonished by the public animosity provoked by this very ordinary remark'.[4] Was it the word 'tawdry' that set people alight? He had asked Celia whether it was appropriate to use in the context of what he was saying. She insisted that it was very apt. Edmund said afterwards that when he'd written the sentence, he'd been thinking about money and the way money was manipulated within families. But the idea that the family, so central to Christian and conservative values, could be a source of misery was anathema to many at the time – and would still be anathema to many today.

Edmund lambasted elderly administrators, the government and the defence industry, and advocated long-term nature conservancy. Here was Edmund the rebel, delighting in the opportunity to unsettle those whom he thought complacent. The reception was certainly critical. He was accused of speaking platitudes '*de haut en bas* as becomes a god, or a provost, in metaphors and parallels which conceal as much as they reveal his meaning'.[5] Other Reith lecturers had raised uncomfortable truths about British society, but Edmund used the role of the anthropologist – that is, the outsider looking at our own society – to pronounce upon class, family and societal values that were – and are – dear to much of the British establishment. He tried to offer an anthropological way of thinking to the wider public.

Rosemary certainly shared and approved of his goal: she was passionately committed to helping others to 'see' anthropologically, to look at themselves as an outsider might do. And she also shared Edmund's view that many of those in positions of seniority – including in universities – were indeed out of touch (as she remarked to Hugh in relation to some of the events following

1968).[6] But she also reacted against Edmund's provocation and his frequent overgeneralisations: 'grains of sense among an often wildly unreliable sermon!'[7] Indeed, these lectures were like a sermon at times, with all the patronising connotations of preaching delivered from a pulpit.

Rosemary was inquisitive about and receptive to – if sometimes sceptical of – those critiques of the society of which she was a part made by both students and feminists. She may have distanced herself from many of the feminist ideas of the period, but she maintained a critical and nuanced view of gender imbalances in both personal and professional situations: in her view, real changes in the position of women were much needed.[8]

Although both Rosemary and Raymond were critical of Edmund's more sweeping generalisations, they valued the public audience he had engaged and the debate that ensued. And significantly for Rosemary, she was now meeting Edmund not just socially but also professionally at ASA conferences.

Raymond was living away, teaching abroad for much of each year, every year until 1975. Nevertheless, Rosemary continued to thrive, though she felt considerable frustration about what she viewed as Raymond's pretence that theirs was somehow a normal arrangement. By the New Year of 1969, she had tolerably adjusted to living alone and was seeing more of her friends. Over Christmas, Rosemary spent two weeks with Raymond in Hawai'i, which allowed them to feel somewhat closer again: she wrote to him to say, 'I think we do in many ways understand each other as we have not for several years. Thank you for that.'[9] On the way back, she met up with her sister Margaret's son Andy Darlington in San Francisco: he was finishing a period of postdoctoral research in genetics at Stanford University and preparing to return to a research post in London.

Rosemary commented in her letters to Hugh about these recurring lengthy periods when Raymond was abroad for his visiting professorial posts. On one occasion, she wrote that Raymond 'is extraordinarily unperceptive and unimaginative most of the time; but I can't do without him, and I am not sure I can stand another period like this last endless six months or whatever it is – really two years of course with small intervals'. On another occasion, she wrote 'I begin to feel a kind of rage at my being asked to keep up appearances of normality. . . . A woman asked me in Exeter at the social workers conference, if I was any relation of Raymond Firth, and I had to bite off the answer, "Yes, I am his widow."'[10]

ROSEMARY'S DIARY

9 June 1967   **Southwood Avenue, London**

I went to see my father this evening: he looked at me with eyes as I have never seen them before and I think these are his last weeks here. He has been sleeping

Figure 17.1. Gilbert Upcott, Rosemary's father, early 1960s. Photograph by John Gay.

on and off all day for the past half week and I think the end is coming. He seems quite peaceful . . .

I sat by his bedside for about 15 mins, watched him quietly. Renee [Renee Goggins, Gilbert's housekeeper] brought some roses for me to take home. I laid them on his bed. He said 'the warm weather has brought them into full flower, hasn't it, in spite of the absence of sun.' Then when I laid my head on his hands on the coverlet of the bed, he said 'Goodnight' and dozed again . . .

ᘓᘎᗡ

Her father Gilbert died on 26 June 1967.

ᘓᘎᗡ

ROSEMARY'S DIARY
28 October 1967   **London**

Three – no four – months since, my father said to me 'in the absence of the sun', 'Goodnight', and I am wrestling with a sense of purposelessness, emotional disintegration, meaninglessness, which I suppose faced others before me, when one of the dearest people in their lives, dies . . .

The hub of the wheel has fallen out, and the wheel's turning seems to have lost all purpose and meaning. Why should I further bother or care about anything?

The past which in his quiet, reserved and undemonstrative way, he made meaningful for me, I can look over again in his letters. In 1952 when I was writing to him about my agonised decision on Canberra, he wrote the most explicit, perhaps only, declaration of love I remember: 'I do not need to tell you, how much I would grieve to lose you.' . . .

He the stationary, sat at the centre, while I roamed and told him of all I did; then waited for me to come home to him.

I need not tell, how much I grieve to lose you, papa . . .

CELIA TO ROSEMARY
24 November 1967   **Provost's Lodge, King's College, Cambridge**

Dearest Rosemary

My life [as provost's wife] has been completely altered, mostly for the better. I'm now in the thick of things whereas before [we moved into the lodge] I felt very left out. All day long people drop in. I like it but I see the danger because private life has all but ceased . . .

Yes, this is not my *own* house. . . . And really the feeling that it's not going to last, that the place with its grandness and marvels doesn't belong, that I'm here temporarily, fits very well with my internal scheme of things. . . . Here I am blessed with material advantages and in a position to lay down the law in a much bigger way than ever before – but very hesitant – very reluctant to become Mrs Provost – which is another mask – and one which like the house, doesn't belong.

. . . So I must go now and deal with this new official life . . .

With love Celia.

ᘓᘎᗡ

Raymond was away at the University of Hawai'i from September 1968 until June 1969. Rosemary visited him briefly at Christmas.

ROSEMARY TO HUGH

31 October 1968   Southwood Avenue, London

Dearest Hugh

Yes, I think it is different living on one's own, and in an empty house. . . . It is a curious thing, that I find I have little time on my own to DO the things I want to do, but much time in which to feel strangely alone, since it is when eating and going to bed, to shop and wash up, that I notice being alone. I therefore plan to be out or see people in my spare time, which really means I have less leisure in the house, for writing, and even for working . . .

Yes, about me, again; I am grim, and for the reason that happiness is relative. . . . I could not be a useful, freely loving wife to Raymond *now*, or for the next five years or more, if I gave up my job and relative independence to run after him. So that although I don't like what's happening to me, to us, I would less like any alternative that I can see. Even going over to visit him for Xmas, would not solve the problem of the days before and after.

I must off to Covent Garden ballet with some old Battersea colleagues.

Love again, Mother.

ROSEMARY TO HUGH

13 May 1969   University of London, Malet Street

Dearest Hugh,

. . . I have with great pain and labour at last finished the attempt to transcribe my feelings over my Malay fieldwork. I have a strong idea it is no good: too long, pretentious even, perhaps boring. . . . I seem always to need a mirror to see the value of what I write, may I ask you to give some time urgently to the immediate, if only cursory attention of this MS? I dare not send [it] to America for publication without some comment. I do not at all mind how critical you are! In some curious way, once I have finished something, it does not seem to belong to me anymore, and I am quite capable of saying, this long labour has produced a still born child, let it die![11]

. . . I had partly the idea in trying this, to see what it might be like to write one's memoirs. I see that it is a rare gift to be able to recall the past as it seemed at the time.

. . . All my love – please send help as requested above!

Mother

RAYMOND TO ROSEMARY

24 May 1969　　　　　　**University of Hawai'i, Honolulu, Hawai'i**

Rosemary dear

. . . I can see that my arrival back will bring problems of readjustment, but I think they are solvable. Disturbance of one's routine *is* a nuisance. But I think this a perfectly natural feeling. Also our very different personal experiences in the last months mean a gap in the things we have shared. But I think this is different from the kind of 'distance of the soul' which you and I *have* experienced at periods in the past, but which I do not feel now. I feel there is now on both sides a willingness to accommodate and understand which was not always there, and for which I am grateful.

Bless you, *au revoir bientôt*,

Raymond.

Notes

1. Rosemary Firth, 1972, 'From Wife to Anthropologist', in Solon T. Kimball and James B. Watson (eds), *Crossing Cultural Boundaries: The Anthropological Experience*, San Francisco, CA: Chandler, pp. 10–32.
2. Rosemary to Hugh, 25 March 1969 and 6 February 1969.
3. Edmund Leach, 1968, *A Runaway World?*, London: BBC, p. 36.
4. He made these comments in the text and footnotes of the published version of *A Runaway World?* on pp. 1, 44, and 83–92.
5. 'Column', *Encounter*, February 1968, 30(2): 51–54.
6. Rosemary to Hugh, 13 May 1969.
7. Marginal comment on the flyleaf of Rosemary's copy of *A Runaway World?*
8. Rosemary Firth, 1995, 'A Woman Looks Back on the Anthropology of Women and Feminist Anthropology', in Wazir Jahan Karim (ed.), *'Male' and 'Female' in Developing Southeast Asia*, Oxford: Berg, pp. 3–10.
9. Rosemary to Raymond, 19 January 1969.
10. Rosemary to Hugh, 22 April 1969 and 2 June 1970.
11. Rosemary's paper was indeed subsequently published, in 1972, as 'From Wife to Anthropologist'.

Chapter 18

Together Again

1969

Anthropology took Raymond away from Rosemary, and anthropology brought Edmund and Rosemary together again. Since Raymond's Tikopia expedition in 1966, Rosemary had felt 'abandoned' by Raymond, her emotional needs ignored. In the intervening three years, her professional prestige and personal self-esteem had grown enormously. Raymond's determination to live abroad for some years after his retirement in 1968 reinforced her sense that she had to be her own woman. And Rosemary was now a regular participant, and an occasional contributor, at ASA meetings. She was meeting Edmund more often in a context in which they both enjoyed the questioning, debate and controversy. This naturally brought them into regular contact.

They both attended the three-day conference of the ASA from 10 to 12 April 1969 in Brighton. At the end of the first day, Edmund and Rosemary spent the night together. During the busy conference the following day, they had no opportunity to talk to each other privately. That night, Edmund nearly joined Rosemary again. Rosemary left early the following morning, as their colleague Joe Loudon[1] had offered to drive her to her cottage in Dorset on his way home to Glamorgan.[2] Edmund, realising too late that she had left, sent her a letter that day.

Then Rosemary heard nothing from Edmund for over eight weeks. She assumed that Edmund had simply forgotten about her or not bothered to contact her, too busy with the rest of his life. Yet going to a public lecture by Eric Ashby[3] at the British Academy in Burlington House, she again saw Edmund. He told her that he had been much more disturbed by their

Figure 18.1. Edmund and Rosemary at a conference in the 1960s. Photograph by J. Lajournard.

encounter in Brighton than he had expected, and it was for that very reason that he had felt a need to avoid contact with her.

Rosemary had known that she had always loved Edmund. It seems that Edmund had not always loved Rosemary, and that he had suppressed or repressed some of his feelings for her for a very long time. 'Shattered' and 'devastated' at how upset he had been, he was apprehensive about meeting her again for fear that he would be unable to let her go.

They made no arrangements to meet up again.

In August, Rosemary flew with Raymond to Vancouver; they spent four weeks together, much of the time with Betty and Cyril Belshaw. Raymond stayed in Vancouver for the rest of the year, while Rosemary returned to London. Alice Dewey, an American anthropologist from Hawai'i, came to stay with Rosemary at their house in London whilst she was working for a time in England. (It was Alice Dewey who had invited Raymond to Hawai'i in 1968–69. She also taught Ann Dunham, Barack Obama's mother, anthropology as an undergraduate, supervising Ann's anthropology doctorate on the craft industry in Indonesia.)[4]

Five months after seeing Edmund in June, Rosemary went to a Royal Anthropological Institute Huxley Memorial Lecture in November. The recipient of the Huxley Medal – the lecturer – was their old friend and colleague Isaac Schapera. Many of her anthropological colleagues were there also. Nevertheless, she and Edmund managed to find a little time alone together and Edmund again talked of his anxiety that he might once more become deeply involved with Rosemary.

Just a week later, Rosemary met Isaac again at a dinner party. It was at Isaac's that Edmund had shown particular attention to her sixteen years previously and at Isaac's lecture that Rosemary and Edmund had found time to talk. Isaac was perceptive. Under the influence of a little alcohol, he began to ask questions about how well Rosemary knew Edmund. Rosemary managed them by sharing what was public knowledge – that she and Edmund had been involved with one another between 1931 and 1933, before she ever met Raymond. More than that she did not disclose.

ROSEMARY'S DIARY

12 April 1969   **Thursday – Saturday**   **Brighton, Sussex**

After thirty years, accident brought us [Edmund and I] once more together. . . . It is, *it is* possible to turn back the clock and momentarily forget our present obligations, to shut out our real loyalties, for brief but deep, deep joy and peace . . .

'There was always something special about us' he said.

But the pain, the ache which follows the joy!

The second night, of weeping, desolation, and loss . . .

14 April 1969   **Monday**   **Holway, Dorset**

Monday morning at the cottage alone, a letter from Brighton in a scrumpled envelope was delivered. It showed ambiguity of attitude but signs of deep feeling and somehow comforted me:

EDMUND TO ROSEMARY

12 April 1969   **Saturday 1.30**   **Brighton, Sussex**

That was not well managed. I hadn't tumbled to the fact that if you left with Joe L. [Loudon] you would be leaving after breakfast. I was pretty sure your door was unlocked last night and I was sorely tempted. But one shouldn't *always* yield to temptations, particularly when bodies are standing about in corridors until well past midnight!

My original intention was childish but virtuous, I wanted to pay you the compliment of a very deeply felt kind, but the outcome was likewise childish – for the feelings are too deep and 'the context of situation' altogether wrong. So I am glad and very sorry at the same time. But it was not well managed.

xxxx

You must *not* write to me. Secretaries open even confidential letters![5] Also this must not be the re-beginning of an 'old affair' or an occasion for searing emotions. It was to show a little love but we should have 'walked and talked' as well as that. I will see you again – don't worry – I think in fact we understand each other.

Thank you

E.

ROSEMARY'S DIARY

April 1969   **Holway, Dorset**

What odd coincidences of the stars cause my great moments of love to fall out upon similar dates!

After thirty years, I have again fallen deep into that pit which was filled over long ago . . .

By his standards, 'it didn't quite work, as usual!' 'I am sorry, and yet I am glad' he said. 'It is really quite simple of course. My body is saying "I am not yours".' 'You had every right to be furious' he told me next evening, 'but because you are so nice, you don't seem to be.' . . .

∽∽∾

After hearing nothing from Edmund for eight weeks, they met again in London.

ROSEMARY'S DIARY

11 June 1969   **Southwood Avenue, London**

Oh joy, unreasonable joy! He also ensnared!

Finding ourselves, each on our own [Edmund and Rosemary in Brighton on 10 April], in the first time for thirty years, yet thrown together professionally, the incredible happened, the barricades came down and forgetting age and obligation for a few hours I experienced joy and a quiet peace that I have not known for years.

[We] came together next evening in a crowd of stranger-friends; I could not bear the public stare on private love and fell into a reactionary despair which was heightened by the belief it was one sided.

A storm of weeping such as I have rarely felt since a girl compressed loss, remorse, anger at scorn.

But walking into Burlington House on a summer afternoon nine weeks later there he was, and seemingly alone. Sitting by him for a brilliant lecture the identical sense of stillness and peace fell on me and I found I could forgive all. To my astonishment, he told me his silence and absence [since 12 April] were due to the fact that he had also been thrown quite 'off balance' – 'to tell you the truth I found I was much more upset than ever I expected to be myself, so I felt I couldn't see you till a cooling off period had elapsed.'

I think I have never before been in a situation where he was the more at a loss, more vulnerable and a-feared than I.

I could have danced or flown home; this makes sense; my love is not a chimera, but has rooted itself in another and has reality enough to be felt in reflection.

One does not love in the same way when each of us is nearer sixty than twenty: but it is just as much the most real, the most meaningful and the most rewarding love that I have ever felt all of my life . . .

13 November 1969   **London**

Walked into the lecture room with Alice Dewey . . . just in time from a whirlwind of activity which had swept in on me both at home and professionally, and gasped almost to find my clansmen – my beloved anthropological colleagues whom I had almost forgotten about as *my* kith too, all ranged there before me.

Searching the rows, of course I soon found a particular one [Edmund]. Then I thought silently: 'Will you come, sweet love, to me?'

But I stirred not myself.

Afterwards he came, laughing, tender, enquiring – 'I thought you were in Vancouver?!'

'So I was – but back again. It's going to go on being like this, married for half the year, separate for half, like Persephone in reverse, I meet my husband in the summer – and am alone every winter.'

. . . He brushed my shoulder lightly with an embracing arm; 'I don't know! Can we, or can't we, do you think?'

So it was time for the dinner and we separated.

Afterwards, there he was again by my side offering to buy me a drink. Tambiah also.[6] 'You know I feel awful not seeing Raymond while he was back. Must think I don't care?' – 'That's alright, we'll arrange it when he comes back for Christmas.'

We were talking in little groups which kept breaking up and being interrupted. At some point, I think I said desperately to Tambiah 'I do want to talk to him'. But I don't know if he heard?

Later I found I had been bought a drink . . . and the three of us sat down together to chat.

His physical presence pressed against me; our talk was filled with asides and double-entendres. Suddenly . . . I found we were alone and without pause or let I found I had started to tell him all of the things I had been thinking in the last seven months.

How I knew this was permissible I'm not sure and the sequence of events is now unclear to me, except that he again reiterated: 'I was shattered to discover how much I had been upset; it was a most disturbing experience, I never expected anything like that to happen to me. Quite devastating.'

I found myself urgently and over and over telling him: 'I love you, I always have loved you, and I will continue to love you. But love at 60 and love at 20 is different. I am bound, and I love another also. So are you. Even if you were free I would not necessarily be. If we were both free, that might be different.'

I found he was telling me: 'I love my wife; no, I have not told her anything but she is very perceptive. I don't want to hurt her. If we were to see very much of each other, I could easily fall in love with you again.'

'I shan't hurt her,' I told him. 'I love you, but I shan't follow you. I don't want to hurt her. I understand all that, we all have complicated obligations –'.

There we were then, perhaps for five minutes side by side and alone, and talking openly of love, and of the fear of what love might do.

Then strangers came; we were separated by the social flow of our anthropological 'clansmen'; and presently he left.

I flew after him as he strode across the room . . . quite unashamed in public, I newly felt, to bid farewell. 'You and Raymond see each other, but I'll stay away, when he comes back,' I said. 'Bless you, goodbye.'

Afterwards in the street I put up my hands before my face and wept.

It is all right to say it does not matter, it will not affect our present obligations. I won't pursue him.

I love him, love him, love him, the same after 40 years. And he still loves me. And fears the growth of that love . . .

He was, as it were, stumbling to say to me, the world and my wife have thrust a multitude of demands upon me, I am not free, but from within this network of hooked obligations, I am miserably aware that you have disturbed me deeply: I know you love me, I am fearful of letting myself love you, (as I have done for a moment) for long and for reality.

I have rarely felt so elated, so fulfilled and at the same time, so aware that the price of looking upon my love in the light, the price of being able to say to him openly 'I love you, I always have loved you, I still will continue to love you' was that probably this means we can't see each other again as we used to do.

But it really is time after forty years that a reality should be acknowledged . . .

20 November 1969   **London**

At dinner with Jo Loudon and Isaac [Schapera] at the Percy Cohens.[7] Ruthie commented how marvellous I was looking. . . . Is this a woman's way of saying: 'I know you are having an affair?'

But Isaac, quite drunk, asked questions of an oddly orientated indiscretion, which I decided I must answer with absolute candour. He asked about my love life before I met R. (!) and whether it were true I knew him [Edmund] before R. did. So I openly told the facts. To cover up the past is surely no way to protect the present? To be willing to talk will show I have no fear . . .

Notes

1. Joe Loudon (1921–99), medical practitioner and social anthropologist, had a particular interest in the social anthropology of medicine, through which he and Rosemary became good friends.
2. Rosemary had learnt to drive as a young woman and briefly learnt to drive again in her early fifties, but she found driving anxiety-provoking and gave up entirely.
3. Eric Ashby (1904–92), botanist, was Vice-Chancellor of Cambridge University from 1967 to 1969, while Edmund was provost of King's College.
4. Alice Dewey (1928–2017) was Professor of Anthropology at the University of Hawai'i from 1962. Ann Dunham (1942–95), who helped develop micro-credit, completed her undergraduate degree in 1967 and her anthropology PhD in 1992. Her PhD dissertation was published posthumously in 2009 as *Surviving against the Odds: Village Industry in Indonesia*, Durham, NC: Duke University Press.
5. Edmund's secretary at this time, June, was devoted to him. She would have been horrified if she had known about the 'tryst'.
6. Stanley Tambiah (1929–2014), anthropologist and biographer of Edmund Leach, with whom he worked in Cambridge between 1963 and 1972. Professor at Harvard from 1976, he is noted for his work on ethnic and religious identities in Sri Lanka.
7. Percy Cohen (1928–99), South African anthropologist who trained at the LSE in the 1950s and became a Professor of Sociology at the LSE in 1971. He and his wife Ruth were good friends of Raymond and Rosemary.

Chapter 19

Only by Change
Can Things Not Die

1970–1978

On 9 January 1970, Rosemary's 27-year-old nephew Andy Darlington, Margaret's younger son, killed himself while staying at his mother's house. He had recently returned to London from California and was suffering from depression. The event was a tragedy for the whole family. For Rosemary, who had lost her much-beloved Uncle Maurice to suicide when she was twelve, as well as her mother to cancer when she was not quite sixteen, it reopened older wounds. Raymond was in London and Hugh in Edinburgh at the time.

Andy's death brought Rosemary and Raymond back together – only for them to be separated again a week after the funeral by Raymond's teaching commitments in the United States until the summer. Raymond was still away in April when Rosemary attended the annual ASA conference – and met Edmund again.

Raymond was away again in the autumn; the next time Rosemary met Edmund was in early November, when she attended a lecture by Claude Lévi-Strauss.[1] Edmund took her out to dinner afterwards. She wrote to Raymond that the 'Lévi-Strauss talk was like watching or listening to a conjuror – clever, fascinating, but really almost meaningless, I do think. Edmund thought so too, I gather.'[2]

Rosemary's relationship with Hugh, now twenty-three, had grown closer as a result of Raymond living abroad. Andy's death, and the renewal of her love for Edmund, set in train a process of reflection and reassessment over the next couple of years. In November, Rosemary wrote an unusually long letter to Hugh, observing how 'death is the last repository of changelessness'. Andy's death in youth emphasised for her how all living relationships must surely change over time, if they are not to die:

> How do we pass from being lovers to spouses? Children to independent adults? From wife to mother, or from student to teacher? A spouse must be partly a lover, a mother must have been also a wife, a good teacher must still be partly a student. The essence of a living relationship is just that it must change; put another way, the essence of loving is that love must die, or change to another kind of love. A mother who always wants her baby to be a baby whom she can love and care for, does not really love the baby, but her own self-image as eternal mother. The man, or woman who wants an eternal lover, loves not the one so chosen, but his own self-image as eternal lover. . . . Only by change can things not die.[3]

Rosemary never mentioned Edmund – but the letter seems to crystallise her changing feelings towards him.

When Rosemary was next alone with Edmund, it was at a Eugenics Society conference in September 1971; her relationship with him had now subtly changed.

Over the next couple of years, Rosemary and Edmund met only one more time when neither Raymond nor Celia were present. By 1974, Raymond was back in London for much more of the year and Rosemary and Raymond were attending conferences together again. Further prestige accrued to Raymond: he delivered the first British Academy Radcliffe-Brown Lecture in 1972, on the value of Karl Marx's ideas to anthropology, and received a knighthood in 1973. Edmund was likewise accorded both of these honours: a knighthood in 1975 and a Radcliffe-Brown Lecture in 1976. Both delivered their lectures in their own idiosyncratic styles. Edmund set up a number of oppositions within which British anthropologists could be situated (conservative/radical; rationalist/empiricist).[4] Raymond explored the contribution of Marxist thinking to social anthropology, but ended with the quotation from Dante Alighieri used by Karl Marx: '*Segui il tuo corso, e lascia dir le gente*' (Follow your own bent, and let people say what they will).[5]

These were successful years for Rosemary too. She published; she emerged strengthened from political infighting at the University Institute of Education; she went on study leave in Ghana, attending conferences on rural agricultural development and education. She had never sought to be a theoretical anthropologist; her main interest was always the use of the anthropological perspective to throw light on one's own society and she wished to show how such a perspective might help others in the fields of teaching, social work and medicine. She had never previously been to Africa; she concluded that she had learnt a lot, and the insights of anthropologists working in Africa would now come alive for her in a different way.[6] (In turn, she influenced some of them, in particular Isaac Schapera, whose study of kinship in Jane Austen's writing was partly the result of Rosemary's 'insistent and persistent encouragement'.)[7]

When, in 1974, Raymond returned from three months teaching in California, Rosemary commented that 'six years of fat independence are over'.[8] Yet she felt 'much more secure in myself and in Raymond . . . [so] that for me the time has irrevocably passed when I could ever possibly forsake Raymond'.[9] When she wrote to Hugh in 1976 (when he was experiencing relationship difficulties), she put forward a view of her relationship with Raymond in which their differences complemented each other in different ways over time.

At the start of the decade, Rosemary and Raymond had separately negotiated six months' leave so that the two of them could travel together to the Australian National University (ANU) in Canberra from September 1972, each of them as a visiting fellow in the School of Pacific Studies. It was the first time she had had the same status as Raymond in an academic setting. For Rosemary, the visit confirmed that she and Raymond had indeed made the right decision not to emigrate to Australia in 1952, despite her bitter regrets at the time. She had little admiration for what she saw as the ANU's lack of original research in anthropology, and she added that Australia is 'too blood rich, and too bloody philistine into the bargain. The more I learn of their treatment of the aboriginals, the more I am inclined to brand the A. [Australians] as the most racist country next to and very nearly up to the S. Africans.'[10] While they were in Australia, Raymond took the opportunity to visit Tikopia settlements in the Trobriand Islands off New Guinea, but he wisely refrained from suggesting another trip to the island of Tikopia itself. Before their return to England, they were also able to attend her father-in-law's Wesley's hundredth birthday in Auckland, which was a source of great pleasure for Rosemary, as she was extremely fond of 'Father'. It was the last time she saw him (Raymond saw him again in 1975); he died peacefully aged 104 in August 1977.

In 1976, Rosemary noted that 'I've had more to do and had "personal" success this last eighteen months, than ever before: many students, some public speaking, publications solicited, reviews and lectures, advice, external examining.'[11] She was ready to respond and protest when her ideas were not met with an appropriate level of recognition: she expostulated in a letter to Raymond (then teaching abroad in Fiji), 'My Dearest . . . E.R.L. [Edmund] rang . . . [sometimes] he has a way of talking to me as if I was aged 16 still – condescension – which I suddenly realised no other anthropologist treats me so! I am snorting as you see!'[12] (At times, Edmund also belittled Rosemary's lack of academic training in anthropology.)

Edmund had been active in King's College politics, espousing and presiding over the introduction of women to King's, and representation for students

Figure 19.1. Raymond and Rosemary at a conference, 1970s. Photographer unknown.

on the College Council. By the close of the decade, both Edmund and Raymond faced a similar decision: whether to extend their careers into retirement with more university appointments. Both acceded to the pleas of their long-suffering wives to refrain from further commitments. In 1979, Edmund and Celia moved from the Provost's Lodge to a bungalow in Barrington, a village about eight miles from Cambridge. Once he had retired as provost of King's College in 1979, Edmund agreed not to pursue any higher-status roles, such as the vice-chancellor of Cambridge University. Raymond now devoted himself to a Tikopia dictionary, a publication on Tikopia songs and an anthropologist's perspective on religion.[13] Aware of how difficult Rosemary found his absences, he finally agreed not to take any further appointments abroad after 1978.

ROSEMARY TO HUGH IN EDINBURGH

11 January 1970   **Southwood Avenue, London**

Dearest Hugh,

We are all dreadfully tired and upset and confused about Andy's death, but it has been a really *good* experience to find how the whole Darlington family have gathered themselves together emotionally as well as physically . . .

I think Raymond is more hurt and bewildered *inside* than he perhaps shows, but I don't know. A death like that does odd things to one – it makes one wonder if one knows anybody at all – ever . . .

But for us all the load is now heavy. For Andy himself he is at peace. Looking at him lying there so calm and natural, I half expected him to open his eyes just to murmur: 'Don't worry about me, I am sleeping and at peace' . . .[14]

Bless you . . .

Your loving Mother. R.

RAYMOND TO ROSEMARY

25 January 1970   **Cornell University, Ithaca, New York State**

Rosemary dear,

. . . I was much touched by your coming to the terminal with me. Despite the tragedy of Andy's death, we *did* have a good experience together this vacation and I feel that we have not merely been brought closer temporarily but have really got to understand each other at a deeper level, on a lasting basis. I feel I can talk with you very frankly knowing that your reactions will be considered; not lacking in warmth thank goodness *or* in swift flashes of rejection or anger sometimes, but essentially sympathetic – with rather than against, as the built-in attitude. And I hope that peevish or ungenerous as I may be – or cold-blooded – sometimes, you feel the same about me . . .

All my love, dear, Raymond.

ROSEMARY TO RAYMOND

5 April 1970   **Southwood Avenue, London**

My dearest,

It was good to find two letters awaiting me on my return from . . . the ASA conference in Bristol. . . . Many people at the conference asked thoughtlessly if you were present or not, and I realised with deep pain that to many people your absence from me is not realised – or perhaps understood.

. . . What can I say to you? I had a long talk to Edmund at the conference, and opined that I found it hard to understand how you could accept to live quite alone in a strange place. He said with E.R.L. type brusqueness that it was probable you were not living alone. Now I really believe that this is not so, but do you realise that in some curious way I appear as a challenge in my position as a woman alone and alive and yet 'safe', in the sense that I am not going to produce children and not likely to demand marriage of anyone who proposes to play love games with me? . . .

My darling . . . I promised you I was always yours even if I should ever be tempted to stray down a side primrose alley . . .

You do care about me nearly as much as about your work and your teaching don't you?

. . . really yours, [Rosemary]

ROSEMARY'S DIARY

18 August 1970   **Holway, Dorset**

. . . Andy, in January, when the days were short and London was cold dark dirty and lonely after California, killed himself. Lonely and alone in his mother's house he lay down by the gas tap and died. The fearful shock reverberated amongst every close member of the family. R., Hugh and I, all three deeply wounded, grew close in seeking comfort. R and I really loved each other again.

Then I once more met E. [Edmund] in Bristol [at the annual ASA conference in April]. He took me out to dinner, in a country restaurant, on a warm spring night, in his car.

Affectionate, detached, slightly quizzically, and sentimental, he put his arm round me as he entered the country house, a ruined castle rebuilt, reminiscent of Cambridge days in 1930s. A great coldness, detachment and sense of unfeeling and aloofness kept me at a vast distance from Edmund. I almost wondered what we would talk about! But he allowed me to mention Andy. I had hardly anything to say in spite of a magnificent dinner and wonderful wine.

Only when he had driven me back to the hotel in Bristol, he suddenly gathered me up again in his great arms, and kissed me, an all-embracing goodnight. I covered his hand, his face, with my fingers and kisses, and then I was vanquished again. As I lay there in the car in the dark it occurred to me, all was undone again: and if he had asked, I would once again have said yes, yes . . .

But he didn't. There were people about. He let me go and I went. We slept each alone, how alone!

So I allow myself to think and think about him, to love and know I am loved, but it all has to do with some long ago, surrendered past. It does not touch today. When R. returned, I ran to him, in tears of love. I belong to Raymond: but oh my god, a little bit of my dead heart has been Edmund's, as his has been mine; now all is over.

෧ඏ෪

ROSEMARY'S DIARY

23 September 1971   **Eugenics Society Conference**   **London**

. . . On this most extra ordinary eve of my 59th birthday, I actually rejected that manifestation of love which I could have had.

Or did I? Did I not simply refuse a manifestation of something less than the love we both – surely both? – still feel for each other? I rejected the idea that love was something which we could give and exchange for an hour or so only; in the belief that love means for me – for us, I don't know? – far more than [mere] bodily contact [which] I refused . . .

Yet, yet, how strange! He [Edmund] looked around for me: he came and sat by me – he caressed me with his eyes, with the tips of his fingers, his arm ostensibly around my chair . . . then came home . . . he had a drink – saying 'I mustn't stay . . .' but staying, and saying 'O you are a temptress!' But I said No. 'No' I said. 'I need your love so much that I must reject this special relationship between us. I have to be able to see you, to meet you, to have ordinary social relations with you – I can't have this if we don't give up this special forbidden relationship . . .'

And he said, 'It's because of the long term relationships' – I think he was thinking only of her [Celia]: but I was thinking of long term relationships on several fronts: of my need of a long term relationship with *him*, but also with R. and also his with C. [Celia] and of my need to feel a friend of C. too.

The extra ordinary thing is that if I had wanted, I might perhaps have had him to myself again once more. . . . Now I have sent him away and alone [to] try to think out why . . .

I have refused what at one time, I wanted more than anything in the world? And why?

What is love? To recognise in what part of a crowded room the loved person is, by a smallest glimpse – by intuition? To feel at marvellous peace, just to sit quietly side by side? To know, as one looks at him, that this is the person I have known intimately the longest period of my life – since 1928 – forty three years? Who longer? No one – but my sisters!!

[. . . One] should also, I think, have some choice. So I made my choice. To know he wanted me, and to say No . . .

24 September 1971   **London**

Not sure at all whether the [second day of the] meeting warranted it and definitely feeling that even if we did meet there again it would be anti-climax, nevertheless I did go . . .

In the afternoon, however, as we sat together again, I still every now and then felt his arms over my chair press my shoulders, his fingers just caress the back of my hand, the minute meaningful contact of love. And yet we could behave otherwise almost as only very old friends. When he walked me home, then bade farewell, I said 'It's better like this, I think this is the better way isn't it?' He said 'Oh anything else would have been absolutely chaotic.'

I took a kiss of farewell and came home curiously a-whirl . . .

ROSEMARY TO RAYMOND IN FIJI

1 November 1975   **Southwood Avenue, London**

My dearest,

. . . There is a new life of Bertrand Russell just out, of numerous wives and mistresses. How complicated are the personal lives of great thinkers – and how little we know of what really goes on underneath a marriage!

. . . Love Rosemary.

ᘯᘵᘯ

Rosemary wrote to Hugh (approaching his thirtieth birthday) at a time when he had experienced the break-up of a relationship.

ROSEMARY TO HUGH

28 March 1976   **Southwood Avenue, London**

Dear Hugh

. . . Making or breaking a relationship is a hard job, and causes one to look deeply into one's own self . . .

The world assumes we mate . . . with people of similar temperament to ourselves. Whereas I think every person . . . seeks a partner . . . to balance him [or her].

. . . A lot of nonsense is talked about altruism and unselfishness in loving. . . . A relationship cannot I feel sure long continue if one party feels really aggrieved at limitations the other imposes . . .

There is also another thing which experience teaches me at any rate. And that is that the hidden quality of a partner, which the world does not know about, may be the most important element we need in that partner. I remember being highly tickled once, about 25 years ago, when a colleague – over wine! – said to me 'I never understood how a lively passionate girl like you could get on with such a cold and intellectual person as Raymond'. And yet in some odd way, Raymond's need for me physically has always been greater than my physical need for him. In some ways, I am more independent of him than he of me emotionally. He supplies my intellectual needs, my anchor. I suppose I supply his need of emotional reassurance. But we have changed over forty years. I was very inhibited and intellectually unsure when I was in my twenties, and I grew to self-assurance under his wing, and grew more outgoing. He was quite a lot more 'extravert' in his young days and more sure of himself, oddly, than he now is. We've each 'taken' from the other: in the middle period having grown different, we nearly needed to separate. But fortunately, something kept us unsure of the value of a break-up, and now I think we've learned to tolerate each other's individuality; are closer socially altho' each more independent at heart . . .

Yr loving mother R.M.F.

ROSEMARY'S DIARY

12 October 1977   **London**

. . . This evening I went to the new premises of R.A.I. [Royal Anthropological Institute] at six o'clock to hear . . . a new members' series of meetings, on medical anthropology. [Raymond was in Cambridge for a conference.] I was early: greeted affectionately by Jonathan [Benthall][15] as usual, and . . . took a seat on my own near front to left. . . . Then, to my surprise, E.R.L. [Edmund] took a seat in a row just behind me in a corner and we spoke a few and casual words, as was my feeling.

But during the talk a note was passed to me. *'Can I give you dinner after this?'* I was astonished at the note but as soon as I'd read it, it seemed the most natural thing in the world, and so I expressed by answering – *'Of course!'* . . .

An interesting discussion followed Jo [Loudon]'s very modest opening talk . . . and I found I had things to say and spoke with ease. . . . At end, E. and I made certain small movements to mask our evident leaving together . . .

He looked for the French Restaurant Marion [Benedict] took me to in 1969 and then we walked a bit till we found a good looking one, as that was no more . . .

So what was it like?

Simply that he is the most pleasant person in the world to spend an evening with: simply that there is no one else who can make me feel so happy, contented, so at ease, so absolutely RIGHT; simply that passion being forgotten, (as I think on both sides?) there is no one whom I know that I *love* as a human creature loves the sunshine as I do him. To be with him is *all* pleasure, as it is to be in the sunshine, to be with him is to stop asking and seek only immediate pleasure, to stop being self-conscious and know I am with a man who fits me as a glove a hand; a man certainly not yet aged or even grizzling as I saw him in February: a man still young, fresh, energetic, loving power, and still *remembering* his *love for me*, if I put it at its basis.

. . . I reminded him laughing that we had known each other fifty years – or so it will be next year – but he laughed that away. But this is not just romantic sentimentality that keeps him warm for me after half a century: I don't glow like this when I meet James [Livingstone], William [MacKenzie] . . . why not I ask?

Is it just that we have never lived together, lived through the experience of his ranging and promiscuous affections for many other women – as I well guess – through his hot/cold shifts, his cruel aspect which I know too well? R is cruel to

Figure 19.2. Edmund, perhaps around 1970. Photograph by Alexander Leach.

me, but his cruelty comes of clumsiness – or of a desire to control and distance me? E's comes of alien passions, or a multitude of other interests? . . . This decade shows me that I can still love, and still be loved, at a level of reality, and absence of sentimentality, which I can shout for joy at. It is an astonishing fact that a girl's passion of 1928 is still a warm living fire in nearly 1978 . . .

And when he left me at Bond St station, he kissed me soundly twice, on the mouth, and on the cheek. It is no accident that he does not kiss me in public as others do.[16] I now realise clearly, when that happens – there will be a changed feeling.

Notes

1. Claude Lévi-Strauss (1908–2009), French social anthropologist, who explored the underlying structures evident in human categories and thought processes. He held the Chair in social anthropology at the Collège de France from 1959 to 1982. He and Raymond had great respect for each other.
2. Rosemary to Raymond, 23 November 1970.
3. Rosemary to Hugh, 22 November 1970.
4. Edmund Leach, 1977, 'Social Anthropology: A Natural Science of Society?', *Proceedings of the British Academy* 62: 157–80.
5. Raymond Firth, 1973. 'The Sceptical Anthropologist? Social Anthropology and Marxist Views on Society', *Proceedings of the British Academy* 58: 177–213. Marx closed the preface to the first German edition of *Das Capital* with the quotation from Dante Alighieri, *Divine Comedy*: Purgatory, Canto 5.
6. Rosemary to Hugh, 2 May 1971.
7. Handwritten dedication to Rosemary in her copy of Isaac Schapera, 1977, *Kinship Terminology in Jane Austen's Novels*, Royal Anthropological Institute Occasional Papers, No. 33.
8. Rosemary, diary entry, undated, August 1974. Raymond spent less time abroad after 1974.
9. Rosemary diary entry, 1 January 1975.
10. Rosemary to Margaret Hardiman, 11 December 1972.
11. Rosemary, diary entry, 31 October 1976.
12. Rosemary to Raymond, 1 November 1975.
13. Raymond Firth, Ishmael Tuki and Pa Rangiaco, 1985, *Tikopia–English Dictionary: Taranga Fakatikopia ma Taranga Fakainglisi*, Oxford: Oxford University Press; Raymond Firth and Mervyn McLean, 1990, *Tikopia Songs: Poetic and Musical Art of a Polynesian People of the Solomon Islands*, Cambridge: Cambridge University Press; Raymond Firth, 1996, *Religion: A Humanist Interpretation*, London: Routledge.
14. Rosemary visited the undertakers to see Andy's body before the funeral.
15. Jonathan Benthall (1941–), British anthropologist, born in India, with a particular interest in Islam and aid agencies; director of the Royal Anthropological Institute 1974–2000. Jonathan and his wife Zamira were good friends of the Firths.
16. 'Does not kiss me in public like others do': Rosemary means that Edmund does not kiss her when other anthropologists or friends are present to notice this demonstration of intimacy. She assumed that no-one they knew would be watching them, at Bond Street station.

Chapter 20

The Dark Side
of the Moon

1978–1979

Edmund and Rosemary retired within a year or so of each other. The first six months of Rosemary's retirement proved eminently successful.

She had hugely enjoyed the last decade of her career, but was tired and needed to prepare for retirement, which she chose to take in June 1978, at the end of a stimulating year of teaching. Raymond had suggested that they both go abroad together again for a period of teaching following Rosemary's retirement. Rosemary was invited to deliver some joint seminars with Ralph Bulmer[1] at Auckland University. Thus, from July 1978 until late February 1979, Rosemary and Raymond were in New Zealand again. It was their last long trip abroad.

Coincidentally, while Rosemary and Raymond were to be in New Zealand, Rosemary's close friend Betty and her husband Cyril Belshaw – who normally lived in Vancouver – were due to come to England for six months. They were on a sabbatical year from their university jobs; Betty was working on a biography of Katherine Mansfield. They had rented an apartment in Montana, Switzerland, for the second half of the year. Rosemary and Raymond invited them to live in the house in Highgate while the Belshaws were in London.

Rosemary wrote to Betty Belshaw in early June 1978 to discuss her retirement, and agree the arrangements for the Belshaws occupying the house in Highgate: 'It is no joke pulling up your roots. . . . I have gone out on the top of a wave, however, thank the gods, very good and very appreciative – with words and with gifts – [from] groups of students, and a backhanded compliment that the dept. is to be enlarged and the status of the head upgraded after

I go!'[2] There was a period of feverish organisation as Rosemary cleared her work and office, and prepared to leave the house and the cottage while they were away for eight months.

At the end of June, the Institute of Education gave her a splendid farewell dinner. The Belshaws dined with Raymond and Rosemary twice in the week following the Belshaws's arrival and before Raymond and Rosemary's departure: once on the evening of 9 July and again at the airport on the day Raymond and Rosemary left England.

In Auckland, both Rosemary's and Raymond's seminars were a success. They visited old friends and stayed twice with Raymond's younger brother Cedric and his wife Bobby. Raymond and Rosemary were uncomfortably aware of a discreet, polite, covert, racist attitude only skin-deep beneath the surface of many friendly, generous, apparently gentle New Zealanders. Cedric talked of 'all this nonsense' regarding Māori attempts to preserve their land, their language and traditional culture. Rosemary perceived it as 'a quite frightening racist chauvinism'.[3]

Raymond and Rosemary visited Māori communities on several occasions. On one of these, Rosemary was presented with a traditional cloak 'to honour our foreign visitor'. On another occasion, after greetings with Māori formality in the Māori language, and having been honoured as 'distinguished and friendly stranger guests', Raymond formally gave back an eighteenth-century jade ornament given to him around 1920; the Professor of Māori Studies in Auckland had traced the living descendants of the owner for the formal return.[4] Rosemary wrote to Betty, conveying her feelings and doings, and reminding her of the times in 1952 when Betty had rescued Rosemary from her loneliness amongst her in-laws and their extended family.

On their way back from New Zealand in February 1979, Raymond and Rosemary paid another brief visit to Malaysia and the village of Bacho'k to see their erstwhile informants and friends. 'On the beach . . . in the evening,' Rosemary noted, 'the long line of the breakers . . . islands on the horizon, the little thatched or brick tiled houses, brought back 1939, 1940 like a rush of pain and mourning. The last days here have been a curious mixture of pleasure and pain: I shall never see this country again, but it's not there either even now: no sailing boats, our friends [from Bacho'k in 1939] died. . . . I feel back here in a place [where] I now realise I was probably as happy, as productive, and learnt as much about myself and the world as at almost any time in my whole life.'[5]

ഇന്

Yet the next two years were to prove, for Rosemary and Raymond, amongst the most traumatic and upsetting of their lives. They were faced with a trag-

Figure 20.1. Betty Belshaw, 1974. Photograph by Jim Banham.

edy whose implications grew steadily more disturbing over time, and which was to test Rosemary's compassion, understanding and loyalty to the limit.

Raymond and Rosemary were still in Malaysia on 9 February 1979 when they received a letter from Cyril Belshaw, who was in Montana in Switzerland, telling them that Betty had gone missing without a trace on 15 January while Betty and Cyril were visiting Paris. There had been no word or sighting of her since.

Betty was one of Rosemary's oldest and dearest friends. Rosemary had first met Betty as Cyril's fiancée when he was one of Raymond's students in 1947. She had lunched with Betty and Cyril on their wedding day and admired

Betty's baby daughter the following year. They had seen each other two or three times a week in London between 1947 and 1949; they saw each other again in Canberra in 1951 and in Auckland in 1952; and they stayed with each other often in the 1960s and 1970s.

Rosemary immediately wrote to Cyril from Malaysia. She and Raymond reached London in late February 1979 and were, from that point on, in regular contact with Cyril by letter. Rosemary wrote to him at least every few weeks. Cyril remained in Switzerland through the spring and returned to Vancouver in the summer.

In April, Cyril visited London on his way to an anthropology conference in York. Leaving no stone unturned, he visited the Salvation Army in London to make enquiries of their Missing Persons unit. He took the Firths to dinner; they met again at the conference in York.

Rosemary also wrote in April to Betty and Cyril's (adult) daughter in Canada:

> At my age every death of a close friend or loved [one] reactivates every other such past bereavement. And my family have been beset with violent death – At twelve, I first saw, horrified, my mother weep in public at the suicide of her brother-in-law, a much-loved uncle. My mother herself died of cancer when I was sixteen. . . . On retirement, if one is realistic, one accepts that death must be somewhere now waiting not so far off, for oneself. Then he strikes in devilish fashion at a younger one [Betty was eight years younger than Rosemary]. . . . Many who were close friends at some time or another have drifted away [for one reason or another] . . . I used to count both your parents as two who had not drifted away an inch. Now Betty has been torn away.[6]

In late August, Cyril wrote from Vancouver to Rosemary and Raymond about Betty's letters and papers. Amongst these he had evidently read something written by Betty in which she expressed some extremely negative feelings toward Cyril. This provoked a constructive discussion between Raymond and Rosemary about how almost every couple feels rage and resentment at times in their lives together.

With no definite news or information of any kind – only continuing uncertainty – it is especially hard to adjust to loss. It is difficult to judge how Raymond's feelings evolved over the next eighteen months or so: he preferred an apparent detachment to sharing his anxieties, doubts or fears. Consequently, it gradually became more challenging for Rosemary and Raymond to talk about what might have happened to Betty.

Rosemary pored over every detail of her relationship with Betty for clues. '[I] always felt that I knew her [Betty] as well as anybody else in the world, and that in some ways we had many things in common which enabled us to identify each with the other without the necessity for overt detailed intimacy.'[7]

Rosemary took everything she knew about Betty – and that which she feared she did not know – to pieces; yet each attempt to come to some plausible understanding led her to a locked door.

ROSEMARY TO TERENCE

10 February 1979   **Kuala Lumpur, Malaysia**

Dear Terence,

. . . Something we are not making known to many yet, but feel I must tell you; Cyril Belshaw and his wife Betty who had looked after our house until December and are two of our very oldest closest friends, went to Paris together in early January, and an unbelievable thing has happened. Betty left Cyril one day, to work at the Librarie Nationale [sic: actually, Bibliothèque Nationale], did not turn up for lunch, and has been totally disappeared since. He wrote to us a fortnight after her disappearance . . . police, embassies, social welfare organisations and all the stops out, but no word, no trace. She suffered some slight depression and perhaps had an amnesia, but they fear even worse things than self-destruction I think. This news has quite shattered us. . . . It is a sort of nightmare or something which one reads about in books. A complete and absolute absence of any evidence at all. Cyril is now in Switzerland, trying by work to banish the squirrelling round and round of his mind. A suicide provides a body sooner or later does it not? Only another can hide the dead seriously for long. . . .

Your loving sister, Rosemary.

ROSEMARY TO CYRIL IN SWITZERLAND

10 February 1979[8]   **Kuala Lumpur, Malaysia**

Cyril dear,

. . . I don't think I have ever received a letter of such a shattering nature. Your dreadful story is one which belies belief – as you say – a non-sense. But such a nightmare . . . of not-knowing, <u>that</u> I cannot imagine. . . . Whatever has, or has not happened, in the meantime before this letter reaches you to make things better or worse, this miserably inadequate letter is sent off at once to bring you the only thing your friends can bring you, floods of thought for you, to support you in anything you may still have to suffer. Something quite primeval in me almost forced me to prayer for her; surely in the world there must be some Grace, some Goodness, some Power who would watch over a person as bright, as warmly loving, as courageous and honest as she is.

. . . I won't say more now, except one thing, which I think you should know, and on which both Raymond and I are firmly agreed. . . . I had a number of letters from her, you know, and they all radiated her content in London, in our house, and in what she was doing. I think you must hang on to that, whatever the upsets or the strains at the cottage in November, she had been happy. God grant she may return to you to be happy again.

. . . It is a bad thing to plan too far ahead; but you will need your friends – perhaps – whatever happens – and if and when you need us of course we will come to see you, in Montana [Switzerland] or wherever.

. . . We are thinking of all four of you constantly.

Rosemary.

ROSEMARY TO CYRIL

13 April 1979[9]   **Good Friday, Holway, Dorset**

Cyril dear

In your own words one of the strange things about our present situation is the disjointedness of our phases. . . . Since talking to you I've had a nasty period of thinking Betty almost cheated me by being so reserved – or that I short-changed her by seeing so little, and I was angry. Anger is one usual phase of mourning. . . . Well on this Good Friday morning I've worked through my anger and realise that one has small right to expect to know any one other person, however close, completely. . . .

I begin to see that of all the terrible alternatives, short of resurrection, an accident which happened *to her*, not one sought by her is preferable. So the most difficult to accept comes to be the most acceptable in the end.

. . . Affectionately ever, Rosemary

ROSEMARY TO HUGH

13 April 1979   **Good Friday, Holway, Dorset**

Dearest Hugh,

. . . Cyril Belshaw rang up, and then came and took us out to dinner. He was in London partly to talk to the Salvation Army Lost or Missing Persons dept., and partly on his way to York for the Anthropology Association's annual meeting where we of course met again. A cruel turn of the screw in York made me wonder greatly at the length a man can remain in uncertainty about his wife, without going mad or becoming hard or cruel. He had a telegram from the Paris Police – but only to ask for more information, not give any.

It is now 3 months since he waited for her at lunch and he knows *nothing*. She has walked off – had a personality crisis, killed herself, had a genuine accident or been done harm to – most horrible of all?

When one does not know how or why a loved one has gone, mourning – a difficult and slow process anyway – becomes a horribly impossible thing to accomplish. The manner of death or desertion cast so many questioning shadows back on what *was* a simple past – What sort of person then was this woman I thought I knew? And every such death – violent to us at least – reactivates all other such past events, too many as you know in my Upcott family history. . . .

Affectionately, Rosemary.

ଓଓ

Cyril wrote to Rosemary and Raymond in late August about a 'personal statement' he had found in Betty papers, in which she had apparently written some very negative, even hateful, things about him.

ROSEMARY TO CYRIL

6 September 1979[10]   **Holway, Dorset**

Dear Cyril

It is always good to get your letters and this one really put us in the picture. It is inevitable that some of your hardest adjustments and choices must be faced now that you are back home [in Vancouver]. I am glad you have some real and good friends. . . .

We talked of [Betty's personal statement] together over the breakfast table where R and I shared your letter. Raymond said to me 'Tell him that we have *all* done this. Hated our spouses, our loved ones, our fate, at some time and taken solace in writing down this hate. But it is important that those who hear of it understand what we DON'T write down, the happiness, the belongingness, the mix of good and bad'.

It started a dialogue between *us*, Raymond and I, that it would have been good for you to hear Cyril. We are OLD; we have each both of us hated the other. I, in particular, have raged against the injustices of being a wife of a famous splendid clever person. R. tells me [he] has raged against my spite, egotism, coldness, as he has seen it. . . .

Now I was going to leave somewhere among my own papers a note for R. to say that much of these angry feelings had evaporated. To my astonishment he said at that breakfast, 'I have often wondered if I should destroy some of the things I have written down about you!' So we became quits over your letter and were able to say, living, to each other, what might have had to [be] read after death. You alas have been left only with the dark side of the moon, and yet you must have suffered from that dark side even when Betty was alive as well as now? Don't be bitter, be angry, but not bitter is what I would like to say. And be remorseful but not guilty if you can see the difference. . . .

Well perhaps I'm just chattering about things you've known for a long time. My only excuse is, that I've lived with suicide all my life. . . . First my father's brother, with whom I now think my own mother was half in love, drowned himself in his forties in Scotland. Then my nephew gassed himself at twenty-seven, in his mother's house. Before that my father's father hanged himself after a bout of depression. . . . The suicide says I care not about you any longer, and probably his suffering and his sickness make that true. . . .

Your loving Rosemary

Notes

1. Ralph Bulmer (1928–88), social anthropologist whose research focused especially on Papua New Guinea.
2. Rosemary to Betty Belshaw, 4 June 1978 (LSE Library, Firth/8/4/1).
3. Rosemary to Hugh, 12 October 1978.
4. Rosemary to Hugh, 12 October 1978.
5. Rosemary, diary entry, written retrospectively on 16 February 1979. The sailing boats of 1939 and 1963 had all been replaced by motorboats for fishing.
6. Rosemary to Betty and Cyril Belshaw's daughter, 13 April 1979 (LSE Library, Firth/8/4/1).
7. Rosemary to Betty and Cyril Belshaw's daughter, 4 August 1982 (LSE Library, Firth/8/4/1).
8. Rosemary to Cyril Belshaw, 10 February 1979 (LSE Library, Firth/8/4/1).
9. Rosemary to Cyril Belshaw, 13 April 1979 (LSE Library, Firth/8/4/1).
10. Rosemary to Cyril Belshaw, 6 September 1979 (LSE Library, Firth/8/4/1).

Chapter 21

Knowing Too Much and Too Little

1979

On 28 March 1979, the melting snow revealed a woman's body below a high, remote road at Le Sépey, Vaux, Switzerland.

The body had been stripped of clothes and jewellery, wrapped in strong plastic bags and tied with twine. Jettisoned down a steep slope, it had been stopped by a tree. Attacked and partially eaten by animals, it was unrecognisable. The discovery of the body was the subject of much attention in the Swiss press. The Swiss police visited Cyril Belshaw in Switzerland in mid-April as part of their attempts to identify the body and asked Cyril to obtain Betty's dental records. The dental records Cyril obtained from Vancouver and passed to them did not match the body.

Three months went by without any match being made between the body found near Le Sépey and any of the missing persons known to the Swiss, the French or police forces elsewhere in Europe. In late July, the Swiss investigators decided to check Betty's dental records again, this time requesting them directly from Vancouver. Canadian officers contacted Cyril on 23 August, now at his home in Vancouver, to ask for the name of Betty's dentist. The following day, Cyril delivered a statement to the Vancouver police admitting that because he 'could not face the psychological trauma of possibly identifying my wife without the presence of family', he had 'altered the charts during the copying process' before giving them to the Swiss police in the spring.[1]

When the Vancouver dental records finally reached Swiss investigators, it was discovered that they were indeed a match for the body that had been found. Swiss police then moved as rapidly as they could. But Cyril had committed no crime on Canadian soil and extradition from Canada to Switzerland seemed unlikely. However, they were able to interview Cyril – with Canadian officers in attendance – in Vancouver on 24 September 1979.

Betty's body had been found at Le Sépey, only forty miles from Montana in the Valois region of Switzerland, where the Belshaws had been living after they left London in December 1978. But the discovery of Betty's body – and where it had been found – were not public knowledge at this stage.

On 25 September, Rosemary received a phone call from Jonathan Benthall, the director of the Royal Anthropological Institute, to tell her that Betty's body had been found – not in Paris, but in Switzerland. He also told Rosemary that British police wished to interview her on behalf of the Swiss police – to provide background for their lines of enquiry. Cyril also telephoned the Firths later that same day to tell them that Betty's body had been found, and that he had been interviewed at length by police the previous day. What he did not tell them was that he had recently admitted to police that he had altered Betty's dental records. Rosemary only became aware from Detective Inspector Bendel, on 2 October, that there was 'some kind of problem' or discrepancy in Cyril's account.

ROSEMARY TO CYRIL

28 September 1979[2]   **Southwood Avenue, London**

Dearest Cyril,

Just a note to endorse our messages over the telephone yesterday and the day before. The nightmare from which you've just awoken seems to have plunged you into an even more terrible reality – but I hope this one won't last so long. To think that we hoped knowing would make things in some ways better!!! I have a curious new feeling of present compassion for Betty, not just for whatever happened on those few days – or weeks – but that she has been the unwitting cause of so much anguish to so many of those she loved best. . . .

[. . . We] send from Raymond and myself our deepest wells of sympathy – from me my real prayers – prayers to some old-fashioned gods of rectitude and truth and justice – surely they will not be forever silent.

With love. . . .

Rosemary.

[P.S.] The outside world is viciously sceptical. . . . I've just read that some collector deposited Virginia Woolf's loving farewell suicide note to Leonard in the B.M. [British Museum], *because rumours were* circulating that Leonard had *invented* it! So no one believes in love in a troubled marriage? – But I do.

ROSEMARY TO CYRIL

5 October 1979[3]   Southwood Avenue, London

Cyril dear,

This is just to let you know that we have had a visit [on 2 October] from Scotland Yard – distressing in the confirmation of details of Betty's death but otherwise in some ways comforting – to me at least – in that the ground of doubt and of what is not in doubt seems clearer.

Det. Ins. Bendel was a very sensitive, straight young officer, who let it be known without actually saying so that the Swiss police methods were not those his force would most approve of. He came to get 'background' material about the case. . . . He made it clear it was all unofficial so to speak and really I just told him the sort of person I thought Betty was and the same about you – emphasising the past history of mental strain after Betty's father died – her earlier fears of air travel after the missed accident and the later odd 'sleeping' behaviour confirmed by [the domestic help] Mrs. Holdsworth's[4] observations of her sometimes seemingly 'confused' condition.

He asked few direct questions and answered those I thought I needed to ask pretty straightly. He had intended to ask me to make a statement . . . but said he decided he would relieve me of that. When I queried had the interview been of any use to him – he had a file of course but took only the most brief note I think – he said 'Yes'. He could see more clearly that the thing was not so simple as he'd thought or something like that. But I gather the Swiss believe there has been some confusion of information somewhere – for reasons they find bad for you – so all I pray is that now you've seen this ghastly red light and have legal support, truth will find its way out into the open and clear up these tragic ambiguities and misunderstandings.

How dense can be the legal mind! But Bendel was really sympathetic – 'Your friend' he said as he left me 'needs someone to talk to'. I hope you've got enough friends at hand and you really can talk openly to at least one among them. . . .

How true now seems your earlier words – we do not know anyone really ever, perhaps [including] ourselves.

I feel ten years older this last week. . . .

Poor Betty that it should all come through her who only wanted to do good to people.

Rosemary

ନ୍ଧର

After her interview with Detective Inspector Bendel on 2 October, Rosemary wrote in her engagement diary: 'A very black day – and many sadder followed.'

Rosemary struggled, not knowing what she should believe. The weeks after Betty's body was identified were exceptionally disquieting and distressing. Her letter to Cyril on 28 September, with its reference to 'love in a troubled marriage', is a clear indication of the direction in which her thinking may have been moving. Her notes (written up subsequently) comment that when Cyril had telephoned her on 25 September, she 'pleaded for honesty'. The long years of trust and friendship with Cyril and Betty meant that she did not want to think – let alone believe – that Cyril might have been involved in Betty's death in some way.

Cyril organised a tribute for Betty in Vancouver on 3 October. It was on that same day that press reports broke in Canada revealing the details of how and where Betty's body had been found in Switzerland. Rosemary wrote again to Cyril and Betty's daughter on 7 October to express her sympathy. In that letter, she felt able to say to her that 'I begin to see some of the pain that your parents must have been through together as well as the love and the happiness'.[5]

Rosemary and Raymond worried over the developments. Yet their differing personalities and modes of expression increasingly led to defensiveness, anxiety and tension between them. Rosemary needed to talk through the doubts and questions in her mind, while Raymond thought it inappropriate to form any kind of judgement given how little they knew, and he fiercely resisted discussion of these painful emotional issues.

Unable to discuss details of the Belshaw case with friends or colleagues for reasons of privacy, and wary and defensive of Raymond's responses, Rosemary's sorrow, perplexity and anger reached bursting point. 'I sobbed and sobbed on Hugh's shoulder . . . and I was allowed to cry and cry and cry, without a word, a challenge, a stop – just an acceptance, an all-embracing supporting life giving acceptance. It was so good, so desperately wanted, so good.'[6]

At the end of October, after several sleepless nights, she wrote a letter to Cyril to set down the issues that concerned her most: '28 October: A very angry night thinking over C.B['s] deceit and use of my trust. 29 October: Made peace with my conscience and the Belshaws.'[7]

The letter she wrote, in anger, to Cyril – but never posted – reads:

ROSEMARY TO CYRIL

28 October 1979[8]   **Southwood Avenue, London**

Dear Cyril

I have written nine letters since Betty disappeared and I suppose you will agree that every one of them has been full of compassion love and trust. This letter will probably never be posted, but it's one even the best friend would dearly like a straight reply to.

1. What behaviour preceded the breaking of the wooden strut in one of our beds in Highgate in 1978?[9]

2. From the fortnight after Betty's disappearance, you have been making very explicit assumptions that her death was *not* self-induced; yet in nearly every letter since the first, you have built up a picture [of] a disturbed, unhappy woman; and in a conversation in York you told me 'She refused to go to a psychiatrist.' Yet on the telephone also about 3 weeks ago you said 'It's not psychiatric but neurological evidence we seek.' How could you change from psychiatric to neurological only after evidence of foul play is made public?

3. How did it come that, after police interviews of 6 April and 13 April in Paris and Switzerland, when we now know a body had been found, you were convinced the enquiries were routine 'a knee-jerk reaction, due to Embassy prodding'. Clearly that was not the case. Yet you at once said you 'could not take any more of that', and arranged to pack up and leave Switzerland before planned?

4. If some reasonable explanation is forthcoming about mistaken dental charts being sent for identification in spring, what led the Swiss police eventually, in September, to query those original charts and get hold of correct ones which led them to make positive identification, by then after eight months, instead of only three months' time?

5. What made you say on the phone [on 25 September], describing the [joint] Swiss and Canadian police grilling in Vancouver on 24 September, for which of course you were unprepared, 'I made a *tactical* mistake'?

If I had straight clear answers to these questions, I would not grieve at not having answers to others, deeper and more impenetrable anxieties. Something fearful, some one person subjected to intolerable provocation, unhappiness, or anger caused Betty's death. We can forgive Betty or any other person without knowing exactly the provocation. But it's not easy to forgive someone one suspects of covering up what should be common sense matters. All the above questions *should* have common sense answers.

I wish you could answer these questions but I greatly fear for the answers.

RMF

☙☙☙

After a day of reflection, Rosemary wrote instead to Betty and Cyril's daughter. Her letter quoted a sonnet by George Meredith,[10] a favourite of Betty's, and Rosemary concluded: 'Perhaps we shall never be certain how your mother met her death, but I am at last able to feel compassion – even forgiveness – for whoever did cause that death.'[11]

Notes

1. Ellen Godfrey, 1981, *By Reason of Doubt: The Belshaw Case*, Vancouver: Clarke Irwin, pp. 31–32.
2. Rosemary to Cyril Belshaw, 28 September, 1979 (LSE Library, Firth/8/4/1).
3. Rosemary to Cyril Belshaw, 5 October 1979 (LSE Library, Firth/8/4/1).
4. Mrs Holdsworth provided domestic help at the Firths' home in Southwood Avenue before, during and after the Belshaws' stay there in 1979.
5. Rosemary to Betty and Cyril Belshaw's daughter, 7 October 1979 (LSE Library, Firth/8/4/1).
6. Rosemary, diary entry, 4 November 1979.
7. Rosemary's engagement diary.
8. Rosemary to Cyril Belshaw, 28 October 1979 (LSE Library, Firth/8/4/1).
9. While Betty and Cyril were staying in the Firths' house in London in 1978, their bed had been broken; Cyril had written to Rosemary to say that it was being mended.
10. George Meredith (1808–1909), novelist and poet. His wife Mary Nichols (1821–61) married Meredith in 1849, but left him in 1858. The fiftieth sonnet, which Betty had marked out, begins:
    'Thus piteously Love closed what he begat:
    The union of this ever-diverse pair!
    These two were rapid falcons in a snare,
    Condemned to do the flitting of the bat.' (Sonnet L, *Modern Love,* 1891).
11. Rosemary to Betty and Cyril Belshaw's daughter, 29 October 1979 (LSE Library, Firth/8/4/1).

Chapter 22

Pity Bolts
Other Doors

1979–1982

On 11 November 1979, Cyril Belshaw flew into Paris to chair a UNESCO conference. As he arrived, he was arrested by French police at the request of the Swiss and held in prison while extradition proceedings commenced. Raymond and Rosemary learnt of this development ten days later. At the end of December, Raymond received a message asking for a character reference. He sent a carefully worded cable in response.

Whereas earlier in the year Rosemary had had to deal with a private grief – in that Betty was not known to most of her friends – now she had to struggle with something else: a private grief subjected to public gaze. The discovery and identification of Betty's body after so many months attracted coverage in the Canadian and Swiss press. Cyril's arrest stoked press interest still further. Anthropologists both in Britain and abroad – such as Rosemary's friend Ralph Bulmer in Auckland – came to hear about the case. A number of them knew that the Belshaws and the Firths had been close friends and contacted Raymond and Rosemary. Communicating with other people, trying to be both loyal and non-judgemental in relation to Cyril, but also truthful, proved a strain: 'R. and I have suffered severely from knowing too much and too little, and having been regarded as a centre for information and reassurance from incredulous colleagues all over the world. I think I have borne a harder brunt in all this because it was she that I knew and loved most, whereas others in anthropological circles outside Canada felt that they knew Cyril best.'[1]

As the days went by, through October and November, Rosemary reflected at length on all she had been told since Betty's disappearance. Her belief grew steadily stronger that Cyril had probably been involved in some way in Betty's death, and complicit in covering it up for eight months.

There was an initial hearing in Paris on 12 December to determine whether Cyril should be extradited from France to Switzerland; then there was a full hearing on 9 January. After some time to consider the legal issues involved, extradition was granted on 30 January 1980. Cyril was handed over to the Swiss authorities on 2 February and 'indicted' for murder and for falsifying dental records. Bail was refused. Under the Swiss system, there follows a period of investigation, which leads to a decision whether or not to formally 'accuse' a defendant – to bring him or her to trial.[2]

In early February, Rosemary was approached on behalf of the Swiss police by Inspector Bendel for a statement, which she completed and signed on 26 February. Maître Paschoud, Cyril's lawyer in Switzerland, also wanted to talk to Rosemary and Raymond. This took much longer to arrange – Rosemary was reluctant to meet him – but they did meet on 22 May. At the end of the lengthy judicial process of enquiry, Cyril was formally accused on 9 October. His trial took place from 3 to 5 December 1980.

The prosecution called few witnesses but did present Rosemary's statement as one of their many pieces of evidence. The statement included reference to the bed that had been broken by the Belshaws and Betty's strange sleeping behaviour while they stayed at Southwood Avenue. Yet, in Rosemary's view, there was more significant evidence that Cyril had possibly been involved in some way in Betty's death. Cyril had alleged that Betty disappeared in Paris, but her body was discovered only forty miles from Montana in Switzerland, where Cyril and Betty had been living. Cyril offered no hypothesis as to why she might have gone missing in Paris only to be found hundreds of miles away in Switzerland. The Firths' housekeeper, Mrs Holdsworth, had reported that sometimes when Betty came to the door to let her in, she seemed in a strangely depressed, unhappy state, and that she had once heard her say, 'I have had enough, I just can't take anymore', or words to that effect. Rosemary wondered whether the bed, broken whilst Cyril and Betty were staying in their house, might have been broken as a result of some struggle. In one of Cyril's letters, he had talked of possessiveness in marriage, of not really knowing ourselves; in another letter, he had said that he had to be a kind of psychiatrist to Betty – a potentially 'dangerous' state of affairs.[3] Rosemary might have wondered whether medication was a part of the reason she had died. And then there was Cyril's behaviour: Rosemary had also gathered – perhaps directly from Cyril – that there had been some 'mislaid or misrouted dental charts'.[4] There had also been his comment, during a telephone call with Rosemary, that he had made a 'tactical mistake' when interviewed by Swiss police in Vancouver on 24 September 1979.[5]

Certainly, by early 1980, Raymond and Rosemary knew that Cyril had deliberately altered Betty's dental records; he had admitted this obliquely in a letter to Rosemary and also in open court in Paris.[6] Especially significant to Rosemary were two conversations she recalled, the first on 1 April 1979, when Cyril met them for dinner just eleven weeks after Betty's disappearance. Cyril had described to Rosemary how he had been to the Salvation Army Missing Persons unit, where someone had, he said, told him that police had managed to identify a naked headless torso thrown into a culvert merely from a gold fountain pen found near the body. But the Salvation Army later told Rosemary they had said nothing to Cyril about a naked torso. Why, Rosemary wondered, had Cyril invented this story?

If, as he alleged, he knew nothing of the body found at Le Sépey on 28 March – despite the headlines all over the regional papers in Switzerland on 29 March – why had he invented such a gory story about a naked torso? Had he actually seen the headlines, with their reports of a naked torso wrapped in plastic bags?

A few days later, at a conference in York, Cyril had said, 'We must have a wake for Betty soon, Rosemary. You must both come over to Vancouver when I get back in July. I will send you the money for the air-tickets.' Rosemary was so shocked by Cyril's offer of money in this context that she never told Raymond about it; she was also struck by the levity with which he talked of a wake.[7]

Three weeks later, in May 1979, Cyril altered Betty's dental records because, so he subsequently said, he could not face the trauma of identifying his wife.[8]

Opinion amongst others was divided. Rumours and evidence that Cyril might have been having affairs before Betty's death were one contributor – he had allegedly been discovered in a compromising position with a woman in a red car.[9] Many people in Canada were inclined to think that falsification of dental records was strong evidence of guilt. There were others who were convinced of Cyril's innocence and who testified in the subsequent court proceedings to that effect, including Kenneth Burridge, head of anthropology at the University of British Columbia, Vancouver. Amongst anthropologists in Europe, many did not know Cyril personally, even though he was president of the International Union of Anthropologists and Ethnologists, as the numbers of anthropologists in the profession had grown enormously in the 1960s and 1970s. Edmund, for example, did not know Cyril personally and largely avoided any involvement in the gossip that circulated once his arrest became known. When professional duty took Edmund to Vancouver, while Cyril was awaiting trial in Switzerland, Rosemary warned him through Celia that there was much vicious gossip about the Belshaws in Vancouver that had absolutely no foundation at all. Both Rosemary and Raymond were equally concerned with evidence, accuracy and fairness, and they were both shocked by some of the things that were being suggested without any basis whatever.

Rosemary felt 'polluted' by Cyril's behaviour. Nevertheless, she recognised that most people commit truly hurtful acts only under great pressure, either from others or from powerful forces within themselves. The Swiss police, once they realised that Cyril had deliberately delayed the identification of Betty's body, were presumably convinced that Cyril had murdered Betty: this was the indictment they brought. The different legal process and traditions of investigation under Swiss and Canadian law, in particular the assumption of a 'right of silence' under Canadian law, meant that the Swiss authorities perceived Cyril's lack of cooperation with their enquiries as further evidence of guilt. The Swiss law distinguished three categories of homicide. The least serious – *meurtre passionnel* – was killing under the influence of passion. Next was *meurtre*: intentional homicide. The most serious charge was premeditated murder: *assassinat*. The Swiss investigation concluded that the charge of *meurtre* – intentional homicide – was appropriate. In deciding which charge to bring against Cyril, they appear to have concentrated on Cyril's alteration of Betty's dental records and anticipated that this fact would be sufficient to secure a conviction. It was only in the closing summary that the prosecution even considered a scenario in which Cyril and Betty might , for example, have had an argument during which Cyril might have killed Betty by accident.

Yet it was just circumstances of this kind – accidents of one kind or another – that seemed most likely to Rosemary. Knowing both Cyril and Betty, and contemplating all the information of which she was now aware, in particular the apparent evidence of strain, pressure, even domination of Betty in the marriage, some sort of accident, argument or fight between them seemed most likely. Rosemary concluded that some unintended event had led to Betty's death, some occurrence that Cyril might have wished to hide from the public, an accident that took place in conditions Cyril would have perceived as deeply embarrassing or potentially incriminating. What those circumstances might have been, she could only guess at.[10] Yet such a scenario seemed most credible to Rosemary and Raymond, whereas the suggestion that Cyril had murdered Betty intentionally did not appear credible to either of them, knowing the two of them as they did.

Between the indictment on 2 February 1980 and the formal accusation on 9 October, the Swiss process of enquiry unfolded in secret. To those awaiting its outcome, it must have seemed interminable.

By contrast, the trial itself, which began on 3 December, was remarkably brief.

CRLO

Despite her best attempts to understand and forgive whatever may have happened between Cyril and Betty, Cyril's lack of openness meant that Rosemary
was unable to continue any further relationship with him. She wrote her last
letter to Cyril when he was still fighting extradition to Switzerland. Raymond
moved to judgement more slowly. He did not write a final letter to Cyril until
after the trial was over – when all the questions about Betty's death were still
unanswered.

ROSEMARY TO RALPH BULMER (her anthropologist colleague in New Zealand)

14 November 1979   **Southwood Avenue, London**

Dear Ralph,

. . . The Belshaw story becomes increasingly incredible. Betty's body was found
on 28 March . . . in Switzerland. . . . There was some inexplicable delay in making
a correct identification, through a mislaid or misrouted dental chart, and although
treating the case as one of murder, no cause of death has yet been established –
or at least announced by the Swiss police. Interpol have been active in Paris, in
London, (they came to see us) and of course in Vancouver. Ghastly for all who
loved *them both*, and for the children. . . . One has to keep one's thoughts tightly
bridled, and ask forgiveness for any escaping doubts. We don't seem ever to
know anything about even our best and dearest friends . . .

Affectionately from both of us,

R.

ROSEMARY TO CYRIL

19 December 1979[11]   **Southwood Avenue, London**

Dear Cyril,

Your letter dated 11 December from Paris [prison] came today, 19 December . . .

I have thought a good deal about your earlier letters, in which you spoke of
seeming to spread a virus among your friends with your bad news about Betty.
The pain and distress which has been steadily mounting among those who loved
you both best, is now darkened and deepened by an obscurity which has sprung
up about many things which before seemed never in doubt. At the moment you
bear the brunt of legal process, perhaps sometimes clumsy, and often slow and
muddled seeming. But for those of us who are onlookers, it still remains a prime
goal to establish, if not what actually happened, then at least to clarify what did
not happen. And I for one have to unwind in tears, as the poet says, my earlier
pictures of Betty seeking her own undoing.

It is easier to bear any kind of truth, horrible howsoever that it be, than not to
know at all. This is one moral certainty which the traumas of the last ten months

have made absolutely certain for me. For how can we begin to adapt until we know what we have to face? Forgiveness follows, for those who tried to unravel the truth as for those who caused the confusions.

Don't get too annoyed with those who seem to be your tormentors, for they are trying to establish the truth in the only way that they can in the structures of our western society . . .

Christmas is the season of new beginnings, growth when all has seemed dead. May the New Year bring you the courage to face not only your immediate difficulties, but also any which the future may bring you, when the storm is over and cost of the struggle, just or unjust, is clear to see.

Affectionately,

Your old friend – and hers

R

ROSEMARY TO CYRIL

28 January 1980[12]   **Southwood Avenue, London**

Dear Cyril

It is exactly a year since you wrote us that sad letter from Montana about Betty. It is not your own family alone, but all your friends and colleagues who have been drawn into a great deal of anxiety, perplexity and suffering ever since. It is time now to think of the living rather than the dead. For this reason your last letter to me of 27 December, which arrived in Highgate on 8 January, gives me some hope.

I am grateful that you let me know that you begin to feel able to face reality more rationally now, although at one time – from the shock of all your suffering perhaps? – you felt that you could not . . .

You know my own feelings about truth . . . there are times when it is only hurtful to tell all the truth, especially to those we love. But there are also times when it is even more hurtful to tell only some of it, and of course worse still to tell untruth. Some of us cannot do it without help from outside, and I hope that if you also need such help, you also will be able to find it . . .

Of course, I know that legal help is also necessary, but there are some things which the best lawyers in the world cannot do. They help us face the outside world, but they are not able to help us face our inner, our own, our most private world; within this sacred place we can be helped to distinguish our 'real thoughts' as you put it, which are 'healthy', and those which are 'unreal', or not so healthy. Raymond and I will not desert you then – it will in fact be easier for us to come closer again.

Rosemary.

[Subsequent note in margin: 'My last letter to C.B: Only Raymond would write again, in Spring 1981.']

ROSEMARY TO CELIA

12 February, 1980   **Southwood Avenue, London**

Dearest Celia,

. . . Reading through my Malayan field notes for professional reasons recently, I found that some time about this month in 1940 you flew to Rangoon and were married to Edmund.[13] Ruby weddings are those of forty years, and no one else much but thee and me seems able to stick by their husbands for so long! So here is a present for you both with love from both of us . . .

I understand that E. is going to Vancouver pretty soon.

. . . That university is filled with real evil about C.B. and perhaps more so with unknown evil thoughts spread abroad by malicious women. I hope E. does not meet it head on. If he does, perhaps he can help the gossipers to distinguish between what can be known and what cannot . . . or at least what a person is charged with in law, and what another only charged with by innuendo. We had a sad, sad letter from Shack,[14] and also from Bulmer about these horrible stories. As if the reality were not horrible enough!

Love & best wishes to you both for another twenty years at least!

R.

ROSEMARY TO RALPH BULMER

26 April 1980   **Holway, Dorset**

Dear Ralph

I have been writing this letter to you in my mind now for so many weeks . . .

I have suffered so intensely in the last three months that I had come to *hate* Cyril. Everything about him seemed ego-centric, mean, calculating, from his aspersions on my beloved Betty and her alleged mental troubles, even to the flood of letters, presents, expensive restaurant dinners and flowers sent me on our return to London which now are shadowed by the sinister suspicion of hush money. You see the household in which the two of them stayed and this cottage which they visited twice has thrown up chilling pieces of evidence which fit too nicely a picture of long calculated terror for her and deliberate wrong doing at various levels from him. The reluctant evidence of an honest daily [Mrs Holdsworth] . . . postal stuff from some pornographic house which I first destroyed, then began to think about, amazed; some evidence of violence: – a broken bedframe, mended by Heals while we were away! – worse still, an evil amalgam of half-truths in a story told [about] the social service dept. of the Salvation Army which came out by accident when I visited them to see if they could help C.B. in prison . . .

So for all these reasons I cannot see Cyril as a man hounded by doubts and regrets as to some past act of passion or indiscretion and an honest wish to protect those he most loves or respects . . .

. . . I was moved by your plea for pitying Cyril and could forgive him if he'd stop being defensive and confess what he has done wrong and under what duress, if any. I have quite strong views on 'deception' of those we love. For instance, it certainly is not always – [or] even often? . . . wise or kind to tell certain truths. But the occasion alters circumstances, and sometimes deliberate untruth, rather than avoidance of whole truth, really undermines the structure of ongoing personal relationships . . .

. . . All the others are concerned about C.B.'s honour. I worry about Betty's honour – and Raymond has got to the age he can't bear to look too long on another's sorrow anyway.

It has been a warming link to hear you talk of fondness for Reo [Reo Fortune, anthropologist, died in November 1979]. I too was fond of him. . . . I remember saying [when we became mildly amorous on a summer's day during the war]: 'I'll be fond of you till the autumn leaves fall Reo, and Raymond comes home!' . . . So, I never *quite* could reverse my feelings when he treated Raymond so outrageously.[15] Come to think of it, I never have been able to *not love* anyone I've once loved, even if active love becomes for social or matrimonial reasons inappropriate. And that goes for deep friendships too.

I suppose what embitters me now is the feeling that I've been led to hate a person I once respected and admired, and [who was] a dear friend loved and trusted. . . . Perhaps this is the last occasion I'll ever weep so bitterly about loss – the loss of a friend – of a faith – and the loss of some psychologically important feeling of the moral sense of the universe.

. . . Write to Rosemary

ROSEMARY TO GEORGE MILNER[16]

22 April 1980   **Holway, Dorset**

Dear George

I thank you sincerely for your long and thoughtful letter. I was evidently as discreet as Raymond would always wish me to be if I only spoke about 'a friend' in trouble in Switzerland, but I have found the whole horrible affair almost more than I can bear to keep to myself, so I am glad news came to you from other sources than mine. R. considers I have become obsessional and worse still 'prejudiced' about matters he still prefers to regard as *sub-judice*. But the plain fact is that Betty was my close friend for over thirty years and altho' Cyril had been regarded as also part of a quartet of friendship with us both, when it comes to the crunch, as it has done only in the last few months, my passions are concerned for justice for *her*, not him.

After the admittal [*sic*] by C.B. of the forgery of Betty's dental chart, I have to say that both of us are now convinced of Cyril's close involvement with, and also deception in concealing, the death of his wife. It has become clear in the course of the fifteen months' correspondence . . . that C. has been dishonest with us. I feel deeply betrayed, both by his wife's death and also by his deceptions in the six – nine months' time in which we were in close correspondence and in personal contact comforting and supporting him in a supposed mysterious loss. My own deep (and perhaps obsessional?) concern is now to discover what could have led up to such a tragedy; in particular as the most horrible stories of sexual abnormalities have been wickedly . . . circulated among his American colleagues . . .

In much gratitude and affection.

R.M.F.

ROSEMARY TO RALPH BULMER

9 August 1980   **Holway, Dorset**

Dear Ralph

It was very good indeed to get your two letters. . . . I don't think C. is a sadist – perhaps in some small area of distorted erotic development he may have been. But as for that, if that was the worm in their marriage relationship – there must be some collusive acceptance on the partner's side, surely? I now think some accident happened in circumstances which the world would regard as shameful . . . and that it was *cowardice*, and *pride*, which ensured all that followed. Raymond keeps on telling me that C.B. was a proud, secret man; and when I met his 'advocate' from Switzerland, in a very strange defensive interview, the only piece of information I could get from him was that Cyril was not a brave man at all. So, in the end, one's scorn and hate does turn to pity. . . . Of course, pity bolts other doors . . .

Affectionately Rosemary

ᏗᎥᏂ

The trial lasted just three days, from 3 to 5 December, and was overseen by the court president. The jury, together with the president, formed their judgement at the end of the trial. The jury and president then set forth their summary, their judgement, their verdict and the sentence.

Three days after the close of the trial, on 8 December 1980, the president announced the judgement. After detailing the 'facts' of the case, the judgement made clear that it did not accept Cyril's explanation that he had falsified Betty's dental charts because he could not face identifying Betty's body. However, on a technicality, he was found not guilty of falsification of evidence.[17] The court moreover concluded that the gulf between the legal traditions of Swiss and Canadian law, together with the (reticent and private) 'character of the accused and his conceptions of justice', meant that there remained a 'very light doubt' on the main charge.[18] On account of his obstruction of the procedures of Swiss justice, he was ordered to pay 30,000 francs – the bulk of the legal costs of the investigation and trial.

He was found 'not guilty' of murder, 'by reason of doubt'.

Following the judgement, Cyril wrote to Rosemary and Raymond. Raymond replied after some thought.

RAYMOND TO CYRIL

18 March 1981[19]   **Southwood Avenue, London**

Dear Cyril,

Your letter of 3 February has gone unanswered for some time because like yours this has been written with difficulty. I would have liked to avoid reopening a painful subject, but I think it necessary in this reply. Your letter was addressed to us both. I am replying in my own terms. But though Rosemary might well put things differently – particularly as a woman for whom Betty was a very dear friend – she and I share the view that our old friendship with you belongs to the past, and if we meet again a new kind of relationship will have to be established.

The essence of the matter is that Betty's death, in itself a most sorrowful event, has been made even more traumatic by the treatment given to her poor mortal remains. The horror of this, when it was eventually discovered, was if anything increased by the long delay in identification of her body – a delay for which you bear some responsibility through your alteration of the record, for reasons which you have explained but which nevertheless held up the enquiry. You have been acquitted by the Court of responsibility for the major events themselves, and I am glad that after the protracted ordeals of imprisonment and trial you are now free again to take up your life professionally and with your children. It must have been a terribly harrowing time for them as well as for you, and Rosemary and I have thought of you all a great deal . . .

But behind all the pain, frustrations and burdens of your experience there still stand the questions: How and why did Betty die? And how did she come to rest in that awful place? When it seemed just that she had disappeared from Paris, a series of logical possibilities lay open – you will remember how we discussed them with you. Some like amnesia, were of relatively mild order, others grimmer, but they were all focussed initially on France. But when her body was discovered within reach of Montana, in circumstances clearly not of her own choosing, a completely different set of logical possibilities opened up. I had hoped that your trial, as well as exonerating you, would have thrown some light on the whole mysterious circumstances of Betty's death and treatment of her body. But nothing emerged, no single suggestion which could explain what happened. So, it is very hard indeed for old close friends such as us to come to terms with the uncertainty, the mystery, the pain – anguish is hardly too strong a word – of these unanswered questions. This must continue to throw a long shadow over the memory of the past pleasures and friendship we all shared and chill the warmth of past relationship.

You may feel this is a harsh and unjustified stand for me to take. If it is unfair, I deeply regret it, but I have tried to express to you frankly what I feel. To change the metaphor – the gulf of those unanswered questions, to which seemingly you cannot supply answers, stretches between us, no matter how much I try to overcome it. If in the course of time, there is some clarification of the whole situation then maybe we can start to build another bridge across this personal gap.

Meanwhile, my best wishes for you . . . in your own rebuilding processes.

Sincerely, Raymond

☙❦❧

This was the last contact between Raymond and Cyril. Cyril died in November 2018.

After Betty's death, Rosemary continued to correspond for a number of years with Betty and Cyril's daughter. In 1982, she asked for Rosemary's recollections of Betty. Rosemary replied, saying:

> I knew her as well as anybody else in the world . . . [we could] identify each with the other without the necessity for overt detailed intimacy. . . . We first learned to help each other in respect of our two small children in Canberra, [and] secondly in our equally precarious positions as intelligent women married to brilliant professional men. In 1952 she became the most important person in my life at a time of the greatest emotional crisis I had experienced up to that time, when ANU had offered Raymond a life-job in Canberra and he had accepted it . . . Betty came to my rescue at once. . . . [In the 1960s] Betty and I used to refer obliquely to the difficult situation our marital obligations often laid upon our professional ambitions and personal desires, but we never criticised either spouse openly or directly. But in our . . . long letters . . . we each knew at some hidden level of the other's difficulties . . . bursting with half-concealed unhappy indignation.[20]

Rosemary concluded: 'If I had anything to offer . . . in the fashion of good fairy godmother magical gifts, it would be: Grow up brave, honest and compassionate to others, but above all learn to value the importance of your own integrity. Without this you cannot have true courage. Without [integrity] you cannot be honest to yourself and others without harming some who are weaker than yourself. Without knowing yourself in depth, you cannot be compassionate to others. The balancing of these three virtues is no mean feat. . . . But I did not learn the central value of self-knowledge and self-respect until at least halfway through my own life, when the lack of it littered me with problems. . . .'[21]

Notes

1. Rosemary to Ken Burridge, Professor of Anthropology at UBC Vancouver, undated, 1980.
2. We are indebted to Ellen Godfrey for many of the details of the legal proceedings against Cyril Belshaw: see Ellen Godfrey, 1981, *By Reason of Doubt: The Belshaw Case*, Vancouver: Clarke Irwin.
3. Rosemary's draft statement for police, 'Memo for self, not used', 9 February 1980, and Rosemary to a friend of the Belshaws in Vancouver, 29 April 1980.
4. Rosemary to Ralph Bulmer, 14 November 1979.
5. Rosemary to Cyril (not sent), 28 October 1979. See pp. 251–52.
6. Rosemary to George Milner, 22 April 1980; Rosemary to a friend of the Belshaws in Vancouver, 1 April 1980.
7. These details are from a draft letter from Rosemary to Jonathan Benthall, undated, summer 1980.
8. Godfrey, *By Reason of Doubt*, pp. 31–32.
9. Godfrey, *By Reason of Doubt*, p. 52.
10. Rosemary to a friend of the Belshaws in Vancouver, 29 April 1980.
11. Rosemary to Cyril Belshaw, 19 December 1979 (LSE Library, Firth/8/4/1).
12. Rosemary to Cyril Belshaw, 28 January 1980 (LSE Library, Firth/8/4/1).
13. Celia had in fact travelled by sea.
14. William Shack, an American anthropologist who was a professor at the University of Chicago and later at the University of California, Berkeley.
15. Reo Fortune was known for his idiosyncratic antagonism towards some of his professional colleagues. It is possible that Raymond's recommendation of A.P. Elkin, rather than Reo Fortune, to succeed him as acting professor at Sydney in 1932 was part of the cause. Raymond's view was that 'Reo Fortune was angry that I had not preferred his name. [He was] certainly a better scholar but almost certainly a less effective head of department' (Raymond Firth, 'Chronology', unpublished).
16. George Milner was a colleague of Rosemary's at the London University Institute of Education.
17. The dental charts were ruled to be technically 'not evidence' in Swiss law under article 110 of the penal code.
18. Godfrey, *By Reason of Doubt*, p. 203.
19. Raymond to Cyril Belshaw, 18 March 1981 (LSE Library, Firth/8/4/1).
20. Rosemary to Betty and Cyril Belshaw's daughter, 4 August 1982 (LSE Library, Firth/8/4/1).
21. Rosemary to Betty and Cyril Belshaw's daughter, 4 August 1982 (LSE Library, Firth/8/4/1).

Chapter 23

Almost Like Brothers

1984–1986

After the trauma of Betty's death, with no warning or by-your-leave from Edmund, Rosemary was contacted in the summer of 1984 by Martha Mac-intyre,[1] who said she had been authorised to be Edmund Leach's biographer. Edmund had skin cancer and was beginning to plan for the future. Despite his protestations that he would prefer 'no posthumous existence', he had recently written a partly autobiographical article[2] and it seems likely that – even if only unconsciously – he wished to retain some control over his post-humous record.

Rosemary took exception to the description of her Martha had been given by Edmund. He had called her his first 'girlfriend' – a term that, among the middle classes of the 1920s and 1930s, carried the connotation of a superfi-cial, purely sexual liaison carried on alongside an already existing marriage, engagement or serious courtship. She also resented Martha's warning that any interview would 'constitute an invasion of her privacy'. There was an exchange of correspondence – tart on Rosemary's side, apologetic but slightly baffled on Edmund's side. To Rosemary, Edmund's behaviour seemed to be a repetition of the self-centred behaviour she felt she had often experienced in the past. However, Edmund still seemed to think the issue was straightforward: 'I am nonplussed. . . . [For] anyone who tries to write an intellectual biography of ERL [Edmund] . . . to get . . . to anthropology *you* are necessarily involved in some degree. . . . I suggest you call it [the interview] off.'[3] Rosemary was furious that Edmund still did not appreciate what he had done. She drafted a parody of the letter Edmund had sent her fifty years earlier, just before he left for China, when he jilted her. His letter then had begun: 'I wonder what you are expecting me to write. It would be pleasant to know because then I could be perverse and write the other thing.'[4] Rosemary copied his 1933 letter word for word except for a few choice substitutions; however, she opted not to send what she had written, choosing instead to repair the relationship. In the course of this exchange of letters, Edmund commented: 'Since I do not keep letters [Martha] will have a job making any sense of my "literary remains".'[5] This was categorically untrue: Edmund was incapable of throwing anything away. He kept piles of letters in untidy heaps in many rooms, including a great many of Rosemary's letters that she had written to him over the years.[6]

Rosemary did eventually agree to talk to Martha Macintyre, and they met in the autumn of 1984. Discussing Edmund as a young man brought Rosemary back to the 1930s and left her reflecting on their relationship over the years.

Early in January 1985, Edmund stayed the night at the Firths'; Rosemary thought his behaviour 'pompous, arrogant, destructive of younger theorists, and plain rude to me'.[7] Afterwards he wrote another letter of apology – but Rosemary shifted their correspondence to a more serious discussion about biographical perspectives, historical truth and the nature of reality. Edmund's views on writing were in line with the postmodernist views of the time: there is no 'reality'; everything is 'illusion'. Rosemary disagreed, believing that different writers offer differing perspectives, each an aspect of some externally existing truth.

Edmund put forward the epitome of his view a couple of years later at the 1987 ASA conference in a characteristically provocative style, with the conclusion that all anthropologists' descriptions of cultures are 'fiction'.[8] He parodied anthropologists' pictures of static, timeless, primitive cultures in contrast to developed western societies, suggesting that Raymond himself had sinned in this manner in writing about Tikopia. Raymond and Edmund debated the issues vigorously. Rosemary wrote a short satirical poem:[9]

Tweedledum and Tweedledee
Agreed to stage a fight
For Tweedledum said Tweedledee
Lacked historical insight . . .
. . . And so they argued – no one won –
If fact or fiction should be done,
Displaying to us all at length
Great funds of controversial strength.
For Tweedledum's the sort of boy
Who often argues to annoy
And Tweedledee will always try
To set aright what is awry.

Edmund's suggestion that Raymond had portrayed Tikopia society as unchanging was certainly rather wide of the mark: Raymond had, after all, published a whole book about social change in Tikopia. Edmund had also published an equally polemical article entitled 'Glimpses of the Unmentionable in British Social Anthropology',[10] alleging that Raymond was guilty of these sins. Rosemary had written to Edmund, chiding him. Raymond had simply scribbled 'Nonsense!' in the margin of his copy of the article.

In their own ways, Edmund, Rosemary and Raymond were each reflecting on their lives and careers. Raymond was pursuing two projects: a dictionary of the Tikopia language and a collection of Tikopia songs; both efforts to preserve aspects of Tikopia culture threatened by change (Solomon Islands pidgin was increasingly replacing Tikopia vocabulary). Rosemary had been reviewing a book of letters from Bernard Deacon, a young anthropologist who died in 1927,[11] and this led her to think about whether she had material in her vast collection of letters that might be worth publishing. Rereading Edmund's letters from the 1930s, in response to Martha's request for an interview, had also made Rosemary reflect on the possible value of preserving her diaries and correspondence.

Edmund's aim in 'Glimpses of the Unmentionable' was serious: to explore the extent to which the social backgrounds of anthropologists affect their careers and their thinking. His analysis of the 'outsiders' (the foreign-born anthropologists who were Malinowski's students, like Raymond from New Zealand and Isaac Schapera and Meyer Fortes from South Africa) was provocative and sometimes wide of the mark. Yet Edmund offered fulsome praise for Raymond's 'deep commitment to the preservation and development of the academic discipline of social anthropology', and his . . . very remarkable' achievements and 'outstanding [political] skill', adding that his 'performance as an academic politician fits in with his anthropological commitment to the concept of "social organisation"'.[12] And in an important autobiographical interview at this time, Edmund was explicit about his relationship with Raymond, which he termed 'a lifelong discipleship'.[13] For Edmund to say this in print was praise indeed.

In 'Glimpses of the Unmentionable', Edmund reserved his commentary for anthropologists older than himself. His article caused a furore; many anthropologists felt they had been denigrated and some refused to have anything more to do with him.

Would Edmund have been able to make links between Rosemary's background and her approach to anthropology? He might have referred to her upper-middle-class origins: she was an 'insider' in British pre-war intellectual culture. As an 'insider', she was able to be challenging, to champion the underdog. So maybe it was to be expected that she would be particularly interested in the position of women. Additionally, perhaps because she was culturally an 'insider' but yet worked as an outsider to the centres of postgraduate academic anthropology training, she felt able to cast a somewhat oblique view on anthropological matters, with her critical glances at fieldwork as initiation and anthropology 'within and without the ivory towers'.[14]

It was no doubt partly as a consequence of the animated discussion and correspondence between Rosemary and Edmund about his post-modernist views that Rosemary came to see Edmund's greatest insult as his earlier 'casting off one who had become so intimate intellectually, emotionally and culturally'.[15] She reflected how 'his overweening ambition and vanity made him find excuses to throw me off in 1933, as in 1938; in 1969 he couldn't manage his own self-deception so easily. But there have been so many good intervening years of friendship . . . that I ought to be able to understand all that. He is a brilliant man, and I suppose the Devil drives most ambition in men. But it is something to put out flags for, that I have been so intimately associated in so different ways, with two of the great anthropologists, two great men, this century!'[16]

Six months later, in July 1986, both men went under the surgeon's knife on the same day: Raymond for prostate cancer, Edmund for the skin cancer that had become aggressive.

ROSEMARY TO EDMUND

31 August 1984   **Southwood Avenue, London**

Dear Edmund,

. . . I was astonished to receive today a letter from one Martha Macintyre. It seems you have given her the names of a number of friends with authorisation to collect material for your life history.

I would consider it a courtesy if we could have some talk about this first. It might be wise for me to know what material she is receiving from you.

I have a great deal of written material myself, letters and diaries from nearly sixty years. As I get older, I have myself been wondering what should be done about much of this. If it is to be used in the lifetime of thee and me, I would prefer to use it myself. If posterity is to have it, what stop should be put on it?

It would be good to lunch with you before Macintyre turns up. . . . Could you telephone about this?

Affectionately RMF

EDMUND TO ROSEMARY

3 September 1984   **The Birk, Barrington, Cambridge**

Dear Rosemary

. . . I am very sorry to find that you have reacted as you have to Martha's approach. I must take the whole blame. She asked me to approach both you and Raymond.

It was I who suggested that she should first approach you direct on the grounds that while you could well refuse her it might be more difficult for you to refuse me. I think you have met Martha but perhaps not. . .

Since I do not keep letters she will have a job making any sense of my 'literary remains' but I have talked autobiographically on tape and will doubtless do so again. What other people reveal about my past is their affair.

What Martha knows about your relevance at present is simply in answer to the question 'But if when you were working for Butterfield and Swire your technical qualification was that of an engineer how on earth did you fetch up as an anthropologist?'

The answer briefly is that having arrived back in England with a lot of notes and pictures from Botel Tobago and knowing that you (a ghost from my past) had married a social anthropologist I got you to introduce me to Raymond who said 'you have asked all the wrong questions but you had better meet Malinowski'.

Martha is very intelligent. She will not think that is all there is to it. But as far as I know her object is to show how my anthropology emerges out of my class background. But there of course you come in again. She knows already that my life model has been Sir Henry Howorth . . . father of Sir Rupert Howorth, distinguished Civil Servant and friend of Sir Gilbert Upcott, another distinguished Civil Servant, etc.

But you are perfectly entitled to say 'nothing doing; that all belongs to a different era; mind your own business' . . .

In general I think that all biographical history is inevitably wildly distorted. It invariably uses hindsight to reinterpret documents which originally meant something entirely different. I would prefer it if I had no posthumous existence at all but it seems that that will not be the case anyway. So as far as I am concerned Martha is my 'official biographer' simply so as to fob off the others.

As to papers about me in your possession burn them or give them to Martha as you wish but if, as you now suggest, you plan to use them yourself (this had not occurred to me as a possibility!) I suggest that you simply tell Martha that there is nothing doing. After all she is not *your* 'official biographer'. She will understand.

Much love

Edmund

ROSEMARY TO EDMUND

22 September 1984   **Southwood Avenue, London**

Dear Edmund,

In your letter of 3 September you say about yourself 'what other people reveal about my past is their affair'. But I think that you have perhaps not fully understood the implications of 'revealing the past', since everybody's past involves other people . . .

Historians have a clever habit of asking questions to which any, or no answer gives clues. Of course, all this is supposed to be some fifty years ago, but it is not quite so simple as that, is it? I believe each of us should burn their own smoke, and I have no right to tell you to do your own homework on your early life, let alone your middle life. But I do not find it easy to tell untruths, or half-truths so I have to do my best . . .

If in the interview my version seems to show you as simply one of a great number of amorous young men, of whom I have very little to say after all these years, you will I hope not contradict this on your bloody tape machine.

Of course, we are still friends. But I did not think you still had so much power to jeopardy my own very personal self-possession.

R.

ROSEMARY'S DIARY

26 November 1984　　　　**See, We Have Come Through!**　　　　**London**

. . . Many terrible things have happened to me since I last wrote here – Betty's cruel death and Cyril's crueller deceptions, Raymond's blundering mis-cues over my misery and humiliation during those years 1979–1980. I got through them without recourse to the solace of [writing in] this book!

Recently a different trauma hit me.

Briefly, I felt betrayed in an outrageously 'public' fashion by being asked for an interview . . . by some Australian woman who was 'commissioned' (or so I understood) to write an intellectual biography (sic!) of ERL. . . . Eventually we [Raymond and I] met and liked her and both talked to her.

But since that letter, in July, and the interview on 23 October, I found I had my past turned up again in front of me, I went back to all the old letters and re-enacted all the old pains, pleasures and disappointments of my earliest interactions with ERL. It raised barriers again between me and Raymond. What obtuseness on E's part! How does he never see the other's likely reactions to his self-centred activities? Self-confessed Egoist he is indeed!

For some weeks recently I've been filled with genuine hatred of Edmund. He even 'cut' me at Audrey [Richards]'s Memorial service in King's College Chapel a fortnight ago.

Then it gradually dawned on me that hatred implies poisoned love: if it had been not so I'd have *mocked* at him, not caring. I still do care, but am still able to keep my balance, I find . . .

[Raymond] would never have treated me as E. did, even though he may often have hurt me in different ways – by not being able always to respond as I wanted;

but he it is who has loved me faithfully and steadily through a difficult marriage; he is the father of our son; he is the husband! Lovers are for youth, fantasy and the past.

Let those things perish. We two, R and I, shall remain.

ROSEMARY TO EDMUND

26 January 1985   **Southwood Avenue, London**

Dear Edmund

. . . We were woken early on the morning of 12 January to hear that [my sister] Margaret had died about half an hour earlier. I was up early intending to visit her.

It was not a good death; a week is long enough for all her children to have been able to visit, but a hell of a long time to fight for every breath, to panic as she did at asthmatic spasms on top of emphysema; to be frightened; and eventually, since Debbie left her at midnight on Friday, to die alone in a strange place. Raymond and I often talk of how it will be when one or other of us is left alone, and I have been thro' many deaths close to me . . . but none has brought home to me so closely what dying is really like – Something each of us – however loved – unless we are believers – must face alone . . .

As for you, I mourned what seemed at some moments terribly like the deliberate killing – by public exposure, – of a relationship which despite all its misunder-standings and pain, had survived from 1928 the storms of 1931, 1933, 1938 and 1969. I believe you (but with increasing effort) that you 'still don't really under-stand what all the hoo-ha is about'. Your inability to see beyond your own expe-rience of a relationship, to the meaning it had for another, has been the cause of all our discontents. Even Martha, whom you must never blame, realised that there was something strange in the animosity some of your professional relations engendered, to your own astonishment as well.

It's perhaps taken me 56 years to disengage from you: but I don't intend to allow anything to weaken Raymond's genuine trust of you –

Now peace be between us.

RMF

EDMUND TO ROSEMARY

29 January 1985   **Barrington, Cambridge**

Dear Rosemary

We both of us send you our sympathy. You have thought about the psychology of mourning much more than I have. I can only hope it helps.

I am very sorry how actions of mine should have made things seem worse. Clearly I erred, but quite unintentionally, though I am not a pleasant person. Maybe I am now too vain to be vulnerable and that I would [have] more pleasure if I were not, but I was vain long before you met me and I was certainly vulnerable then!

Anyway let there be peace between us. I am sorry for my sins. Do not mourn too long.

Love E.

ROSEMARY'S DIARY

1 July 1985   **London**

I'm writing this 6.30 am summer morning because I've been awake several hours, and feel old, old, depressed. Margaret died on 12 January: I felt cut in half, or as if a limb had been amputated. Now there seems no one who really knows me, as an equal, except Raymond . . .

How I wish I could predecease Raymond! Old now, he still has more *intellectual* energy than I, more physical strength . . . less emotional energy or liveliness certainly. But on the eve of our golden wedding, all the disasters and despairs of the last years which have found their solace in the writings of this diary shrink to no more than the bedrock for a deep irreplaceable companionship and trust between us.

If anyone reads this after our deaths, I hope they read this page first for context.

ROSEMARY TO EDMUND

22 July 1985   **Holway, Dorset**

My dear Edmund,

. . . I have recently had for review Deacon's letters to Margaret Gardiner . . . this has forced me to consider what place personal letters really should have in the public image of a well-known figure. Is curiosity legitimate about the early background and temperament of people who have later made their mark in the world of thought? I wondered a lot about this when going through your own letters for Martha Macintyre last year. But I also have a great many letters of my own to kith and kin, as well as diary records for over fifty years, and latterly I have been seriously reconsidering whether I should try to put some of this together for later publication. Many people, especially younger women colleagues, have long been suggesting I do this, and I suppose that I have been an interested onlooker, at the least, over a very productive period of anthropological development. . . . I wonder what you think, you who say you keep no private papers yourself? . . .

Best wishes, let's discuss it sometime. Rosemary.

EDMUND TO ROSEMARY

29 July 1985   **Barrington, Cambridge**

Dear Rosemary

. . . About diaries, letters and all that. Since I don't have any[17] it is hard to hold any opinions. . . . I don't think anyone can ever know 'what really happened', not even if he/she was an actual participant in 'events' and wrote it all down at the time. This clearly is a very extreme position. To explain what I mean I attach an extract from a current 'work in progress' paper which is concerned amongst other things with the relationship between myth and history:

> . . . For example the prominence given to military victories and voyages of exploration in the school history books which I had to digest in my child-hood certainly had far more to do with how the British middle class of the period perceived their role in the world than with any objective assessment of the past as it really happened. . . .

. . . Publishers like biographies because there is a category of fantasy dwelling readers who like reading them; but they are not 'true'. . . . Letters and diaries may give the illusion that somehow they reveal the authentic author as distinct from the poseur who exhibits himself/herself on the public stage. But you might argue just the other way round . . .

As you can see I am at heart a Buddhist! Everything is illusion.

. . . Love Edmund

ROSEMARY TO EDMUND

19 August 1985   **Holway, Dorset**

[Dear Edmund]

. . . I had yesterday scrawled you [but not sent] a long and contentious reply to your assertions about what constitutes a 'good historian' . . .

What is of more interest to me at the moment are two things. One, most impor-tantly perhaps – that having been pretty angry with you for about a year, I have come to see that it does not do to forsake those with whom friendship at the least has managed to exist for half a century and more. And come to think of it, re-reading your letters, I was myself surprised to discover how warm was our cor-respondence during the war and how friendly I had come to be to one who had treated me (as a young woman) even more selfishly than she thought at the time, not being sufficiently detached then!

. . . You see, I don't believe, either, that there is some, one, 'really true' picture or record of what is, or of what was. I see our own professional writing, and also that of biographers, historians and even perhaps artists, as a presentation of one

aspect of what is 'reality' – what is outside there. . . . A number of different people, as you say, in the field, in looking at a landscape, or observing the behaviour
of those around them as Trollope or Jane Austen did, will each notice different
things of interest and each will rate different things in importance and so on. But
still there is the same thing at which they are all looking outside of them. . . . For
surely, Edmund, it is the height of arrogance to believe, because each of us as an
individual self-conscious Ego is not enduring, that nothing else is so, that everything is illusion? . . . you are not really Buddhist . . .

The reason I am moved to write about my own life is most certainly, in my own
mind, to get some control, by perspective, to get some pattern and some sense,
some comprehension of my own Ego; for my own satisfaction of course, but all
personal satisfaction of human beings is partly in the interaction with others . . .

Recently I have had a lot to do with clearing up papers, letters, and personalia
from friends and kin who have died. And I have discovered that after death, in this
way one meets a different and often unknown aspect of that person. . . . BUT this
does NOT mean that one is true and the other not true. It is simply that there are
so many aspects of a character that any person will show in response to another.
I have been surprised – perhaps I have said this before – at different pictures her
friends had of my own sister [Margaret], whom I thought I knew quite well. The
reality is richer, nearer to the 'truth' than one thought: it does not destroy, but
enlarges one's knowledge of that person.

Well, I must stop now . . .

[Rosemary]

EDMUND TO ROSEMARY

21 August 1985   **Barrington, Cambridge**

Dear Rosemary

. . . By my own lights I do not exaggerate. I try to say what I believe I believe . . .

As far as my views of 'writing' are concerned I am conditioned by current fashion.
I read a lot of 'Lit. Crit.'. . . . Authors write things down to please themselves;
some may envisage a reader, others may not. . . . What matters for the reader is
not the author but the text. The text is like the back wall of a Five's Court. The
reader throws his 'interpretations' against the wall and they bounce back at unexpected angles. The text on the printed page remains the same; what the reader
gets out of it differs according to the reader. There is no 'correct' interpretation.
The author's intention (if we knew what it was) is not privileged.

. . . Love

Edmund

FROM ROSEMARY'S DIARY

12 January 1986   **London**

. . . Edmund . . . came for a night. . . . Horribly mutilated by further open raw holes in his head from this recurring now eight year old skin cancer, he seemed to me, at first, to have moved into a completely closed world of senile self-concern and isolation – talked without interruption of his family's history in quite unwanted detail, laid about him theoretically, which provoked me to exclaim: 'You are a fool, Edmund!' – which shocked Raymond into a curious defensive position for the rest of the evening, as if he felt the two men alone were sensible but facing 'this stupid little woman' together! E. ate and drank my excellent food and wine greedily and unnoticing – or so it seemed; and when – after my carefully rehearsed friendliness over coffee and Armagnac to end the evening – he had retired, I went to bed almost in tears of sorrow and regret at his transformation.

But next morning I came down early to breakfast. . . . We had a good talk about his early religious upbringing, which had led him to so thorough a knowledge of the Bible that he naturally came back to that as text for his recent 'structural' interpretations of myth and history[18] . . .

So . . . that my old feelings for him – for the past year soured to bitterness – were reinstated, and I can accept a situation in which my love for him bears no relation to my present obligations, to any past insults, or any future fantasies of recipro-cated passion . . .

Raymond returned from their mutual attendance at a British Academy meeting very happy – 'E was very gentle to us I thought' he told me – 'as if he were a brother. It was a good time together.'

That is as it should be. If R and E feel as brothers I need not exactly explicate the tangled roots of my own very deep feelings for each of them over half a century and more . . .

Notes

1. Martha Macintyre (1945–) is an Australian anthropologist who has specialised in the impact of development in Papua New Guinea.
2. Edmund Leach, 1984, 'Glimpses of the Unmentionable in the History of British Social Anthropology', *Annual Review of Anthropology* 13: 1–23.
3. Edmund to Rosemary, 25 September 1984.
4. Edmund to Rosemary, 10 September 1933, reproduced in chapter 3, pp. 41–42.
5. Edmund to Rosemary, 3 September 1984.
6. Unfortunately, they were destroyed sometime after Edmund's death.
7. Rosemary, diary entry, 12 January 1986.
8. Edmund Leach, 1987, 'Tribal Ethnography: Past, Present, Future', *Cambridge Anthropology* 11: 1–14.

9. Rosemary Firth, 1987, *Anthropology Today*, 3(3): 15.

10. Leach, 'Glimpses of the Unmentionable'.

11. Bernard Deacon (1903–27) was studying the Malekula in what is now Vanuatu when he died of Blackwater fever. His letters to Margaret Gardiner were published by her in 1984 as *Footsteps on Malekula*, Edinburgh: Salamander Press.

12. Edmund Leach, 1984, 'Glimpses of the Unmentionable', pp. 13–14.

13. Adam Kuper, 1986, 'An Interview with Edmund Leach', *Current Anthropology* 27, 375–82. Adam Kuper (1941–) is a South African anthropologist who taught at Makarere, University College London, Leiden and Brunel universities.

14. Rosemary Firth, 1972, 'Wife to Anthropologist', in S.T. Kimball and J.B. Watson (eds), *Crossing Cultural Boundaries: The Anthropological Experience*, San Francisco, CA: Chandler, pp. 10–32; and Rosemary Firth, 1971, 'Within and Without the Ivory Towers', *Journal of the Anthropological Society of Oxford* 2: 74–82.

15. Rosemary, diary entry, 29 January 1986.

16. Rosemary, diary entry, 29 January 1986.

17. This is false. His literary executor – his daughter Loulou Brown – has a number of diaries Edmund wrote, along with very many letters written to him and some copies of letters he wrote to people. Also, there are many letters written and received by Edmund Leach, together with a few diaries, at King's College, Cambridge.

18. Edmund Leach and Alan Aycock, 1983, *Structural Interpretations of Biblical Myth*, Cambridge: Cambridge University Press.

Chapter 24

Who Was That Woman?

1986–1997

Edmund was not in good shape in May 1986. The skin cancer he had developed in the late 1970s – probably as a consequence of his exposure in Burma during the war – was progressing, and he was periodically undergoing both radiation treatment and skin grafts. Edmund and Celia were nevertheless able to attend Rosemary and Raymond's golden wedding anniversary party at the end of June 1986.

The previous decade had been full of both sorrow and joy for Raymond and Rosemary. In the year that Cyril Belshaw was charged and tried for murder, their son Hugh married Melinda Shaw: their marriage gave Rosemary the daughter she had always wanted alongside her son. Rosemary cherished her relationship with her daughter-in-law, with whom she shared many of her sorrows as well as her delights: 'When you are due to come and stay, [and] when you walk in, I have a lift and think how nice. When you are both here, I enjoy it so much I don't think about it. But when you have gone . . . auch, that is another matter. . . . The next morning is *horrid*. Bless you both anyhow, nice d-in-law.'[1] Rosemary's final prayer, to become a grandmother one day, was indeed granted. Both Raymond and Rosemary were delighted at the birth of their grandson Nicholas in 1985 and their granddaughter Emma some three years later. Raymond and Rosemary were able to see them both grow into their teenage years.

By July 1986, Edmund required major surgery to deal with his skin cancer. Raymond needed a more minor operation for his prostate cancer. Four weeks after the operations, Rosemary wrote that Edmund had become a 'familiarly confident voice over the telephone telling me that he looks nothing like his passport photograph, and that his appearance frightens the wits out of his daughter Louisa. . . . He's to "go in" to be "tidied up somewhat" later.'[2] Rosemary worried about which of them – Raymond or Edmund – would 'get into real trouble the soonest'. In recent years, Rosemary and Raymond had already lost many of their oldest and closest friends, including Greta Redfield, Raymond's lifelong friend Munia Postan and their colleagues William Stanner, Meyer Fortes, Audrey Richards and Lucy Mair. Rosemary wrote to Edmund in May 1986 to say that 'We've been thinking of you both quite a lot recently. . . . You know that there is now no one that Raymond and I feel so fond of as you and Celia. May we all last a long time more!'[3] Rosemary reflected that Edmund was the living person who had known her almost the longest: 'In sorting and throwing away early papers and things recently I came across a photograph of a girl of sixteen looking over a bridge in Ederyn, Wales, in 1928! – Do you realise that – apart from my estranged little sister, Elizabeth – there is now no one at all alive today who remembers me from that time excepting you?'[4]

Despite repeated surgery, Edmund remained remarkably vigorous and active intellectually for more than a year: it was in the spring of 1987 that he delivered his lecture to the ASA in which he audaciously insisted that all anthropologists' characterisations of other cultures were 'fiction'. Raymond made a good recovery from his surgery for prostate cancer and did not need more surgery. But ten days after they had all attended the ASA conference, Rosemary became alarmed when, over Easter 1987, Raymond developed a cardiac arrhythmia – he collapsed and was left weak and breathless. Rosemary fearfully summoned her son and daughter-in-law, who promptly travelled down to London. With palliative treatment, Raymond gradually improved. Yet Rosemary was now worried that she might very likely lose both Raymond and Edmund before long, and, feeling her age, was becoming increasingly concerned about what life would be like for her as a widow.

Throughout this period, Rosemary and Raymond visited Edmund and Celia regularly, either on their own or together. On some of these occasions, Edmund and Rosemary were alone and able to share some of their thoughts and feelings about their relationship over the years.

By the autumn of 1988, friends and colleagues observed that Edmund was no longer his former self, 'diminished both physically and mentally'.[5] In October, he travelled with Celia to Lisbon in Portugal to deliver a lecture. Much of it was incomprehensible to the audience. Celia and Edmund returned home the following day.

ROSEMARY'S DIARY

25 May 1986   **Southwood Avenue, London**

Bank Holiday weekend: Celia [Edmund's wife] rang up to 'warn' us that E. was now seriously ill: she had a long talk to R. [Raymond], and I only had a short talk and so upset I can't exactly remember all she said. But deeply humiliated to find R. inadvertently became aware of a prolonged weeping fit which shook me after talking to C.

Next day [the] Adeney family[6] came and lunched on our patio. Talked to Ann about illness, and radium treatment and its effects 'on a sick man whom I knew and was worried about'. She asked 'how old is he?'

'He is 75' I answered.

'Surely then they might let him in peace without treatment?' she replied.

Something jumped up inside my mind and shouted – 'It's not true. That man I know and am worried about isn't 75! He is 40, no, 30, no, 21. How could you tell such an untruth, Rosemary? Too old to treat?'

So where is Reality? Is all of Edmund just in my imagination, my heart: as he once said *I* was but a dream lady, without reality, for him to talk to? . . .

3 October 1986, Friday   **Visit to Edmund [at his home in]**
Barrington, Cambridge

. . . Autumn was golden and warm. No blackberries; but a wren sang along the tree lined lane we [Rosemary and Edmund] trod in peace, and talked quietly together of a past we both remembered and yet let it go.

He smiled and said: 'Yes. We used to write letters to each other every day . . .!' Never before has he alluded directly to that past . . . and kissed me. . . .

28 November 1986   **London**

Old age is rum. Outside we grumble about the unresponsiveness and awkwardness of the body. Inside we regress to the sunlight and joy of youth – at least in the unconscious, as revealed in dream.

[In a dream] last night, I, an old lady as now, met James [Livingstone] – a slim and loveable young man – in Edinburgh. I touched his arm and said 'You didn't notice me – don't remember me?' He turned with a most loving expression and said in his good Scots voice, 'O yes I do: but I thought *you* might have changed' (He was young, I old, remember in this scenario!). 'I haven't changed at all in my feelings for you' I replied, 'just the same mixture of love, and doubt.' . . .

The same night I also dreamed of my other love [Edmund]. We were staying in the same house, and he came to bid me goodnight. I was transfixed with joy at his loving and sensitive attention: but his face was disfigured and as he bent over me for a sort of a butterfly kiss he warned 'Not to touch him for fear of contamination.' He was nearing death. . . .

5 May 1987   **London**

I [. . . now have to face] a new phase of possible greatest slowing down in all Raymond's activity, and I feel a great tenderness and sadness for him. So strange and sudden a change [his heart arrhythmia and breathlessness] after an apparently good recovery from the surgery of 10 months ago, is quite unexpected. . . .

Weather entrancing – first of summer warmth over Easter brought out everything in the garden at once. . . . Visit from Hugh – talking to Hugh of my early married life, the Firth parents, and other such things.

17 May 1987   **Sunday: Raining**   **London**

I feel as if I've been living in a long dark . . . tunnel crawling slowly to an ever smallening [*sic*] hole with light of exit at the end, through what seem to have been weeks and weeks of dull but frightening sameness –

Now I've come out at the other end of the tunnel but the scene is quite different from what even it had ever been before. A closed, dusky landscape without future distant view – without companionship perhaps.

And we are each too cross and scratchy with it all – there's the irony: inevitable narrowing of vision to one's own personal comfort, increased self-concern, lack of patience, humour, and tolerance each to [the] other: it's shaming – terrible.

I never expected the valley of the shadow of death to be like this. I expected it to be quite different. A sick, stoical man, yes. But a short-tempered angry woman – no.

Figure 24.1. Raymond and Rosemary, 1984. Photograph by Joe Loudon.

Angry at the Great Reaper I suppose – scapegoated onto those nearest at hand. *There's* the sting – there the confounded victory. . . .

21 August 1987   **Alone in Dorset**

. . . Today, I let R. go on his own to London to greet [his niece] Greta from N.Z. [New Zealand] and the break from his quiet unobtrusive company came as a great, unacceptable shock. O dear, how shall I manage if – when? – I am really widowed, I who have suffered so, from grass widowhood when I was younger?

Since our bodies have been allowed to acknowledge a permanent end to erotic attachment (dignified for him by R.'s operation and now erratic heart rhythms) we get on excellently well in a very quiet way; and I feel a great surge of protective and embracing affection for him now – he who has been so good to me and so committed for over half a century. . . .

23 September 1987   **London**

Barrington: Lunch [with Edmund] in sun, picnic fashion, and a drink for *two* only, good talk, too. [Celia was on a well-earned break away.]

14 May 1988   **Dorset**

Five fine summer days at Holway, all pleasant and easy within doors, but sprouting weeds and tangled briars, clinging ivy, stinging nettles, and grass which chokes with weeds, while roses reek amok . . . chores that cry out for attention grow more and more difficult to tackle with arthritis, and an ageing and stiffening body. . . . The mind darts and longs to go, to go, to keep order as before. . . .

10 October 1988   **London**

Celia rang: E. 'rapidly deteriorating'; 'Portugal visit and talk a disaster'. He cannot drive car, or write, or read. . . . G.P. . . . won't give clear diagnosis. . . .

Raymond commented very sadly and quietly – 'the lights are going out one by one'.

13 October 1988   **London**

Celia rang: E. is in hospital, tumour on brain. Operation impossible. Radium being tried. The beginning of the end? . . . We keep lovingly in touch, long talk also to Louisa next day. Another pot plant sent [to] them: just 'to remind them of our love and concern'.

19 December 1988   **Barrington**

[Took the train from] Kings Cross 8.15 . . . [to Cambridge].

Celia opened the door in agitation: 'He fell last night. You can only see him for a short time.' 'Of course' I said. There lay a transfigured man on the bed, the weight of age fallen away, the face of the young Edmund I knew in the thirties. We talked. He laughed. 'They certainly nearly "called me" yesterday!'[7] He pressed my hand tightly as I sat. As I left, he lifted his head, his mouth offered to me for a kiss.

ᘘᘙ

Edmund Leach died on 6 January 1989.

ᘘᘙ

The funeral service for Edmund was held in the chapel of King's College. Afterwards, Rosemary found herself immersed once more in the 1930s, with all the angst of that period reawakened again. However, she was soon approached to contribute to a special issue of *Cambridge Anthropology* about Edmund. She chose to focus on aspects of his family history, particularly some of his thoughts and feelings about both his mother and his father, which Edmund had shared in his early letters to Rosemary. Writing the piece on Edmund enabled her to work through her grief and move towards a considered view of each of her relationships – with Edmund and with Raymond.

Rosemary was seventy-six when Edmund died. Despite the ravages of old age – Raymond's atrial fibrillation and her own arthritis – they had another dozen years each. Raymond, who published a significant book on religion at the age of ninety-five and two academic journal papers the year before he died,[8] became steadily more relaxed as he grew older, taking greater pleasure in visits from nieces and nephews and delighting in grandchildren. He lived to within a month of his hundred-and-first birthday. These were years that were, for both of them, characterised by enjoyment, but also much grieving and sadness. Just seven months after Edmund's death, Rosemary's niece Debby took her own life, nearly twenty years after her elder brother Andy. The final decade of their lives saw nearly three dozen of their colleagues, friends and relatives die, including Raymond's younger brother Cedric and Rosemary's younger sister Elizabeth and her stepbrother Terence.

Rosemary was finally able to reach a more rounded perspective on both the travails and the joys of her relationships with Edmund and Raymond. She reflected on what a rich and rewarding life she had led and came to think that Raymond had made a far better spouse than Edmund would ever have made. Although in the past she had often felt that Raymond was wedded to his work rather than to her, he had remained committed to her for almost sixty years; she knew, by contrast, how inconstant, fickle and unpredictable Edmund would have been. What Rosemary now understood was that she and Edmund shared many attributes that had attracted them to each other – a romanticism, a strong dislike of dishonesty or insincerity, an impulse to question, to challenge, to play the rebel. For the two of them, this generated great emotional tensions; but although in some senses they both wished to be fiercely independent, each of them needed someone else to provide them with a certain security, some 'earthing', an 'anchor'. And each of them had found

Figure 24.2. Rosemary in later life. Photograph by Hugh Firth.

someone who provided that grounding: in Celia, Edmund had found someone who was seemingly cool and composed; while, in Raymond, Rosemary had found someone who – for the most part – was confident, open-minded and, like his own father Wesley, calm, thoughtful and reflective.

ROSEMARY'S DIARY

12 March 1989   **London**

Several times, and last night the vividest [sic] of all, I dream of him [Edmund] – nearing death, sick, recovering – being tended by, being tender to me. This morning I awoke from such a long dream I wept aloud long and openly, before Raymond brought us a cup of tea at 6.30. But I managed still to keep drawn the veil over the pain that my past simply won't lie down.

19 May 1989   **London**

... On 19 December [the previous year] ... there lay the young man I fell in love with, sixty years ago. Age, bulk and experience seemed to have left him; from a thin innocent, fragile body he raised his face – offered his mouth for me to kiss. To kiss good-bye, he thought. But for weeks, months, after, I myself was back in those thirties and passionately reliving, regretting, the failed fruition of a once so great love –

Why did he reject me: not once but twice? Why did not I wait? But of course I could not – I needed and I had a rich love life apart from him: and isn't it something extraordinary that we managed to have half a century of rich warm developing relationship ... which never managed to break the seamless garment of our loyalty despite all minor hurts?

So he really did need someone so strangely alien, cool, unprovocative and detached to *stabilise* him? Celia was perhaps the *earthing* device for his equivocal and contrary energies.

... So many *ifs*: intellectual curtailment – emotional expansion, but surely also the everlasting price [I would have paid] of pain and uncertainty from that great cruel, egoistic angel.

July 1989   **London**

Requested 'to write something' about E.R.L., as I have known him for so many years ... [for] a special number of *Cambridge Anthropology*. ...

I couldn't write 'about Edmund' as an anthropologist I decided: but consented to try and let him speak for himself as a young man, by editing extracts from his early letters to me.

So I ploughed through the hundreds of pages and rigorously winnowed out all personal and passionate passages; till I had a harvest of some five thousand words, shown to Raymond ... first, then ... to Percy Cohen,[9] and to Ann Adeney, all of whom found the text a fascinating early picture of the great man he later became.[10]

For me it was a wonderful cathartic. I came face to face with our past and forgave all his earlier hurts for later love.

Nearly May – 1990   **London**

The eighties in view for me. Raymond already into his ninetieth year, much has changed not only for each of us separately, but also, more surprisingly, as between us. I suppose the things I earlier needed in the partnership, control and intellectual stimulation, are now needed less, have been absorbed or acquired elsewhere in my professional life and from later contacts. While the less tangible needs, literary, musical, sensual and so on are not available *thence* any more.

Curiously, I am conscious of strength yet loneliness, altho' I am not alone as I may soon have to be; but it seems as if those cold winds of widowhood already send little cool preliminary warnings to me, as we each retire in small ways into each his shell. All the ageing old do this sooner or later I am sure, and need to do so. But the pace is unequal between us now, and that is saddening to me.

10–12 April 1991   **Cambridge**

[. . . I have just] spent three days at an ASA meeting at Corpus Christi college in [the] new University centre [at] Cambridge. The Cambridge of 50/60 years ago is gone – physically choked with hordes of tourists. . . . The spirit of the place has – almost . . . vanished for me. The heart still remembers but the bodily ache has gone and the memories are now rather quizzically detached.

. . . Only the chapel seems still strangely beautiful, timeless and filled with memories of that lone long coffin and its ring of blue and white wreathed flowers.[11]

Who was that woman who carried her girlhood passion so deep and so far into her married life – who managed so wide a rift between domestic happiness and professional partnership – and inextinguishable early commitment and passion?

4 October 1991   **Friday night ten o'clock**   **London**

Mair Livingstone rang me, up late waiting for Hugh to return for the night from a conference in London.

'I think you should know, James has gone.' He felt faint, saying goodbye to her for a meeting in town, collapsed, and died quite unexpectedly later in [the] Royal Free [Hospital]. A splendid release for him, but for us? – for me, unbelievable!

I feel cheated, that he went before me and no farewell. He is the last of my old love life, now only . . . Raymond, Anthony C. [Clay][12] from before the war. . . .

3 May 1993   **Dorset**

Timor mortis perturbat me [Fear of death disturbs me] . . . I am 80. He is 92.

And a great sadness for all that is lost; yet a strange longing for me not yet to lose it all, as I look up at the moon each night, see the trees greening, the quiet and the friendliness of this country life. . . .

Mid-April 1995   **Dorset**

. . . Our last dinner party I think. Few people, about nine of us altogether. . . .

I seem to have had premonitions of fewer cottage visits before: but this ravishingly beautiful fortnight of fine fresh even warmish weather over Easter, has again made me wonder.

All is so hard now – stiff, forgetful, slightly deaf and sight frequently misleading me, either in recognition of village friends, or in loss of papers, mistakes of writing – yet here, away from London and ignoring world horrors and violence, it is beautiful.

So, I'll be sorry to go. Hope I may not be left to depart alone too long . . .

ROSEMARY TO MELINDA

29 January 1997   **Southwood Avenue, London**

Dearest Melinda,

Thank you for your gentle, healing touch.

The burden of bodily handicap, and the sting of mental longing, is what hurts us. Most elderly people find the changing world difficult to adjust to: but altho' such desolation may be exacerbated by inevitable domestic disagreements from time to time, more often it is alleviated for us by the companionship of a long-trusted partnership.

We often say to each other, how blessed we are in a loving son and daughter-in-law. We are luckier than some others here. And I'm not *so* often *so* miserable!

Yesterday we had a lovely short sunlit walk on Kenwood. Daffodils are coming out in a vase downstairs.

We are both tired, and perhaps I long for *real bedtime* – when it comes, be glad for our long lives – grieve only for yourselves.

Ever your loving,

Rosemary

അഃ

Rosemary died on 8 July 2001.
Raymond died seven months later on 22 February 2002.

അഃ

Notes

1. Rosemary to her daughter-in-law Melinda Firth, 21 February 1982.
2. Rosemary to Melinda, 6 August 1986.
3. Rosemary to Edmund, 10 May 1986.
4. Rosemary to Edmund, 10 May 1986.
5. Stanley Tambiah, 2002, *Edmund Leach: An Anthropological Life*, Cambridge: Cambridge University Press, p. 487.
6. Martin Adeney, journalist, who became the BBC's first industrial editor in 1982, and his wife Ann. Their garden backed on to the Firths' garden. They were good friends.
7. This was some three weeks before Edmund died: his powers of speech were failing, and the 'talk' and 'laugh' were probably minimal on Edmund's part. Rosemary was, however, good at making a connection with people with communication difficulties.
8. Raymond Firth, *Religion: A Humanist Interpretation*, London: Routledge, 1995; Raymond Firth, 2001, 'Tikopia Dreams: Personal Images of Social Reality', *Journal of the Polynesian*

Society 110(1): 7–29; Raymond Firth, 2001, 'The Creative Contribution of Indigenous People to Their Ethnography', *Journal of the Polynesian Society* 110(3): 241–45.

9. Percy Cohen (1928–99), a South African-born anthropologist and sociologist who was a good friend of Rosemary and Raymond.

10. The text was published as Rosemary Firth, 'A Cambridge Undergraduate: Some Early Letters from Edmund Leach', *Cambridge Anthropology*, 1989–90, 13(3): 9–18.

11. Rosemary is here referring to Edmund Leach's coffin.

12. Anthony Clay (1914–97), of whom Rosemary had been very fond in the 1930s. He subsequently married Rosemary's younger sister Elizabeth.

Selected Bibliography

Background Material

Bank, Andrew. 2016. *Pioneers of the Field: South Africa's Women Anthropologists*. Cambridge: Cambridge University Press.

Berg, Maxine. 1996. *A Woman in History: Eileen Power 1889–1940*. Cambridge: Cambridge University Press.

Bell, Diane, Pat Caplan and Wazir Jahan Karim (eds). 1993. *Gendered Fields: Women, Men and Ethnography*. London: Routledge.

Brookes, Stephen. 2000. *Through the Jungle of Death: A Boy's Escape from Wartime Burma*. London: John Murray.

Callan, Hilary, and Shirley Ardener. 1984. *The Incorporated Wife*. London: Croom Helm.

Duskin, Gerald L., and Ralph Segman. 2005. *If the Gods Are Good: The Sacrifice of HMS Jervis Bay*. Manchester: Crécy.

Engelke, Matthew. 2017. *Think like an Anthropologist*. London: Pelican.

Gardiner, Juliet. 2004. *Wartime: Britain 1939–1945*. London: Headline.

Godfrey, Ellen. 1981. *By Reason of Doubt: The Belshaw Case*. Vancouver: Clarke Irwin.

Karim, Wazir Jahan (ed.). 1995. *'Male' and 'Female' in Developing Southeast Asia*. Oxford: Berg.

King, Charles. 2019. *The Reinvention of Humanity: A Story of Race, Sex, Gender and the Discovery of Culture*. London: Bodley Head.

Kuper, Adam. 1986. 'An Interview with Edmund Leach', *Current Anthropology* 27: 375–82.

———. 2015. *Anthropology and Anthropologists: The British School in the Twentieth Century*. London: Routledge.

Kynaston, David. 2007. *Austerity Britain: 1945–51*. London: Bloomsbury.

Larson, Frances. 2021. *Undreamed Shores: The Hidden Heroines of British Anthropology*. London: Granta.

Lewis, Helen. 2020. *Difficult Women: A History of Feminism in 11 Fights*. London: Jonathan Cape.

Mills, David. 2008. *Difficult Folk? A Political History of Social Anthropology*. Oxford: Berghahn.

Oakley, Ann. 2014. *Father and Daughter: Patriarchy, Gender and Social Science*. Bristol: Policy Press.

———. 2021. *Forgotten Wives: How Women Get Written out of History*. Bristol: Policy Press.

Overy, Richard. 2021. *Blood and Ruins: The Great Imperial War 1931–1945*. London: Allen Lane.

Shankman, Paul. 2021. *Margaret Mead*. Oxford: Berghahn.

Sheridan, Dorothy (ed.). 1990. *Wartime Women: A Mass-Observation Anthology 1937–45*. London: Heinemann.

Tambiah, Stanley J. 2002. *Edmund Leach: An Anthropological Life*. Cambridge: Cambridge University Press.

Wayne, Helena (ed.). 1995. *The Story of a Marriage: The Letters of Bronisław Malinowski and Elsie Masson. Volumes 1 and 2*. London: Routledge.

Wilson, Elizabeth. 1980. *Only Half-Way to Paradise: Women in Post-War Britain 1945–1968*. London: Tavistock Publications.

Young, Michael. 2004. *Malinowski: Odyssey of an Anthropologist 1884–1920*. London: Yale University Press.

Audiovisual Materials

Forge, Anthony, 1982. *Rosemary and Raymond Firth*. Retrieved 26 April 2022 from https://www.youtube.com/watch?v=irgftuasayi.

Macfarlane, Alan (dir.). 1982. *Edmund Leach* (Interviewed by Frank Kermode). BBC. Retrieved 26 April 2022 from https://www.youtube.com/watch?v=3hnj0wifpqk.

——— (dir.). 1983. *Raymond Firth*. Retrieved 26 April 2022 from https://www.youtube.com/watch?v=w1ha1kmu3yk.

——— (dir.). 1983. *Rosemary Firth*. Retrieved 26 April 2022 from https://www.youtube.com/watch?v=p1jc3votibe.

Selected Publications by Rosemary Firth

1966 (1943). *Housekeeping among Malay Peasants*. London: Athlone Press.

1969. 'Examination and Ritual Initiation'. In Joseph Lauwerys and David G Scanlon (eds), *The World Year Book of Education: Examinations*. London: Routledge, pp. 235–42.

1970. 'The Social Images of Man and Woman'. *Journal of Biosocial Science*, Supplement 2: 85–92.

1972. 'From Wife to Anthropologist'. In Solon T. Kimball and James B. Watson (eds), *Crossing Cultural Boundaries: The Anthropological Experience*, pp. 10–32. San Francisco, CA: Chandler.

1977. 'Routines in a Tropical Diseases Hospital'. In Alan Davies and Gordon Horobin (eds), *Medical Encounters: The Experience of Illness and Treatment*. London: Croom Helm, pp. 143–58.

1977. 'Cooking in a Kelantan Fishing Village, Malaya'. In Jessica Kuper (ed.), *The Anthropologists' Cookbook*. London: Routledge, pp. 183–90.

1978. 'Medical Sociology and Anthropology: A Necessary Dialogue', *Social Science and Medicine* 12b: 235.

1978. 'Social Anthropology and Medicine – a Personal Perspective', *Social Science and Medicine* 12b: 237–45.

1990. 'A Cambridge Undergraduate: Some Early Letters from Edmund Leach', *Cambridge Anthropology* 13(3): 9–18.

1995. 'Prologue: A Woman Looks Back on the Anthropology of Women and Feminist Anthropology'. In Wazir Jahan Karim (ed.), *'Male' and 'Female' in Developing Southeast Asia*. Oxford: Berg, pp. 3–10.

Selected Publications by Raymond Firth

1957 (1936). *We, The Tikopia: A Sociological Study of Kinship in Primitive Polynesia*. London: Allen and Unwin.

1975 (1938). *Human Types*. London: Sphere Books.

1966 (1946). *Malay Fishermen: Their Peasant Economy*. London: Kegan Paul.

1959. *Social Change in Tikopia*. London: Allen and Unwin.

1969 (with Jane Hubert and Anthony Forge). *Families and Their Relatives: Kinship in a Middle-Class Sector of London*. London: Routledge and Kegan Paul.

1964 (with Basil Yamey; eds). *Capital, Saving and Credit in Peasant Societies*. London: Allen and Unwin.

1973. 'The Sceptical Anthropologist? Social Anthropology and Marxist Views on Society', *Proceedings of the British Academy* 58: 177–213.

1990 (with Mervyn Mclean). *Tikopia Songs: Poetic and Musical Art of a Polynesian People of the Solomon Islands*. Cambridge: Cambridge University Press.

1996. *Religion: A Humanist Interpretation*. London: Routledge.

Selected Publications by Edmund Leach

1954. *Political Systems of Highland Burma: A Study of Kachin Social Structure*. London: Athlone Press.

1961. *Rethinking Anthropology*, London: Athlone Press.

1961. *Pul Eliya: A Village in Ceylon: A Study of Land Tenure and Kinship*. Cambridge: Cambridge University Press.

1968. *A Runaway World?* London: BBC.

1970. *Claude Lévi-Strauss*. Chicago: University of Chicago Press.

1984. 'Glimpses of the Unmentionable in the History of British Social Anthropology', *Annual Review of Anthropology* 13: 1–23.

2001. *The Essential Edmund Leach. Volume 1: Anthropology and Society*, eds Stephen Hugh-Jones and James Laidlaw. London: Yale University Press.

2001. *The Essential Edmund Leach. Volume 2: Culture and Human Nature*, eds Stephen Hugh-Jones and James Laidlaw. London: Yale University Press.

Index